ENVIRONMENTAL PSYCHOLOGY

ENVIRONMENTAL PSYCHOLOGY

A Psycho-social Introduction

Mirilia Bonnes and
Gianfranco Secchiaroli

translated by
Claire Montagna

SAGE Publications
London • Thousand Oaks • New Delhi

English translation © Sage Publications 1995

First published in English 1995

Originally published in Italian as *Psicologia Ambientale*
© La Nuova Italia Scientifica, Rome 1992

SAGE Publications Ltd
6 Bonhill Street
London EC2A 4PU

SAGE Publications Inc
2455 Teller Road
Thousand Oaks, California 91320

SAGE Publications India Pvt Ltd
32, M-Block Market
Greater Kailash – I
New Delhi 110 048

British Library Cataloguing in Publication data

A catalogue record for this book
is available from the British Library

ISBN 0 8039 7905 3
ISBN 0 8039 7906 1 (pbk)

Library of Congress catalog record available

Typeset by Mayhew Typesetting, Rhayader, Powys
Printed in Great Britain by The Cromwell Press Ltd,
Broughton Gifford, Melksham, Wiltshire

Contents

Preface

The purpose of this book is to outline a psycho-social introduction to the field of environmental psychology, which has developed over the past twenty years and is now well-established at the international level (see Stokols and Altman, 1987).

This volume points out that environmental psychology is first of all a frontier field in psychological research aimed at collaborating with other fields, both disciplinary and technical, involved in organizing, changing and managing the human physical environment, such as architecture, geography, ecological natural sciences (biological and physical), economy, law, etc.

The first aim of the book is to bring the specific demands existing outside psychology within the psychological tradition. In particular, it is pointed out that many of the main questions environmental psychology is trying to answer today have a long tradition of research in psychology. Special reference is made to two main theoretical traditions: the psychology of perception-cognition, on the one hand, and social psychology, on the other.

It is emphasized that this second tradition seems to provide the most appropriate conceptual and methodological tools for the development of environmental psychology and for bringing psychological research into the 'real world' so often indicated as one of the major objectives of environmental psychology.

It is also pointed out that environmental psychology has been moving towards the psycho-social perspective since its inception. This perspective is also indicated as the most appropriate one for enabling environmental psychology not only to answer 'external questions', but also to become a theoretically relevant reference point within the psychological field for overcoming the misleading opposition between 'basic research' and 'applied research'.

This volume gives an informative picture of the main working themes of environmental psychology today and investigates the psychological tradition to discover how this new domain of psychological research can develop with both external and internal relevance, finally putting into practice the well-known Lewinian intention of carrying out research that is at the same time 'theoretically meaningful and socially useful.

PART I

THE ORIGIN AND THEORETICAL ROOTS OF ENVIRONMENTAL PSYCHOLOGY

1

The Origin of Environmental Psychology

The main 'founding stages' of environmental psychology

A new area developed within the field of psychology at the end of the 1950s, and during the 1960s which was termed 'environmental psychology' in the United States. Definition of this new field of psychological research proceeded with some effort; initial interest in the physical characteristics of the environment (Proshansky et al., 1979) developed into the larger issue of 'the interface between human behaviour and the sociophysical environment' (Stokols, 1978; Stokols and Altman, 1987) (see pp. 63–8).

Many factors, originating in many different countries, contributed to the emergence of this area of study. However, from the very beginning, environmental psychology (e.p.) found its homeland in the United States due to the many and systematic initiatives taken there which were aimed at its foundation and development.

One of the most important initiatives was taken in 1958 with the formation of a research group by William Ittelson and Harold Proshansky at the City University of New York. Financial support came from the United States National Institute of Mental Health. The purpose of this group was to study how the spatial/architectural setting of a psychiatric hospital can affect patients' behaviour. One of the first works produced by the group was entitled 'Some Factors Influencing the Design and Function of Psychiatric Facilities' (Ittelson, 1960). Ittelson also introduced the term 'environmental psychology' for the first time in New York in 1964 at the Conference of the American Hospital Association on hospital planning. His presentation was entitled 'Environmental Psychology and Architectural Planning'.

Over the next eight or nine years, the group continued to work in this area; it aimed at expanding its interest beyond the study of the physical setting of the psychiatric hospital to include the relationships between behaviour and the physical environmental setting in general. In 1970 the group's first volume was published, edited by Proshansky, Ittelson and Rivlin. The term e.p. was explicitly used in the title (*Environmental Psychology: Man and His Physical Settings*). Besides presenting the group's work on the relationship between the physical setting of the psychiatric hospital and patients' behaviour, this volume presented various studies on the problem of the relationship between human behaviour and physical characteristics of the environment.

Two introductory articles on e.p. also appeared in 1970. Their titles seemed to sanction the new area of study (the chapter by Craik, [1970] in *New Directions in Psychology*, entitled 'Environmental Psychology', and the article by Wohlwill [1970] in *American Psychologist*, entitled 'The Emerging Discipline of Environmental Psychology').

The Environmental Design Research Association (EDRA) was established in 1968 and began holding annual conferences in 1969, which were generally followed by publication of the Proceedings. In 1981, its European equivalent was established, the International Association for the Study of People and their Physical Surroundings (IAPS). This name has recently been changed to the International Association for People–Environment Studies; its conferences are held biennially. Moreover, in 1976 the American Psychological Association formed a new division, 'Population and Environmental Psychology'.

In 1969, *Environment and Behavior*, the first and foremost American journal specializing in this type of study, began publication (Winkel, 1969); soon after, this was followed by another new journal, *Non-Verbal Behavior and Environmental Psychology*, which published for only a few years under this name. In 1978 a journal specializing in this area, *Population and Environment*, began publication and continued until 1987. Then, in 1981, a new journal appeared in Britain, the *Journal of Environmental Psychology* (Canter and Craik, 1981) edited by David Canter of the University of Surrey (Guildford).

In 1973 the *Annual Review of Psychology* dedicated its first review article, by Kenneth Craik, to the emerging field of e.p.; approximately every four years other review articles were published by equally important authors in the area: Stokols (1978), Russell and Ward (1982), Holahan (1986), and Saegert and Winkel (1990).

In 1968 the City University of New York opened its graduate school in e.p., directed by Ittelson and Proshansky. Similar, more multidisciplinary programmes were started and still exist at other universities in the United States: Clark University, Cornell University and the University of California at Irvine. Furthermore, in Britain a Master's Degree in e.p. was established at the University of Surrey (Guildford), directed by Terence Lee and David Canter.

As the culmination of this long preparation and foundation of e.p. as a new field of study within psychology and as a specific sub-disciplinary area, the enormous *Handbook of Environmental Psychology* (Stokols and Altman, 1987) was published in two volumes, with a total of 1,654 pages. Its preparation had taken seven years. Those who contributed either as authors or as referees included almost everyone working in the field at the international level not only in the United States but also in the major European (Britain, Sweden, Holland, Germany, France, Italy, Russia) and non-European (Japan, Australia, Latin America) countries.

The origin of the field: the importance of external factors

On the one hand, the previously described events can be considered as primary stages in the foundation of e.p. as a specific area of study within the field of psychology; on the other, it must be kept in mind that these were prominent stages in a very large and diverse process going back to the origin of e.p.

Within this perspective, e.p. is linked to many forces, internal and external to the field of psychology, which converged both prior to and after the 1970s. Thus, the birth of e.p. must be seen primarily as the outcome of a progressive convergence of interests. In the following sections, we will attempt to outline and reconstruct these interests both internal and external to the field of psychology.

It must be kept in mind that the origin and development of this new area of psychological research can only be understood by looking at both these sides, in order to understand the most recent developments in the field and the difficulties in finding a theoretical identity which goes beyond the general designation of 'applied psychology'.

The many interests progressively maturing outside the field of psychology can certainly be attributed a determining role in delineating the field and its rapid development in the United States and in other European countries. This was mainly due to the needs of disciplines initially rather distant from psychology, such as architecture and environmental planning, geography and bio-ecological sciences.

Here we will first examine the interests of these areas outside of psychology which, for many reasons, can be considered as primary factors in the emergence of the field; then, we will examine interests and problems within the psychological tradition, singling out possible factors of 'theoretical availability' within the field for responding to these 'external' demands.

The interest of the architectural field and architectural psychology

The attempt by Ittelson and Proshansky's group in the United States to study the relationship between architectural design and the behaviour of patients in psychiatric hospitals was not an isolated one. At the same time, other psychologists and psychiatrists were involved in similar research projects both in the United States and in other countries. In particular, the work begun at the end of the 1950s in Canada by Humphrey Osmond – 'a psychiatrist with research interests', as Proshansky (Proshansky and O'Hanlon, 1977, p. 105) defined him – and the social psychologist, Robert Sommer, must be cited. One of the first publications of this group was entitled 'Function as the Basis of Psychiatric Ward Design' (Osmond, 1957). This work presents Osmond's theory on the existence of 'sociofugal' spatial settings, aimed at discouraging social interaction, or, rather, 'sociopetal' settings, able to encourage social interaction. Following Osmond's suggestions, Kyo Izumi (1957) attempted to incorporate these psychological indications into the design for a new psychiatric hospital. The subsequent work of Robert Sommer developed from these first studies. Also studying behaviour on geriatric wards, Sommer developed the concepts of 'human territoriality' and 'personal space', destined to find a remarkable following in psychology in general and environmental psychology in particular (these concepts will be more fully discussed in Chapter 4) and in the sciences of architectural design ('Personal Space: the Behavioral Basis of Design' is the title of the specific volume published in 1969).

At the same time in Europe, the French psychiatrist Paul Silvadon began a research programme in collaboration with architects on the role of the design of the psychiatric hospital for the improvement/healing of patients. In 1969 the results of this study were published in a monograph supported by the World Health Organization (Baker et al., 1960).

Thus, in various countries at the end of the 1950s, the problem of design/planning of buildings destined to house psychiatric patients represented a typical impetus for the formation of research groups with interests often progressing in time towards programmatic, cumulative and even broader aims. The activity of Ittelson and Proshansky's group represents the best example of this. However, it must be kept in mind that these study groups, based on the collaboration between psychologists and architects, were not isolated events; they must be considered as emerging factors in a much broader and diffused movement in various countries in the architectural planning sciences, starting in the 1950s.

This movement manifested itself in architecture schools and in large architectural design firms, primarily in Anglo-Saxon and Northern European countries; they were pushed both by the revision imposed by the modern movement of the first part of the century and by contingent historical and social factors encouraging the world of architectural design to collaborate with the social and human sciences and, in particular, with psychology. This multidisciplinary area of study, centred primarily on the collaboration between architects and psychologists, immediately assumed the name of 'architectural psychology' both in the United States and in Europe and, in particular, in Britain and Sweden.

In 1956 the Research Commission of the American Institute of Architects (AIA) presented a proposal to the National Science Foundation

(NSF) to hold a conference, which took place in 1959 at the University of Michigan; the main topic was the relationship between the physical, biological and social sciences with regard to the problems of creating optimal environments for human activities (Magenau, 1959). Prior to this, at the 1958 convention of the AIA in Cleveland, a preliminary seminar was held on the topic; participants included architects, civil engineers, urban planners, psychologists and sociologists.

As a result of these meetings, in 1958 one of the first collaborative agreements took place between an architect (Miller) and a psychologist (Wheeler) for the construction of several students' dormitories at the University of Indiana. These buildings were then subjected to a post-occupancy evaluation study. Collaboration between psychologists and architects became more systematic over the years through the organization of conferences and through publications. In 1961 the first conference of architectural psychology was held at the University of Utah, followed several years later (1966) by another one at the same university organized by the architect Roger Bailey and the psychologist, Calvin Taylor; the latter was responsible for the publication of the presented papers (Bailey et al., 1961; Taylor et al., 1967). In 1967 the University of Utah (Archea, 1967–9) began publication of the *Architectural Psychology Newsletter*, dedicated to the diffusion of works on this topic and destined to become part of the new *Man–Environment Systems* journal in 1969 (Archea and Esser, 1969).

Similar initiatives to increase collaboration between psychology and architecture can be found during these same years at other universities in the United States, such as the University of Kansas, Pennsylvania State University, Clark University and the Massachusetts Institute of Technology (MIT).

Studies begun at MIT at the end of the 1950s by the urban planner Kevin Lynch played a determining role in the development of this type of collaboration. In this case they led to the 1960 publication of *The Image of the City*, which gained immediate fame.

This book presented a study carried out in three different large cities in the United States (Boston, Jersey City and Los Angeles). The author presented an approach to urban planning which can be considered revolutionary from many points of view. He proposed that the basis of thinking about the city and its planning should be the 'image' of the city or, better, the 'imageability' of it in the minds of its inhabitants/users. The use and the images inhabitants have of urban space as a result of its design and their daily experience of it are proposed as the points of reference for every planning decision.

In this perspective, Kevin Lynch, Donald Appleyard and John Meyer began a research programme on the aesthetics of urban design to study how urban highways are seen by motorists and their passengers in order to establish the modalities to use for planning highways (Appleyard et al., 1964).

Gary Moore (1987, p. 1367), coming from the planning side in the 1960s and one of the most well-known environmental psychologists in the United States, says:

> Formed in 1966 at the end of a conference at the University of Waterloo in Canada by myself and others, the Design Methods Group held its first conference in June 1968 at The Massachusetts Institute of Technology. Dissatisfaction with planning and design methods divorced from the content of architectural psychology led to a series of annual conferences sponsored by the newly formed Environmental Design Research Association.

Thus, in the architecture sector, there was growing dissatisfaction with design, which was defined as 'egocentric', seen as primarily aimed at satisfying the aesthetic self-affirmation needs of the architect/designer, who constructed 'personal monuments' rather than buildings centred on the needs of their users.

On the other side, after the Second World War, the sciences of architectural planning faced increasing difficulty due to the progressive complexity of society and the growing requests of governments and private organizations, which were faced with enormous building construction and reconstruction programmes.

The need to plan for building complexes rather than for single buildings became increasingly frequent; in general, the users of these complexes were far removed from the planner and little known; they were often differentiated or even 'specialized' in the typology of use. The case of planning for a psychiatric ward is a good example in this sense and it often brought about collaboration between architects and psychologists.

On the one hand, egocentric design was explicitly rejected and, on the other, it was increasingly clear that planning for people, or considering the design 'as if people mattered' to use the title of a recent book by Claire Cooper Markus and Wendy Sarkissian (1986), could not be entrusted exclusively to 'intuitive' acts, but required a real change in the modalities for approaching and carrying out the planning and design process.

It should be noted also how the same approach between architectural planning and psychology, which we have outlined up until now in the most salient aspects for the United States, was equally systematic in various European countries, in particular in Sweden (Kuller, 1987) and in Britain (Canter and Donald, 1987), where architectural psychology also developed.

In Britain, the first real interest in this direction occurred immediately after the Second World War. Large-scale post-war reconstruction with limited resources led to the need for optimizing planning choices; the social sciences were contacted directly and became involved in this process.

One of the promoters of this collaborative approach between planning and psychology was Winston Churchill (Canter and Stringer, 1975). In this area, he showed himself to be particularly shrewd and far-sighted. As an example, recall Churchill's words as he opened debate in the House of Commons, which had been destroyed by bombardments: he said that 'we give shape to our buildings and they, in turn, shape us' (quoted in Hansard, 1943).

Parts of the same speech referring to the House of Commons are still quoted today because they demonstrate Churchill's awareness of the importance of paying attention not only to functional aspects but also to the maintenance of some 'inefficiency' as an integral part of the building destined for the parliamentary government. He pointed out several characteristics that the architectural setting of the House of Commons should present following its reconstruction. In particular he stated that 'it should be large enough so that it cannot hold all of its members at once, at the same time without giving the impression of overcrowding (quoted in *Hansard*, 1943).

With Churchill's words the concept started to develop that rebuilding should not be guided exclusively by functional criteria but also by the need to save those shapes which were complementary to the social and psychological processes of the relative institutions.

With this viewpoint, the British government stimulated and financed numerous studies at that time to deepen the connections between the architectural setting of the environment and human behaviour. The result of several of these studies served to institute legislative provisions in environmental planning in Britain and elsewhere. Chapman's study on the lighting of homes with daylight (Chapman and Thomas, 1944) is an example of this.

At the end of the post-war reconstruction, interest in these types of studies waned; however, strong interest re-emerged in the 1960s and again the term 'architectural psychology' was used. In 1969, one of the first European conferences was held in architectural psychology in Dalandhui, near Glasgow (Scotland); this was immediately followed in 1970 by one in Kingston (Honikman, 1971). In 1970 David Canter published a volume with the same title (*Architectural Psychology*) based on the contents of the first conference.

In Britain, as well as in the United States, the schools of architecture were the most active in stimulating this type of interest, although, as Appleyard (1973) observed, a certain difference could be recognized in the way in which this interest was developing in Britain and in the United States. In the latter the sector developed primarily under the sponsorship of academic institutions whereas in Britain the same phenomenon was directed towards the resolution of professional problems.

Following the architectural debate in the 1960s regarding the need to introduce new design methods into practical and professional training, the proposed model (Broadbent and Ward, 1969) was divided into three major phases: analysis, synthesis and appraisal. This model was adopted both in the work plan of the Royal Institute of British Architects and in other guiding civil norms for the design of buildings, such as the Department of Health, called 'Capricode'.

The important conclusion extracted from this type of work plan and destined to have direct implications for psychology was that the appraisal phase should require the examination of users' reactions to the buildings. Users' appraisals were seen as a necessary component in a systematic design, and psychologists were called in to conduct them. British architectural psychology initially developed in this direction.

The Building Performance Research Unit (BPRU) was established in 1967 in the Faculty of Architecture at the University of Strathclyde and the Building Research Unit (BUR) at the University of Liverpool. Their aim was to develop systematic empirical procedures for evaluating buildings.

The underlying idea was to make the evaluative phase more active within the design process, developing standard instruments which could be easily used for appraising the various aspects of buildings. In this type of research unit, the work groups were strongly multidisciplinary. Participants included psychologists, civil engineers, architects and even physicians. Some of the most noted British environmental psychologists took part in these groups, such as David Canter. He subsequently went with Terence Lee to the University of Surrey (Guildford) to create and then direct the environmental psychology group. The work carried out in these units had a strong technical orientation, which raised some dissatisfaction among its members.

In the 1960s, the group of psychologists around Terence Lee at the University of Surrey tried to advance a type of research which followed the interests of architecture but was less determined technologically and more oriented towards psychology. It was in this spirit that Canter and Lee published a collection entitled *Psychology and the Built Environment* in 1974, in view of the upcoming Congress of architectural psychology. In this volume the authors insist upon the need to overcome architectural determinism and move on to a more interactive study of the individual–built environment relationship.

According to them (Canter and Lee, 1974), the Congress should examine research on the relations between environmental-physical variables and actions, thoughts and feelings of human beings and emphasis should be given to research clearly oriented and empirically based on precise theoretical formulations destined to enrich or promote this research.

Canter extended his examination of the modalities of cooperation between psychology and architecture and published a specific manual for use by architects: *Psychology for Architects* (1972). The image he outlined for architectural psychology was primarily one of necessity; he observed that architects and designers, willingly or not, should always take into account the psychological implications of their design decisions.

On the other side, also considering the norms which regulate buildings, he observes that even though not based on psychological science, they are guided by assumptions about the psychological impact of the shapes of these buildings. The sole fact of creating a physical shape taking into account the visual effect which its perception will provoke involves, according to Canter, implicit assumptions – generally not verified at the scientific level – about the relationship between characteristics of the physical stimulus and the corresponding psychological response. Thus, the role of architectural psychology is that of giving a scientific foundation to these implicit assumptions.

From this standpoint, Canter pinpoints several critical aspects, in particular:

(a) the need to distinguish the exigencies of 'functional adequacy' of buildings (if differentiated in relation to many variables) from those relative to their shape;
(b) the complexity of the design process, in which no one (architect included) designs or constructs for him/herself, and the resulting usefulness of psychological research, which can provide an invaluable contribution.

Thus, psychology began to take shape as a possible bridge between concrete-operative problems and the identification of optimum solutions not only from the aesthetic-visual point of view but above all from that of functional adequacy of environmental architecture with respect to the needs and expectations of the building users.

The deterministic assumptions implicitly underlying the initial research of systematic relations between architectural aspects of the built environment and human behaviour modalities within it were increasingly recognized by Canter as limited and theoretically inadequate for facing problems of an interactive nature which connect people to the built environment.

This was primarily discussed by Canter and Lee (1974), who also attempted to pinpoint the basic information psychology can provide for designing the environment. This was identified in reference to three categories:

(a) people's activity – what types of activities are carried out, where and how are they carried out, how do they change;
(b) differentiated appraisals – what are the hierarchies of priorities existing among these both from a practical point of view and in terms of values;
     the behaviour–environment relationship – not only to know people's reactions to architectural variables, but also to discover the reasons for these relationships in an interactive perspective.

In this context, the contribution of psychology to the process of architectural design is seen as differentiated in relation to the various design stages:

(a) ideation – when several general findings can be employed originating from psychological research concerning architectural characteristics and behaviours;

(b) specification – when specific influences can be singled out from the physical characteristics of the environment as well as equally specific psychological aspects, for example relations between environmental luminosity and insomnia or between environmental noise and work output, etc.,

(c) appraisal – when an analysis is made of the existing, also considering the resulting, psychological effects, to identify inadequacies or possible directions for improvement of a current design or future ones.

These types of indications were at the base of British architectural psychology in the 1970s and, from many points of view, also that of the 1980s, since in Britain the term 'architectural psychology' is still used along with that of 'environmental psychology' to indicate the same type of studies, whereas in the United States these are defined by the single term 'environmental psychology' or with even broader terms such as man–environment relationship, person–environment relationship or behaviour–environment relationship. In certain cases, these definitions are preferred by researchers coming from areas other than psychology, such as architects, geographers, anthropologists and sociologists, who are equally active in the field.

The European association corresponding to EDRA in the United States (now called IAPS – International Association for People–Environment Studies) still publishes and distributes a newsletter edited by Kingston University (formerly Kingston Polytechnic) entitled *Architectural Psychology Newsletter*.

In this context, we must note the specific cultural situation of a European country such as Britain with a long, strong history of urbanization, where interest in environmental design remains focused on the built architectural environment; this is very different from a country like the United States where the strong presence of natural environments as well as built ones led initial architectural interests to expand immediately towards broader issues. Canter and Lee (1974) noted the marked interest in natural as well as built environments of the emerging environmental psychology in the United States, whereas the pressing interests in natural and primitive environments are linked to the vastness of natural resources and the size of undeveloped spaces in a human sense, characteristic of North America, that is, like the pioneer tradition, to which this type of environment refers.

What happened in Britain also happened in Sweden: collaboration began between design and the social sciences in the 1940s, as a result of a vast government rehousing programme for the population. Here, as in Britain, this led to the development of architectural psychology during the 1960s. In 1967 the first congress on this topic was held at the University of Lund; in 1969 the Swedish Committee for Architectural Psychology was established. The development of this new area of psychological research in

Sweden had characteristics analogous to those previously described for Britain. Here also the sector expanded and was consolidated according to various study directives; particular attention was given to the design and arrangement of work environments as well as dwellings. Specific development occurred in research on the psychological implications of physical aspects of the environment, such as colour (Johansson, 1952; Hard, 1975), light (Tangenes et al., 1981), thermal comfort (Lofstedt, 1966), etc. 'It is not an exaggeration to say that what is today known as environmental psychology was already at the end of the 1960s, well established in Sweden' writes Kuller (1987, p. 1244) in the part of the *Handbook of Environmental Psychology* reserved for the presentation of the development of the field in various countries. Thus, cooperation between the sciences of the physical/built environment and psychological research developed very early in Sweden; moreover, as Kuller demonstrates, this cooperation still proceeds, and in an increasingly systematic way, through the establishment of specific institutions primarily created by the government to promote these types of studies.

Besides the above-described developments in Britain and Sweden, in other European countries there were also occasional examples of cooperation between architecture and psychology starting in the 1950s. (For further information on this, see the appropriate parts of the *Handbook* dedicated to the emergence of architectural psychology in various countries; Stringer and Kremer [1987] for Holland; Niit et al., [1987] for the Soviet Union; Kruse and Grauman [1987] for Germany; and Jodelet [1987] for France.)

The interest of the geographic field and behavioural geography

Other disciplines outside of psychology, which contributed greatly towards the emergence of environmental psychology, are represented by the sciences of the physical-geographical environment and those of the ecological-naturalistic one; by the end of the 1960s they showed a growing and increasingly specific interest in the so-called 'human' or 'anthropic' factor, considered an inseparable component of the physical-natural processes, the traditional interest area of these disciplines.

In the next chapter, we will present a more detailed discussion of the ecological-naturalistic sector; particular attention will be paid here to the geographical field, which has been prolific in the last decade, often tending to overlap with environmental psychology.

Corresponding to the progressive shift in the field of geography towards human geography, proposals had already appeared in the 1940s regarding the need to investigate the psychological components connected with geographical research. In particular, the American geographer Wright proposed 'geosophia' as a new field of study for geography. With this term, he meant the exploration of the images people have about geographical environments; he names these '*terrae incognitae*', that is 'the worlds that are in the minds of men'. In his 1947 address as president of the Association of American Geographers, he affirmed that the most fascinating *terrae incognitae* of all are those that lie within the minds and the hearts of men.

This proposal referred back to the works of the first cultural geographers of the Berkeley school, which appeared in the first half of the twentieth century. Carl Sauer (1925), founder of the school, pointed out the need for studies on the morphology of the landscape to consider the social and cultural components characterizing the inhabitants of the territory as determinants of the physical features assumed by the landscape over time; essentially, the central role played by sociocultural factors in directing human spatial behaviour was recognized and through this the geographical configuration of the landscape.

Wright's proposal, even though it had few followers at the time, re-emerged much more systematically and consistently several years later in the work of several geographers (Lowenthal, 1961; Saarinen, 1966; Downs, 1970; Gold, 1980; Saarinen et al., 1984) and landscape naturalists (Jackson, 1951–68, 1970).

Geographers tend to speak of the foundation of a new branch of geographical studies termed 'behavioural geography' (Gold, 1980; Arca Petrucci and Gaddini, 1985) or, more often, 'perceptual geography' (Downs and Meyer, 1978; Bianchi, 1980; Bailly, 1981).

In the United States, the publication of the new journal *Landscape*, the work of James B. Jackson (1951–68) – 'careful observer of the American landscape, both natural and human made', as Moore (1987, p. 1364) defined him – was for many years an important point of reference for comparisons and discussions among exponents of various disciplinary viewpoints around the topic of the perception/appraisal of the environment. Jackson became an active promoter of contributions by researchers from various disciplines destined to become representative figures of environmental psychology: Rapoport (1964–5), Stea (1967) and Tuan, who has a phenomenological orientation and became famous for his concept of 'topophilia', which he first presented in *Landscape* (1961) and which was subsequently expanded into a book with the same title (1974) (see pp. 164–6).

Gold (1980), in his introductory book to behavioural geography, stresses that this new branch of geography is characterized by a conception of man–environment relations much more complex than that traditionally employed by geographers. The behavioural geographer recognizes that man shapes and at the same time responds to the environment and that man and environment are dynamically correlated. Man is seen as a motivated social being whose decisions and actions are mediated by his cognition of space. According to behavioural geographers interpretations of behaviour are based on a comprehension of the way in which cognition of space develops, of the nature of cognition of space and of the ties between cognition and behaviour; these interrelated areas constituted the object of their investigations.

Gold (1980) believes also that this new branch of geography had already arrived at the second stage in its development as a new academic discipline: the phase following the first pioneering steps and various inside controls which passes on to verification of proven disciplinary validity.

Frankly, for a psychologist reading this type of literature, it is very hard to believe it refers to geography and not to psychology, even if modalities are used which often seem peculiar.

An examination of the problems treated and methodologies used would seem to bring that field of study directly into the field of environmental psychology, if by psychology we mean the discipline that assumes the psychological processes occurring in the individual as the unit of analysis and if by geography we mean the discipline concerned with physical-geographical space. *Behavioural geography* or the geography of *perception*, since it is concerned with a represented/perceived or acted space at the level of individual and collective psychological processes and only indirectly with physical-geographical space, seems to want to call itself geography rather than psychology for the sake of academic territoriality rather due to disciplinary content.

On the other side, it must be noted that among geographers concerned with psychological phenomena, there is a frequent disciplinary extraneousness to problems treated, which often leads them to display ingenuity and excessive simplification when observed from a more psychological point of view. Gold (1980) observes that the recognition that the problems treated by behavioural geographers transcend academic confines, leads them to look for an explanation of behavioural processes in the literature of the social and behavioural sciences. In the first years this was primarily in one direction, but more recently a reciprocal exchange of ideas has developed. He notices that now it is frequent to find references to geographical sources in the work of environmental psychologists and sociologists, and this tendency is probably destined to increase. According to Gold, if the situation of behavioural geography could be improved by bringing geographical practice more in line with psychology and the sciences of behaviour this union should be guided by discrimination i.e. behavioural geography should develop a complementary and non-competitive role with respect to other approaches.

In these considerations we find the implicit admission of the difficulty in which the new area of geographical studies finds itself; simultaneously it seems to want to concern itself with psychological phenomena and also preserve a programmatically geographical, non-psychological perspective. The solution adopted by other researchers in the area of geography seems more plausible; for example, Reginald Golledge, Ervin Zube and various others, recognizing that they were working completely within in the new field of environmental psychology, ended up trying to provide relevant contributions to the sector not so much in the geographical sense but in the psychological one.

The ecological-naturalistic field, environmental problems and the UNESCO MAB (Man and Biosphere) programme

In reviewing the principal factors outside of psychology which contributed to the origin and development of environmental psychology, the importance that so-called 'environmental problems' have taken on in various parts of the world during the past twenty or thirty years cannot be ignored; nor can we ignore the growing interest they have aroused in various scientific and decision-making areas.

One of the most significant events at the international level was the launching of the UNESCO programme on ecological-environmental problems at the beginning of the 1970s. This programme was termed MAB (Man and Biosphere). Conceived and launched from a privileged observation point, such as the United Nations and UNESCO in particular, today it still presents characteristics at both national and international levels which are innovative due to the modalities proposed for confronting environmental problems and looking at ecological-naturalistic problems.

Overall, the programme is a specific political/cultural proposal with implications for both scientific and political decision-making praxis. It is defined as an 'international programme of applied research on the interactions between man and his environment; source of scientific knowledge needed by decision-makers for managing natural resources' (UNESCO-MAB 1988, p. 12). Further, with regard to method, it proposes the need to face problems in an integrated way, not separately and partially, indicating the method for constructing this environmental knowledge/praxis in cooperation/exchange: 'a collective effort of natural and social scientists, planners, managers and local populations; an education and training effort linked to field research projects' (ibid.: 12).

Above all, the programme is defined as 'helping to establish the scientific bases for sustainable development and for assisting countries in developing their human resources' (ibid.: 11)

MAB was established in 1971 as an initiative of UNESCO's Division of Ecological Sciences. The ecological-naturalistic interests, were redefined within this new programme from, for that time, a highly innovative viewpoint.

The programme began as development/evolution of the preceding international programme of biological sciences (IBP). MAB was innovative compared to IBP because it recognized the need to assign to the human factor – defined in this case as 'man' – a central role in the ecological-naturalistic approach. What in the previous programme had been generically and simply defined as the 'anthropic factor' became the primary referent of every ecological-naturalistic topic in the new MAB programme. The term 'man and biosphere' assumed by the programme is symbolic in this sense: man, that is, the human being, taken in his wholeness as biological and cultural being, is at the centre of the biosphere. The human being is considered as the central constituting element of bio-ecological processes and, thus, is seen as the eminently active and intentional actor of physical-biological phenomena occurring in the biosphere.

The innovative importance of this proposal led ecologist Valerio Giacomini – who was one of the first and most enthusiastic proponents of this programme in Italy – to speak of the advent of a Ptolemaic revolution in the world of the natural sciences (Giacomini, 1983).

As the first programmatic result of this change in perspective, the programme began with the intention of developing, as far as possible, integrated knowledge/interventions on the environment; that is, interventions which should be multidisciplinary right from the start and should become increasingly pluridisciplinary and, finally, interdisciplinary (Whyte, 1984).

The primary need for integration proposed by the programme is between the sciences of the physical-natural environment (biological and physical-chemical) and the sciences of man (human and social sciences: psychology, anthropology, sociology, etc.). This programmatic aim led, at the level of theoretical-methodological reflection, to the singling out of a new unit of analysis, different from that of the preceding international biological programme, and represented by the 'ecosystem' or 'ecological system', typical of the biological-naturalistic approach.

The new unit of analysis, selected as more appropriate for the new aims of the programme of promoting integration between different disciplinary fields, is no longer the bio-ecological system, but the human-use system (di Castri et al., 1981); it is different from the preceding unit of analysis because of the central role assigned to psychological-environmental phenomena alongside physical-biological ones.

Three primary dimensions are held to characterize every human-use system (ibid.):

(a) the spatial dimension;
(b) the temporal dimension;
(c) the environmental perception dimension.

The first two dimensions characterize the physical-biological aspects and relative forces of nature defining the 'abiotic' and 'biotic' aspects of the system; the third dimension specifically concerns the human component of the system and characterizes the human 'forces' or actions which concur to define in a psycho-social sense the physical-biological features of the system.

The term 'environmental perception' is used here in a very broad sense, tending to combine the modalities with which social psychology began to use the term 'perception', especially for identifying the complex of phenomena defined by 'social perception' (Asch, 1952; Allport, 1955; Heider, 1958), with the terminology used by behavioural geography for its environmental perception studies. Here, this term means all psycho-social phenomena regarding both cognitive and affective processes aimed at representing – perhaps it would be better to say than perceiving – the environment and its features at both the individual (psychological) and collective (socio-cultural) level. These processes will be discussed in more detail in Chapter 4.

Processes of environmental perception or representation are considered by the MAB programme as constitutive (in the preparatory sense and in the sense of continuous adjustment) of environmental human actions/ activities, that is, of human actions aimed at shaping the way each human-use system is produced and changed. Thus, consideration of the environmental perception dimension relative to a specific human-use system becomes central for comprehending the functioning of the system, above all with regard to the possibilities of predicting the evolution/change of the system over time. Since this perceptual dimension is considered the constitutive part of every human-use system characterizing the component of active human forces within the system, the MAB programme underlines the need to consider that this perceptual dimension is differentiated within the system in relation to the various possible human actors present.

In terms of the human forces which mould it, the features a specific human-use system presents in time can be considered the result of three main categories of actors, corresponding respectively to three main environmental roles.

1   The environmental decision-makers, institutionally in a position to decide – through approval, promulgation, application of norms, projects, plans – about the environmental system in question: local (town, provincial, regional), state or national authorities.

2   Environmental technicians/experts, having specialized environmental competencies (scientific-disciplinary or technical preparation): planners, architects, engineers, researchers and technicians of various environmental sciences, generally called in by decision-makers to provide know-how and appropriate proposals for directing the relative environmental decisions.

3   Users of the environments in question, who occupy or use the environment in a physical sense (live or work there) or in a normative sense (owners or rights to use): on the one hand, they have the need/ intention to use the properties/characteristics the environment in question presents as a means/resource for achieving/satisfying specific environmental needs (aims/needs of residential recreational, productive life, etc.); on the other hand, they constitute, or should represent, the referents/ addressees of the environmental decisions of the former, as well as the environmental analyses/appraisals formulated by the latter (environmental technicians/experts).

At any rate, it should be kept in mind that the modalities with which systems of environmental representation/perception are constructed in users, during the course of daily environmental practice and experience, are substantially different from those used in the specialist area. In the first case, they proceed with impressive/molar modalities entrusted to psychological processes characterized by tight integration between cognitive and affective processes: the term which most appropriately identifies this type of process is 'environmental perception/representation'. In the second case, the formulation of specialistic representations is, instead, entrusted to analytic-systematic procedures. Here the term 'environmental evaluation' can be better used to indicate the peculiarities of these processes of specialistic representation, thus distinguishing them from the users' perceptual/representative ones.

In this perspective, every initiative for examining and understanding the relations between these two systems of environmental perception/ representation may become of crucial importance, above all keeping in mind that the analyses/evaluations of experts have a preparatory and orientative role for environmental decision-makers, that is, for those who decide about the setting and management of the environment (Bonnes, 1987).

The position of each of the three principal environmental actors described above, as well as the relative modalities of intending and carrying out the environmental role, are increasingly problematic today both at the level of role systems (the reciprocal possibilities and modalities of interaction among the various actors) faced with the increasing complexity of our society and at the level of environmental problems emerging in local and planetary environmental systems. On the one hand, within each category of environmental actors, we find a further differentiation and variety of sub-actors in positions tending towards compartmentalization – separate with limited possibilities of reciprocal communication and oriented towards considering only limited and partial aspects of the environmental system in question – and possibly conflict, for example between various users who have different and incompatible aims, such as the aim of use/consumption or the conservation of specific environmental aspects/resources.

The problem of similarities/differences – or of congruencies/incongruencies – of environmental perceptions/representations relative to the environmental system in question, on the part of human actors performing differently within the system, becomes a fundamental problem for the dynamic of the system and for every prediction of stability/instability of the system over time.

At the same time, we find a tendency towards separation among the three main categories of environmental actors mentioned above; there may be frequent absence or general difficulty in reciprocal communication and comparison of respective environmental perceptions/representations, with relative difficulty/inability with regard to acquiring information/knowledge about the problematic aspects each category of actors encounters in carrying out its environmental role as well as the real possibility of cooperation/exchange among the various actors in view of processes of environmental decision/change.

Further, a particular gulf seems to exist between the first two categories of actors (environmental decision-makers and environmental experts), on the one hand, and the third category of actors (environmental users), on the other, especially with regard to sub-actors in the environmental role of 'inhabitant', that is, everyday users of the resources of the environmental system in question for achieving/satisfying life goals and daily well-being (such as residence, health, work, relaxation, etc.). The environmental actor in the latter category should really be considered not only as generating 'environmental needs' but also as bringing specific environmental competencies (or environmental perceptions/representations), acquired in pursuing these needs, derived from daily experience in the environmental system in question and aimed at orienting the relative environmental practices/activities or performances.

In this picture, it becomes crucial that the various processes of environmental analysis/planning/decision-making keep in mind the environmental perception/representation component of users/inhabitants regarding these same environments as a means of predicting the stabilization of these environmental processes over time.

On the other hand, the possibility of environmental decision-making processes taking into account the users' perceptual-representative dimension seems to depend only on the existence and promotion of means for allowing the bringing together of these various environmental actors. This bringing together should be understood both in a cognitive sense, based on the existence of communication and reciprocal information exchange between actors, and in the sense of 'action', with a cooperative/participatory meaning, destined to be effective at the level of modalities and contents of environmental decisions in play.

Thus, in both perspectives, the knowedge approach initiatives will be encouraged on the part of the first two environmental actors with regard to the above-mentioned users' component and all possible means will be promoted for making users more informed with greater participation in environmental processes and decisions (Bonnes and Bagnasco, 1988; Bagnasco and Bonnes, 1991).

The MAB programme has proceeded on the basis of this theoretical framework, singling out a series of specific topics, primarily corresponding to 'human-use ecosystems', which present particular problems from the point of view of their functioning and maintenance (for example, tropical and subtropical forests and insular ecosystems, mountain ecosystems, urban systems, etc.). Further, MAB encouraged the launching – on national and local levels, with the support of the net of international connections – of specific projects operating at the scientific level, with the hope of also being able to affect and direct management and decision-making levels.

Over the years, the impact of this programme at the national and international level has been considerable (di Castri et al., 1984). In Italy, Valerio Giacomini began to propose and apply the programme in various types of national human-use ecosystems, such as natural parks (Giacomini and Romani, 1982) and urban ecosystems, with particular reference to the MAB project for the city of Rome, which he started at the end of the 1970s (Giacomini, 1980, 1981; MAB Italia, 1981; Bonnes, 1984, 1991, 1993).

Overall, through the proposal of the human-use system and the central position assigned to the dimension of environmental perception, the MAB programme not only advances specific proposals regarding the modalities for confronting environmental problems, but is also interested in promoting the development of psychological-environmental research for considering these problems.

In fact, out of the fourteen initial topics for particular projects, the MAB programme included one specifically dealing with perception of environmental quality; in this regard, numerous contributions were made over the years at the international level (UNESCO-MAB, 1973; Craik and Zube, 1976; Whyte, 1977; Zube, 1980). The most recent approach is to encourage the development of this line of research within the other specific projects, in accordance with the more general aims of the programme.

This is also the direction we have taken recently in our studies on perception/representation of the urban environment (Bonnes, 1986, 1990, 1993). At the beginning of the 1980s, we were invited to collaborate on the MAB project for the city of Rome (Bonnes and Secchiaroli, 1981b). Work on the project has continued and has taken new directions (Bonnes, 1987, 1991; MAB Italia, 1990; Bagnasco and Bonnes, 1991), in spite of the unexpected death of its founder in 1981. Subsequently, this work will be presented in more detail (see pp. 180–5 and 192–7).

2
Environmental Psychology and Psychological Tradition

The spatio-physical environment in the psychological tradition and the 'ecological demand'

The increasing calls in the 1960s and 1970s for psychology to take a specific interest in the spatio-physical environment have to be considered against the tradition of studies developed until that point on the problem of the relationship between psychological processes and the environment.

On the one hand, psychology has been continuously concerned with the environment in general – an example is the long-standing controversy over the 'heredity/environment' problem – and, on the other hand, there has been an almost complete absence of specific and systematic attention to the spatio-physical characteristics of the environment where the considered behaviour occurs. According to several authors (for example, Canter, 1986), it is the tradition of laboratory research which has kept psychology far away from this interest, since the laboratory is, by definition, a 'non-environment'.

If we exclude the studies of the psychology of perception, which involve a very specific interest in the spatio-physical characteristics of the environment, up until the 1960s very few studies gave systematic attention to this aspect of the environment.

During those years a few isolated studies were carried out, often by groups tending to present themselves as dissidents with respect to the direction of orthodox psychology; the case of Barker et al.'s studies, which we will present in more detail later (see pp. 45–53), is a typical example of this. However, it must be noted that at the beginning of the 1960s, due to the influence of studies in adjacent fields such as ethology (Ardrey, 1966; Hinde, 1974), anthropology (Hall, 1959, 1966) and sociology (Goffman, 1959, 1963; Garfinkel, 1967), the emergence of specific interests was also noted in the field of psychology. This interest was directed in different ways towards considering the spatio-physical aspects of human behaviour; for example, ethological studies on the theme of territoriality (Ardrey, 1966; Lyman and Scott, 1967), Goffman's (1959, 1963, 1971), sociological studies with a dramaturgic approach and Hall's (1959, 1966) anthropological studies on proxemics pushed psychological research towards the study of the spatio-physical aspects of human behaviour, especially in terms of communication. In fact, studies in the area of non-verbal communication gained impetus from this type of interest and they are still thriving today. It must also be noted how these interests combined in present-day environmental psychology, particularly in the area of 'spatial behaviour' (dealt with in Chapter 4).

On the one hand (as pointed out in Chapter 3), the development of e.p. was primarily based on psychology's awareness of the lack of attention to the spatio-physical characteristics of the environment where behaviour occurs; on the other hand, this 'internal' awareness achieved by psychology was largely stimulated by the many emerging interests, external and adjacent to it, which seemed to 'force it' to act upon this shortcoming.

As soon as this awareness matured, the main problem for psychology became the individuation of adequate theoretical instruments for developing environmental-psychological research with not only external relevance (that is, for the non-psychological sectors which had made the specific requests) but also internal relevance for the psychological tradition.

Since we believe that this has always been, and still is, the most crucial problem in e.p., we feel it is important to pause and consider in detail the main theoretical traditions in psychological research that this 'new' interest in spatio-physical features of the environment has to face.

Overall, beyond the general or episodic view adopted by psychological research in considering the spatio-physical environment, these external requests primarily face two different theoretical traditions in trying to conceptualize the environment and its features in a specific way with respect to the psychological processes studied. On one hand is the tradition of the psychology of perception, which defines the environment mainly in physical-perceptual terms, and, on the other, the tradition of social psychology, characterized by a more molar viewpoint.

We will pause to consider each of these in detail, examining the main theoretical contributions which seem to have most directly faced the problem of the relationship between psychological processes and environmental characteristics, with reference – pre-eminently (in the case of psychology of perception) or concomitantly (in the case of social psychology) – to its physical characteristics. With regard to the tradition of the psychology of perception, we will consider several main theoretical contributions of the so-called 'New Look' schools of the United States, with particular reference to Egon Brunswik's probabilistic theory, James J. Gibson's ecological theory and the contributions of the transactional school of the Princeton group (Ames, Kilpatrick, Cantril and Ittelson). We will point out the specific modalities used by each of them to pose the problem of the relationship between psychological-perceptual processes and physical characteristics of the environment, providing points of departure for subsequent e.p.

For a discussion of the tradition of social psychology, we will pause first of all (as an obligatory step) at Kurt Lewin, emphasizing how his theoretical reflections are surprisingly up-to-date and pertinent for present-day e.p. Following Lewin, we will consider the contributions of two other major authors who followed the Lewinian tradition: Roger Barker, now recognized as one of the primary founding fathers of e.p., and Urie Bronfenbrenner, not directly linked to current environmental-psychological research even though we believe, along with other authors (for example, Stokols, 1978), that he provides several interesting theoretical insights.

Further, almost all of the authors we will discuss have the common tendency to use the term 'ecological' to support their theoretical proposals or to identify the characteristics of the proposed approach. We will see how the use of this term, coined in the area of biology, returns systematically in the works of these authors, providing a sort of common denominator. Brunswik's problem of 'ecological validity', Gibson's 'ecological theory' of perception, Lewin's 'psychological ecology', Barker's 'ecological psychology' and Bronfenbrenner's 'ecological' approach are all examples of this.

Beyond the various meanings and perspectives applied to the term 'ecological' by each author, the systematic return to it can be primarily considered as an indicator of a common concern in considering psychological phenomena as a result of the concurrence of both individual and environmental/situational factors, including the spatio-physical aspects.

The various uses of the term 'ecological' correspond to different modalities in translating this common 'environmental concern' into different specific theoretical proposals. In any case, this concern tends to unite a wide variety of authors and schools (beyond those examined here), and we will discover how many of the aims of the ecological concern have become part of the most recent e.p.

The spatio-physical environment in the tradition of the psychology of perception

From the Gestalt school to the 'New Look' schools

All of the psychology of perception revolves around the problem of the relationship, or the correspondence, between psychological processes (with particular reference to perceptual/cognitive ones) and characteristics of the physical environment, that is, what Floyd Allport (1955) defined as the 'inside–outside problem'.

The problematic relationship between these two factors emerged particularly in the United States in the studies of the so-called 'New Look' schools on perception. This term 'New Look' was used in particular because of the common aim of these schools to propose a different modality for considering the perceptual phenomenon in comparison to the dominant perspective of the European school of psychology of perception, represented by Gestalt psychology (Köhler, 1929, 1940; Koffka, 1935; Wertheimer, 1945).

At the end of the 1940s, the 'New Look' studies in the United States developed both in response and in opposition to the European Gestalt school; they essentially proposed an inversion in perspective, in functionalist terms, in the study of perception, which until then had been dominated by the phenomenological viewpoint of the Gestaltists.

The main problem of the perceptual phenomenon, and in particular of the 'inside–outside correspondence', tended to be ignored by the Gestaltists through the primacy assigned to the 'phenomenic' world, that is, the perceived world, with respect to the physical-objective one: on the basis of the theory of 'isomorphism', a character of necessity is implicitly affirmed for every perceptual event.

Koffka (1924) stated that the physical world exists for the organism in the form of his own environment, which is his 'phenomenic world', although for the organism that environment is a perfectly real environment.

Due to the phenomenological orientation of the Gestalt school, the problem was not so much that of understanding the correspondence between characteristics of the physical environment and perceptual experience, as it was that of explaining why perceptual experience is presented according to the observed modalities. The physical environment is only what appears through perceptual experience; any question about the possibility of greater or lesser correspondence between these two aspects is completely ignored by the phenomenological orientation. Reality is essentially 'what appears'; outside of this 'perceptual world' and its laws it is irrelevant to ask ourselves about the characteristics of the 'real world'.

Koffka (1935) made the distinction between 'geographical environment', represented by the environment existing in reality, and 'behavioral environments', represented by the environment experienced by the person; he then emphasizes, that only the behavioural environment has to be considered relevant for behaviour and it is the only reference system which enables us to describe behaviour.

Actually, Koffka's major preoccupation was to reaffirm the primacy of the 'phenomenic environment' – defined as behavioural in opposition to the physical-geographical one – for examining and explaining individual behaviour, rather than proposing the problematic correspondence between the two, that is, between geographical environment and behavioural environment.

For the Gestaltists, the latter problem seems hardly relevant since they believe that the geographical environment tends normally to become part of the individual's experienced behavioural environment. The theory of isomorphism, which the Gestaltists place at the root of the perceptual phenomenon, denies any hypothesis of individuals' idiosyncratic interpretations of the perceptual experience. This theory affirms the existence in all individuals of innate neurological mechanisms which, in some way, tend to ensure the correspondence between the two types of environments.

The cultural climate of the United States in the 1940s, when the 'New Look' studies developed, was certainly not propitious for sharing the Gestalt phenomenological dictates, even though it was undoubtedly influenced by this school. At that time in the United States, the behaviourist school was still in full triumph, characterized by a clear 'environmentalism', based on the assumption of a world composed of objective 'stimuli'; for this school, every possibility of explaining observed behaviour, or, better, individual responses to the environment, had to be traced back to these stimuli.

At the same time, both the paradigm of adaptation dominating psychological investigation and the influence of pragmatic philosophy moved the investigation of the perceptual phenomenon towards a theoretical perspective which assumes the individual as an active subject in the environment, not only in a cognitive sense but primarily at the level of activity and actions. In this perspective, the person is viewed as continuously involved in reconciling his/her own needs and goals with environmental requests and limits.

In the cultural climate of the 1940s, the studies on perception in the United States in response to the success of the Gestalt school, on the one hand, showed a specific interest in considering the physical-objective characteristics of the environment in the study of perceptual phenomena; on the other, they stressed the active role (in the sense of behaviour oriented by goals and needs) of the subject in the environment. Thus, we can affirm that through the 'New Look' schools in the United States both the physical-objective environment (and, thus, the spatio-physical one) and the activities and actions of the subject in the environment recover their full dignity as objects of investigation; this had been essentially negated by the Gestalt school.

It can be said that with the 'New Look', the perceptual phenomenon was released from the dynamic of 'forms', to which the Gestalt school had relegated it, to be anchored instead to the goals and needs of the subject of perception (Postman et al., 1948). With the 'New Look' schools, the perceptual 'inside–outside' problem acquires new problematic perspectives, particularly with regard to the modalities for understanding the individual–environment relationship.

It will be shown how the various main theoretical positions examined in the following pages tend to consider the relationship between these two elements differently, aiming alternatively at assigning them a different reciprocal pre-eminence. In this regard, Brunswik's 'lens model' theory is the most direct counter-proposal to the Gestalt isomorphic theory and the most balanced theory for restoring equal dignity to the physical-environmental and subjective factors in the perceptual process. In order to stress these aims, this theory – for the sake of contrast – defined the perceptual process as 'raziomorphic' rather than 'isomorphic'; later this will be discussed in more detail. It will also be shown how the other two perceptual schools discussed represent different tendencies to stress, on the one hand, the role of physical-environmental factors (in the case of James J. Gibson's ecological theory) and, on the other, the role of subjective/ individual factors (in the case of the transactional school).

Brunswik's probabilistic theory: the 'lens model'

Egon Brunswik (1947, 1957) can be considered the first psychologist in the United States to specifically face the problem of the correspondence between perceived reality and characteristics of the environment; he focused on this problem, defined by him as the 'ecological validity' of perceptual cues and 'functional validity' of the entire perceptual process, and he affirmed the probabilistic nature of the perceptual experience itself. Brunswik, influenced by both the European school on perception (Helmholtz, 1866), the Gestalt school and the climate of pragmatism in the United States, tends to redefine in functionalist terms many of the questions already raised by the European school; in this context, he outlined the 'lens model' of the perceptual process (Figure 2.1). Brunswik's (1957, p. 6) first concern is to return the attention of psychology in general and perception in particular to the characteristics of the environment:

> Both historically and systematically psychology has forgotten that it is a science of organism–environment relationship, and has become a science of the organism [. . .]. This preoccupation of the psychologist with the organism at the expense of the environment is somewhat reminiscent of the position taken by those inflatedly masculine medieval theologians who granted a soul to men but denied it to women; our point, then, is to restore or establish the proper equality or standards in the treatment of organism and environment – that is, the equality of subject and situation (or object) in which equal justice is done to the inherent characteristics of the organism and of the environment.

Brunswik's call to dedicate attention to the characteristics of the environment is precise with regard to the psychology of perception; he defines this as the need to consider the physical-objective characteristics of the environment, which he calls 'ecological environment': 'With environment we mean the measurable characteristics of the objective surroundings of the organism rather than the psychological environment of life space, in the sense in which Lewin has used this term. We may specify the sum total of these objective surroundings as the "ecology" of an individual or species' (1957, p. 6).

He further specifies: 'If there is anything that still ails psychology in general and the psychology of cognition specifically, it is the neglect of investigation of environmental or ecological texture, in favor of that of the texture of the organismic structures and processes' (ibid.).

It can be seen how this proposal to 'recover' the environment and its physical characteristics in the tradition of the study of perception was in opposition to the phenomenological Gestalt tradition (in this case Brunswik cites Lewin as a fellow of the phenomenological orientation). And, still in controversy with the Gestalt isomorphic theory of perceptual functioning, Brunswik proposed the lens model and the probabilistic theory of the perceptual process, which, for the sake of contrast, he defined as 'raziomorphic'.

According to the lens model, perceptual experience escapes from phenomenological immediacy, where it exclusively relies on the principles of the dynamic of form (Gestalt), to become, instead, the result of a process of 'probabilistic learning', based on treatment of the cues provided by the environment. Here we must note another innovative aspect of Brunswik's contribution to the psychology of perception, which has remained as the foundation of subsequent cognitive psychology: the abandonment of the concept of stimulus with regard to environmental data in favour of that of environmental cues. With Brunswik, the perceptual process began to be considered as a process of utilization of cues or information coming from the environment.

Brunswik's proposal is aimed not only at bringing the role of the physical-objective environment back to the fore, under the form of 'ecological texture', in the perceptual process, but also at restoring to the individual the active and central role within that process, which the Gestalt school had completely delegated to form. By means of the lens model of the perceptual process, both aspects were affirmed, further, the non-immediate, processing nature of perception was shown, relying on 'probabilistic' judgements continuously formulated by the subject concerning the ecological characteristics of the environment in view of the perceptual achievement, that is, viewed as a problem of 'functional validity' of the final response with respect to the 'distal' focus.

According to the lens model (Figure 2.1), the perceptual process is an arch of achievement, including a series of problematic correspondences which go from the environment – where the distal variables are found – to perception, constituted by the central response variables. The first portion of the arch, defined as the 'ecological' portion, is characterized by a divergent type of process regarding the so-called 'intra-ecological' correspondences, in particular the correspondence between 'distal variables' and 'proximal variables'. The second portion, defined as the 'organismic' portion, is instead characterized by a convergent type of process regarding the so-called 'intra-organismic' correspondences, in particular the correspondence between 'peripheral' and 'central' processes; this regards the phase of cue utilization, relying on probabilistic judgements or hypotheses. The other problematic correspondence between proximal variables and peripheral processes is found between these two portions of the perceptual arch.

In this model, where the subject is seen as continuously involved in probabilistic judgements or hypotheses about these problematic correspondences, the problem Brunswik defines as the 'ecological validity' of environmental cues becomes particularly crucial, that is, the problem of the correspondence between 'distal' variables, concerning the physical characteristics of the environment, and 'proximal' variables, concerning

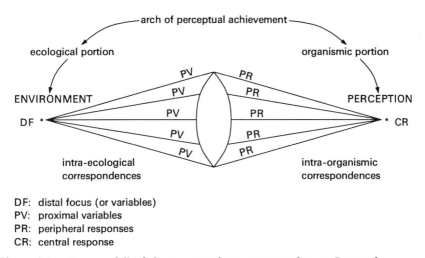

Figure 2.1 *'Lens model' of the perceptual process according to Brunswik*

the modality with which the physical characteristics of the environment are presented as sensory input.

According to Brunswik (1957, p. 7):

> Both thing-perception and social perception involve cognitive attainment of 'distal' variables that are to a certain extent independently variable of the corresponding 'proximal' or sensory input. The measure size of a physical body and the tested intelligence of a person are examples of distal variables, while the size of the retinal impact and the geometric relations in the face or photograph of the person whose intelligence is to be intuitively appraised are examples of relatively proximal variables.

Since environmental messages vary in terms of their 'ecological validity', that is, messages can provide more or less accurate representations of the environment, 'we will have to treat cognition as based on equivocal rather than univocal sign-significant relations, as [. . .] based on insufficient evidence' (ibid., p. 16) and, thus, 'our treatment of the cognitive problem must be probabilistic' (ibid., p. 12).

The individual, faced with the ambiguities and inconsistencies of sensory cues he/she receives from the environment, must construct a repertoire of probabilistic judgements about it, taking on the task of sampling environmental cues originating from the variety of existing environmental conditions; the impossibility of sampling all possible environments necessarily leads to the formation of non-absolute probabilistic judgements. The individual then tends to verify the accuracy of the probabilistic judgement by experiencing its functional consequences through actions in the environment.

Thus, by means of this model, both the importance of the 'ecological environment', considered as physical-objective reality outside the individual, and the active role of the subject, continuously involved in the perceptual process, are affirmed. This last aspect is assumed for the individual not only at the cognitive level (by means of probabilistic judgements) but also through action. Finally, the control of the perceptual achievement or the 'ecological validity' of the probabilistic judgements relies on individual action in the environment.

Gibson's ecological theory

According to James J. Gibson (1950, 1960, 1966, 1979) and his ecological theory of perception, the perceptual phenomenon should be considered as the direct result of 'ecological characteristics' of environmental stimuli. For Gibson as well as Brunswik, a problem defined as ecological exists in the perceptual phenomenon in the correspondence between stimuli and 'natural sources', that is, physical characteristics of the environment. Gibson (1960) also begins with a critical revision of the concept of stimulus as generally used by experimental psychology and, especially, by behaviouristic psychology at that time; he points out that use of this concept is basically extraneous to the psychological tradition. In particular, he criticizes the concept of 'empty stimulus', that is, 'meaningless', at the basis of a great deal of psychological research at that time:

> This theory of the meaningless stimulus has been an accepted doctrine for a long, long time in the study of the senses. It leads to the notion of the sense datum – the bare sensation, or raw, crude sensory impression – and then to the persistent problem of how animals and men can be supposed to perceive objects, places, events, and one other. (Gibson, 1960, p. 699)

Soon after, he also observes that 'students of behavior, however, without questioning the doctrine of the empty stimulus, often act as if they did not believe it [. . .]. Stimuli must specify something beyond them, and they cannot be empty of meaning.' In this regard, he proposes the concept of 'informative stimulus': 'the stimulus provides information for the perceiver [. . .]. The question is to what extent does the stimulus specify its source, and how does it do so?' (ibid.).

According to Gibson, 'The problem of the connection between stimuli and their natural sources has not been taken seriously by psychologists' (ibid.), and the 'unanswered question is: do stimuli carry information about their sources in the world, and how do they specify them?' (ibid., p. 700). 'We need to know the laws of stimulus information' (ibid., p. 702). In this regard, he proposes considering stimuli not in a 'molecular' but in a 'molar' sense: the stimuli defined by him as molar stimuli – analogous to what the Gestalt school had proposed in relation to the molar experience – are represented by 'what an organism is responding to, and not by what excites all the little receptors' (ibid., p. 700). In this sense, for Gibson, perception is a holistic phenomenon since it is turned towards the perception of meanings and not of simple stimuli or geometric configurations/forms, as in the case of visual perception.

In this regard, Gibson formulates an explicit criticism, which has been taken up by present-day environmental psychology (Ittelson, 1973b), concerning the entire previous tradition of experimental studies on perception; he defines it − with particular reference to visual perception − as exclusively aimed towards considering what he calls 'snapshot vision':

> Vision is studied by first requiring the subject to fixate a point and then exposing momentarily a stimulus or a pattern of stimuli around the fixation point [. . .]. The investigation assumes that each fixation of the eye is analogous to an exposure of the film in a camera, so that what the brain gets is something like a sequence of snapshots. (Gibson, 1979, p. 1)

In opposition to this approach, he proposes the one he defines as ecological since it is concerned with what he calls 'ambient vision', characterized by considering how it occurs naturally:

> We need to see all the way around at a given point of observation and to take different points of observation [. . .]. The single, frozen field of view provides only impoverished information about the world. The visual system did not evolve for this. The evidence suggests that visual awareness is in fact panoramic and does in fact persist during long acts of locomotion. (ibid., p. 2)

He adds:

> Moving from place to place is supposed to be 'physical' whereas perceiving is supposed to be 'mental', but this dichotomy is misleading. Locomotion is guided by visual perception. Not only does it depend on perception but perception depends on locomotion inasmuch as a moving point of observation is necessary for any adequate acquaintance with the environment. So we must perceive in order to move, but we must also move in order to perceive. (ibid., p. 223)

Gibson continues by proposing 'a radically new way of thinking about perception' (ibid., p. 2), primarily supported by the systematic analysis of the environment and its informative characteristics in view of the relative perceptual results.

> First of all, it is necessary to describe the environment: what has to be perceived must, in fact, be stipulated before beginning to speak about perception.

However, this strongly environmentalist position tends to keep its distance from 'physicalistic' reductionism, thanks to the approach defined as ecological: 'This is not the world of physics but the world at the ecological level' (ibid.); 'the total environment is too vast to describe even for an ecologist, and we must select those aspects of it which are perceptible by animals, which we are' (ibid., p. 36).

> I have been assuming that ecological reality (as distinguished from physical reality) consists of substances, the medium, the surfaces that separate them, and the varieties of surface layout. (Gibson, 1978, p. 416)

> The process of perception must be described. However, this does not consist in the processing of sensory input, but in extracting the invariants from the flow of stimuli. (Gibson, 1979, p. 2)

In this sense, Gibson considers perception as a direct and immediate phenomenon, primarily carried out by the informative capacities − in the molar sense – of environmental stimuli. Persons perceive significant patterns of environmental stimuli rather than separate points of stimuli. He holds that how much people need to perceive of environmental information is already contained in the pattern of stimulation coming from the environment. The meaning is directly perceived in the environmental stimuli and does not require the intervention of processes of reconstruction and interpretation by the perceiver.

For Gibson, perception consists in 'picking up the information available in the environment': 'Substances, media, surfaces, layouts and events are what there is to perceive, that is, known directly. Perceiving is extracting the information in ambient light, sound, odor and mechanical contact' (Gibson, 1978, p. 416).

In this sense, Gibson puts himself in a clearly critical position with regard to more mentalistic, constructivist approaches to perceptual phenomena.

> The doctrine that we could not perceive the world around us unless we already had the concept of space is nonsense. It is quite the other way around: we could not conceive of empty space unless we could see the ground under our feet and the sky above. Space is a myth, a ghost, a fiction for geometers. (Gibson, 1979, p 3)

This position of strong environmental realism proposed by Gibson is mitigated by the evolutionary perspective of the ecological approach, which affirms the existing correspondence between organism and environment established through the process of phylogenetic adaptation of every species to its environment, including the perceptual one.

Thus, perception is viewed as an adaptive function, in the sense that the external world must provide information capable of guiding the relative adaptive behaviours in a functional way. The theory emphasizes the capacity for active exploration of the environment by the individual, who in perceiving is turned towards gathering the 'properties of functional invariance' of environmental objects.

Therefore, meanings are directly perceived from the environment in relation to the properties of functional invariance which the objects themselves present: the concept of 'affordances' allows Gibson to specify what is at the same time a peculiarity of environmental objects and a correspondence between them and the expectations/hypotheses of individuals who behave in relation to those objects and perceive. Gibson (1979, p. 127) explains this concept:

> The *affordances* of the environment are what it *offers* the animal, what it *provides* or *furnishes*, either for good or ill. The verb *to afford* is found in the dictionary, but the noun affordance is not. I have made it up. I mean by it something that refers to both the environment and the animal in a way that no existing term does. It implies the complementarity of the animal and the environment.

> Affordances are properties of things *taken with reference to an observer* but not properties of the *experiences of the observer*. They are not subjective values. (ibid., p. 137)

He provides the following example:

> If a terrestrial surface is nearly horizontal (instead of slanted), nearly flat (instead of convex or concave), and sufficiently extended (relative to the size of the animal) and if its substance is rigid (relative to the weight of the animal), then the surface *affords support*. It is a surface of support, and we call it a substratum, ground or floor. It is stand-on-able and run-over-able. It is not sink-into-able like a surface of water or a swamp, that is, not for heavy terrestrial animals. Support for water bugs is different. [. . .] Terrestrial surfaces, of course, are also climb-on-able or fall-off-able or get-under-neath-able or bump-into-able relative to the animal. Different layouts afford different behaviors for different animals, and different mechanical encounters. (ibid., p. 128)

Further, 'The *affordances* of the environment are permanent, although they do refer to animals, and are species-specific' (Gibson, 1972, p. 410). And again:

> The *affordances* of something are assumed *not* to change as the need of the observer changes. The edibility of a substance for an animal does not depend on the hunger of the animal. The walk-on-ability of a surface exists whether or not the animal walks on it (although it is linked to the locomotor capacities of that species of animal, its action system). The positive affordance of an object can be perceived whether or not the observer needs to take advantage of it. It offers what it does because it is what it is. (ibid., p. 409)

Researchers in the Gibsonian school cite numerous experiments in support of the immediate nature of direct perception, depending on the ecological characteristics of environmental information; among these experiments is the famous one conducted by Elinor Gibson et al. on the 'visual cliff' phenomenon in the child (Gibson and Walk, 1960). The visual cliff consists of a flat surface drawn to give the illusion of the presence of a sudden drop-off starting from what seems to be the edge of the surface. Researchers have found that animals that can walk from birth, for example kid goats, avoid the edge right from the first days of life; however, a child does not manifest the same type of fear before the age of walking on all fours. Thus, these results provide evidence in favour of the ecological theory of perception, demonstrating the existence in both animals and man of immediate perceptual ability – that is, not entrusted to experience and, thus, learning – based on repertoires of responses predisposed from early infancy in relation to the environmental species-specific necessities of the organism. In the child, as well as in the kid goat, the ability to perceive information about the visual cliff appears together with the acquisition of physical mobility in the environment.

The Gibsonian ecological approach to perception is still a much practised theoretical direction in perceptual studies. For example, there exists a specific scientific association (the International Society for Ecological Psychology) which holds conferences biennially; there are also entire series of books dedicated to the topic, such as *Resources for Ecological Psychology*, edited by Shaw, Mace and Turvey (Reed and Jones 1982).

Furthermore, recent cognitive psychology has shown specific interest in attempting to integrate the Gibsonian ecological approach into the cognitive viewpoint, as advanced by Ulric Neisser (1987, 1990). His proposal is primarily based on the importance of distinguishing between perceptual-visual processes (seeing) and perceptual-cognitive processes (thinking, that is, categorizing), consequently assuming different psychological modalities of functioning for the two types of processes, represented in the first case by 'direct perceptions' and in the second by 'theory-dependent categorizations' (Neisser, 1987, p. 9). He distinguishes 'between perception and categorization. The former is based on the direct pickup of objectively existing information, while the latter goes beyond that information on the basis of beliefs about the world. [. . .] Seeing is one thing, thinking another' (ibid., p. 4).

According to Neisser, in this way it is possible to uphold that the first case, that is, perceiving considered as seeing, is above all the direct result of the ecological characteristics (in the Gibsonian sense) of the environment, and, thus, of the characteristics of the available environmental information; however, the second case, that is, thinking/ categorizing, relies on typical inferential processes of cognitive functioning and is anchored to the socio-cultural characteristics of the context.

Neisser's more recent positions are interesting because for a long time, especially after the publication of *Cognition and Reality* (Neisser, 1976), he was considered one of the most authoritative exponents of the constructivist approach to cognitive phenomena, which for many reasons is antithetical to the Gibsonian position of 'ecological realism'. The attempt to integrate the two perspectives, which he most recently proposed, is in fact resolved by a reaffirmation of their opposition; however, this is particularly interesting because it is a sign of the fascination and vitality of the Gibsonian proposal, even when compared to theoretical traditions basically extraneous to it. Even recent e.p. shows specific interest in the Gibsonian ecological school, attempting to propose and reformulate its concepts (Heft, 1981, 1988; Landweher, 1988) within the field.

Of particular interest for e.p., especially for the area interested in dialogue with the architectural side, is the physical realism proposed by the Gibsonian perspective. In particular, following this approach it becomes possible to specify and differentiate between the informative characteristics of the various environmental settings; an example of this is the systematic examination of 'textures' of surfaces, which Gibson himself is involved in.

However, many difficulties remain with regard to the complete assumption of the Gibsonian ecological model within e.p. due to the modalities this ecological approach considers perception.

On the one hand, the Gibsonian approach to the perceptual environment seems to agree with many of the assumptions of e.p.: first of all, the attempt to study psychological phenomena dealing with the physical features of the environment by considering as much as possible the modalities with which these phenomena occur naturally, that is, according to the modalities of the everyday context.

On the other hand, the proposed physical-biological immediacy in treating the perceptual phenomenon tends to preclude the extension of the ecological approach to the understanding of more complex environmental-psychological processes, that is, when not only immediate perceptions are implicated – and above all sensory receptors – but also the most complex cognitive and affective functions. Not by chance, these have been made central to the perceptual phenomenon (Postman et al., 1948) in many 'New Look' studies. In particular for this perspective, the assumption of a psycho-social viewpoint seems difficult; it means taking into specific consideration the social and historical-cultural aspects of the environment, where both the physical-perceptual and the individual are placed.

In this regard, we can share what Landweher (1988) observes; according to him, the environment taken into consideration by the Gibsonians is essentially 'what this environment is for humans as an animal species, not what it might be to them as a cultural society' (ibid., p. 33).

The transactional school

The transactional school of perception began in the mid-1940s with Adalbert Ames's first experiments; it continued in subsequent years with the work of other main representatives of the group at Princeton University: Hadley Cantril, Franklin Kilpatrick and William Ittelson.

These researchers took up the term 'transaction', initially adopted by Dewey and Bentley during their long correspondence and joint work *Knowing and Known* (1949), to indicate a particular modality for understanding the relationship between subject and object of perception. Attention is directed to the process of exchange existing between these two elements rather than to their specific features. The term 'transaction' adopted by 'the Princetonians' – as Brunswik (1957) defines them – was aimed at pointing out that the perceiver and reality are part of the same process. There is no simple reciprocal modification or interdependence between these two terms, to the point where it is possible to consider them separately; they are both aspects of the same transaction, which involves them in a unique process defined as transactive.

The transactionalists start with a criticism of the 'objectivist' viewpoint of perception, which, as Kilpatrick (1961) observes, 'reasoned from object to organism'; 'stimuli or stimulus patterns are treated as though they exist apart from the perceiving organism. Mechanical or interactional relationships between the organism and the "objectively defined" environment are sought' (ibid., p. 2).

Kilpatrick illustrates how the transactional school poses the problem of perception, with particular reference to visual perception:

> . . . in visual perception one is faced with the fact that any given visual stimulus-pattern can be produced by an infinity of different external conditions, and this

holds true for both monocular and binocular vision. But we never see an infinity of configurations; we see just one. This means, of course, that perception cannot be 'due to' the physiological stimulus pattern; some physiological stimulus probably is necessary, but it is not sufficient. There must be, in addition, some basis for the organism's 'choosing' one from among the infinity of external conditions to which the pattern might be related. Thus, any notion concerning a unique correspondence between percept and object must be abandoned, and a discovery of the factors involved in the 'choosing' activity of the organism becomes the key problem in perceptual theory. (ibid., p. 3)

In contrast with every objectivist position that starts from the consideration of the reality of the environmental stimulus as object of perception, the transactionalists propose a complete inversion of perspective which, in some ways, recalls the phenomenological-Gestaltist one and which starts from a consideration of the modalities of the perceiver for reaching the perceptual result; thus, physical reality is considered as result and not as cause of perception, or, in Ittelson's words, 'the environment we know is the product, not the cause of perception' (Ittelson et al., 1974, p. 105).

Unlike the Gestalt school, which singles out the principal regulator of this creative process as form, transactionalism – true to its pragmatical matrix – assigns the explicative principle of every perceptual result to the individual's behaviour in the environment, that is, to his/her activity oriented by goals. As Kilpatrick (1961, p. 4) observes,

. . . the search for absolute objectivity is a vain one. Apparently, the correspondence between percept and object is never absolute. Instead, perception is of functional probabilities, of constructs which emerge from the consequences of past action and serve as directives for furthering the purposes of the organism through action [. . .]. Perception is that phase of the total process which is an implicit awareness of the probable consequences of purposive action with respect to some object. Man never can know more of the external world than those aspects which are directly relevant to the carrying out of his purposes.

In this sense, the transactional school, although focusing on the perceptual phenomenon, tends to consider the perceptual problem as part of the more general problem of the relationship of the individual with reality, that is, as 'part of that total process which links the individual to the surrounding world'. Kilpatrick (1961, p. 4) affirms:

By perception, then, is meant that part of the transactional process which is an implicit awareness of the probable significance for action of present impingements from the environment, based on assumptions related to the same or similar impingements from the environment [. . .]. Assumptions function as probabilities which are built up by action, checked by action, and modified by action as the consequences of these actions are registered in relation to purposes. Taken altogether, our assumptions form our 'assumptive world' which we bring to every occasion and on which our perceptions are based; therefore, the only world we know is determined by our assumptions.

As support for their theoretical position, the transactionalists present a large number of experimental studies, or 'demonstrations', as they call them – designed *ad hoc* and generally based on phenomena of perceptual illusion since they are aimed at showing the active and constructive role of the individual in the perceptual process. It was Dewey who cited them as proof of the transactional nature of the perceptual phenomenon, based on his direct knowledge of Ames's first demonstrations (Ratner et al., 1964, p. 164).

Ames's first experiments involved the observation of perceptual functioning in subjects wearing special distorting aniseiconical eyeglasses. It was found that in these cases not all objects were perceived according to the distortion predicted by the principles of optical physiology; in particular, several distortions did not appear immediately but developed gradually through continuous observation.

For Ames, this indicates that the perceiver is not a passive participant, but is actively involved in the perceptual process in the formulation of the final percept. All the experiments of the transactionalists are designed to make the role of the perceiver particularly prominent (Ames, 1955). Every experiment presents a configuration of stimulation of the retina which appears to be created by the external configuration but which in reality is the result of another and unusual configuration of the object of perception. It is not by chance that Brunswik (1957) defines these experiments as 'experiments with negative ecological validity'.

One of the most famous experiments created by Ames involves the use of a distorted room. The walls of the room have trapezoid-shaped walls of varying dimensions; when the room is seen from a specific vantage point, it seems to have a normal rectangular shape. Kilpatrick (1954) used the distorted room for an experiment in which subjects, looking from that vantage point, had to perform activities such as throwing balls and touching parts of the room with a stick. In this way, he was able to demonstrate that the subjects, after a bit of practice, not only actually saw the room as distorted but, more importantly, saw a similar rectangular room as distorted and not rectangular. The study shows the crucial role of the subject's action in the environment to orient the perceived result; further, it was shown how, through experience based on action in the environment, the perceiver begins to doubt the validity of the perceptual cues provided by simple visual investigation.

Along these lines, Ames (1960, p. 3) is able to affirm that 'it is more likely to consider past experience as the cause of the visual impression rather than the object, which actually serves as catalyst for the percept'. In this sense, even though the transactionalist school primarily relies on studies of the perceptual process, it aims at presenting itself with implications that go beyond the simple perceptual phenomenon, that is, as a real psychological school with its own specific proposal on how to look not only at the perceptual process but also at human beings in general and at their relationship with reality.

The concept of environment is considered in a broad sense which goes beyond the consideration of simple physical-perceptual characteristics. For example, Cantril (1950, p. 59) explains the transactionalist position as follows:

> Each transaction of living involves numerous capacities and aspects of man's nature which operate together. Each occasion of life can occur only through an environment; is imbued with some purpose; requires action of some kind, and the registration of the consequences of action. Every action is based upon some awareness or perception, which in turn is determined by the assumptions brought to the occasion. All of these processes are interdependent. No one process could function without the others.

Overall, the modalities of the transactional school for looking at the relationship of the individual with the physical-perceptual environment and with the environment in general are very close to those of Lewinian social psychology. Nor does it seem chance that Dewey and Bentley, in choosing the term 'transactional', also considered the term 'field', which was adopted by Lewinian psychology at the same time (Ratner et al., 1964, p. 167).

Actually, the definitions of the transactional school for the concept of transaction and occasion seem very close to those of Lewinian psychology for the concept of 'psychological field'; on the other hand, the transactional view seemed destined from the beginning to find one of its areas of greatest involvement and development in American social psychology. The various studies of 'social perception' which developed in the 1950s and 1960s seem like examples of the intersection between these two areas of psychological research: we find, on the one hand, the direction developed by Heider (1958) on the subject of 'naïve psychology' and person perception, and, on the other, the intercultural approach to problems of perceptual illusions. Examples of the latter are the studies conducted by Allport and Pettigrew (1957), in more or less 'angular' cultures, on the perceptual distortion of a trapezoidal window, one of the most famous demonstrations of the transactional school. They discovered how this illusion, in which a rotating trapezoid seems to oscillate back and forth, is found less in individuals from the Zulu culture, where squares and rectangles do not exist and round forms prevail.

An analogous example can be found in Segall et al.'s (1966) experiments on the perceptual illusion of Müller and Lyer's darts; the illusion is more or less accentuated depending on whether the subjects belong to more or less angular cultures, that is, based on physical environments primarily constructed with squared corners.

All of these types of research are oriented towards demonstrating the effect of previous perceptual experience on the individual perceptual result, in these cases determined by the characteristics of the specific cultural context. In this way both the constructive nature of the perceptual process and the 'plastic' nature of individual perception on the basis of previous experience in the environment are emphasized.

Considering these theoretical transactional positions, it is not surprising that William Ittelson, the important representative of the transactional group, was among the first to meet requests in the 1960s from the architectural side to form with Proshansky the first environmental psychology group in the United States.

From many points of view, the transactional positions seem particularly adequate for providing useful conceptual instruments for psychologists interested in the problems of the individual–spatio-physical environment relationship. And it is not surprising that the first introductory volumes in the new field, primarily the work of the initial group of the City University of New York, tend to propose – especially through Ittelson – the transactional perspective for conceptualizing the individual–environment relationship.

In this case, the theoretical proposal tends mainly to focus on the problem of 'environmental perception', again thanks to Ittelson (1973b); on this occasion, with the attempt to provide adequate theoretical tools for the new field, he makes a basic contribution by outlining a very critical revision of the studies of psychology of perception, defined as mere perception of objects and not of the environment.

However, it seems important to observe that if the transactional orientation prepares the way for many subsequent psycho-social and psycho-environmental studies, the strictly pragmatic matrix, on the one hand, and the perceptual-individual one, on the other, tend, especially in the beginning, to orient environmental-psychological research towards the individualistic psycho-social perspective rather than the social one. In this sense, we are taking on the distinction proposed primarily by European social psychology in order to oppose these two orientations (Doise, 1976; Tajfel, 1984; Moscovici, 1984b).

The authors of the transactional school propose the following modalities for looking at the perceptual phenomenon:

> Each man's perceptions are therefore his own, unique and personal. (Kilpatrick, 1961, p. 4)

> Perception is the process by which a particular person, from his particular behavioral center, attributes significance to his immediate environmental situation. (Ittelson et al., 1974, p. 105)

The individual–environment relationship which figures in this theoretical perspective, although very much oriented in the holistic and constructivist sense of social psychology, tends to have primarily individualistic characteristics, centred on determining individual idiosyncracies rather than on socio-cultural intersubjectivity; on the contrary, the latter is often at the core of social psychology today, particularly in Europe.

It has been the task of more recent e.p., primarily in the work of Irwin Altman and Daniel Stokols (Stokols and Altman, 1987), to position the transactional orientation within a specifically psycho-social perspective; this was accomplished by means of a direct link with the founding fathers, Dewey and Bentley, rather than by passing through the mediation of the transactional school of perception (Altman and Rogoff, 1987).

As specifically discussed on pp. 152–61, the term 'transactional' has been taken up again, proposing what Altman defines as 'the transactional view of reality' to indicate a theoretical orientation more clearly characterized in the psycho-social direction, as we will point out later (see Chapter 5 below).

The abandonment of the concept of environment considered exclusively as spatio-physical environment in favour of socio-physical environment (Stokols, 1978), the direct reference to the holistic-systemic approach of Barker's ecological psychology originating with Lewin (Stokols, 1987), and the substitution of the concept of 'place' for 'behaviour setting' (Stokols, 1981; Altman and Rogoff, 1987) seem to be the principal factors characterizing the recent transactional orientation of e.p. in a psycho-social sense; more will be said about this in Chapter 4 and 5.

The spatio-physical environment in the tradition of social psychology

Kurt Lewin and psychological ecology

Field theory and psychological ecology Kurt Lewin (1890–1947) was initially trained in Europe in the phenomenological orientation of the Gestalt school; he then moved to the United States, where he became involved in the pragmatistic climate. Lewin still remains a fundamental reference point for every psychology which attempts to approach the problem of the relationship between psychological processes and environmental characteristics in a 'total' way, not in a general or in a solely spatio-physical way. The famous equation of Lewinian theory, $B = f (P \times E)$, foregrounds the environment (E) as determining behaviour (B), with exact equivalent importance of the factor always implicitly favoured by the psychological tradition, represented by the person (P).

The emphasis of Lewinian theory on the environmental factor does not remain at the level of simple affirmation of a principle, but, with the support of 'field theory', provides the conceptual tools for a non-generic but systematic consideration of environmental factors, including the spatio-physical aspects of the environment.

Field theory, defined by Lewin (1951, p. 45) primarily as 'a method of analyzing causal relations and of building scientific constructs', aims essentially at explaining, or deriving, behaviour in relation to the so-called 'situation' in which it occurs; thus, the determination of the character of the situation at a given time, also defining this as 'property' of the 'psychological field in a given time' (ibid., p. 43), becomes crucial for understanding the psychological phenomena.

In this regard, Lewin explicitly cites the spatio-physical aspects determining the 'situations' to be considered:

We are dealing in psychology with 'situational units' which have to be conceived of as having an extension in regard to their field dimensions and their time dimensions. If I am not mistaken, the problem of time-space-quanta, which is so important for modern quantum theory in physics, is methodologically parallel (although, of course, on a more advanced level) to the problem of 'time-field-units' in psychology. The concept of situations of different scope has proved to be very helpful in solving a number of otherwise rather puzzling problems. (ibid., p. 78)

Still with the intention of clarifying the concept of 'psychological field', he observes that since 'the boundary conditions of a field are essential characteristics of that field' it must be kept in mind that 'the problems of *physical* or social action are legitimate parts of psychology proper' (ibid., p. 57; emphasis added).

In this way, Lewin, in the final years (1943, 1944), was able to define a specific problematic area for psychological research, primarily for understanding the situation or the psychological field at a given time; he defined this research area 'psychological ecology':

Within the realm of facts existing at a given time one can distinguish three areas in which changes are or might be of interest to psychology:

1. The 'life space;' i.e., the person and the psychological environment as it exists for him [. . .].
2. A multitude of processes in the physical or social world, which do not affect the life space of the individual at that time.
3. A 'boundary zone' of the life space: certain parts of the physical or social world do affect the state of the life space at that time.

Lewin (1951, p. 57) continues, exemplifying:

. . . the process of perception, for instance, is intimately linked with this boundary zone, because what is perceived is partly determined by physical 'stimuli,' i.e., that part of the physical world which affects the sensory organs at that time. Another process located in the boundary zone is the execution of an action.

On the basis of these premises, he points out the need to continue with studies which define 'psychological ecology', as aimed at investigating points 2 and 3 above, in order to arrive at a greater understanding of point 1. In essence, these studies are aimed at analysing the relationship between data – in this case defined as 'non-psychological' – relative to point 2 and data, considered psychological, typically represented by point 1, through the examination of the dynamics of the 'boundary zone' between the above-mentioned points represented by point 3.

Lewin specifies:

Theoretically we can characterize this task as discovering what part of the physical or social world will determine, during a given period, the 'boundary zone' of the life space. This task is worth the interest of the psychologists. I would suggest calling it 'psychological ecology'. (ibid., p. 59)

Thus, in Lewinian field theory, through the proposal of psychological ecology, the physical environment is placed explicitly next to the social environment as a component of psychological investigation. However, it should be noted that Lewin, parallel to his claim of the importance of including the physical characteristics of the environment in the psychological investigation, openly criticizes what he defines as the 'objective' or 'physicalistic behaviorism' of much research which he believes has been erroneously defined as psychological:

> Many psychologists, particularly those who followed the theory of conditioned reflex, have confused this requirement for operational definitions with a demand for eliminating psychological descriptions. They insisted on defining 'stimuli' superficially in terms of physics. One of the basic characteristics of field theory in psychology, as I see it, is the demand that the field which influences an individual should be described not in 'objective physicalistic' terms, but in a way in which it exists for that person at that time. (ibid., p. 62)

He continues in this regard, observing how

> Gestalt theory has much emphasized (perhaps overemphasized in the beginning) certain similarities between the perceived structure and the objective structure of the stimuli. This does not mean, however, that it is permissible to treat stimuli as if they were inner parts of the life space (rather than boundary conditions), a common mistake of physicalistic behaviorism. (ibid., p. 90)

In essence, even though Lewin affirms the importance of considering the physical characteristics of the environment as components of psychological processes, he stresses that they must appear in the psychological investigation as psychological, not purely physical-objective data, that is, they must be present – as they are perceived/known – in the psychological field considered.

It is interesting to note how Lewin emphasizes the difference of his position from Brunswik's 'probabilistic' perceptual theory. From Lewin's point of view, Brunswik 'wishes to include in the psychological field those parts of the physical and sociological world which, to my mind, have to be excluded' (ibid., p. 58). Further,

> Brunswik, however, is correct in assuming that I do not consider as a part of the psychological field at a given time those sections of the physical or social world which do not affect the life space of the person at that time. The food that lies behind doors at the end of a maze so that neither smell not sight can reach it is not a part of the life space of the animal. If the individual knows that food lies there this *knowledge*, of course, has to be represented in his life space, because this knowledge affects behavior. It is also necessary to take into account the subjective probability with which the individual views the present or future state of affairs, because the degree of certainty of expectation also influences his behavior. (ibid., p. 57)

In essence, Lewin confirms the importance of maintaining the phenomenological viewpoint, with the pre-eminence of perceived reality over physical-objective reality, as the indispensable perspective of psychological investigation; in this same perspective, he encourages consideration of the problem of 'probabilistic judgment', posed by Brunswik at the centre of his perceptual theory:

To my mind the main issue is what the term 'probability' refers to [. . .]. If an individual sits in a room trusting that the ceiling will not come down, should only his 'subjective probability' be taken into account for predicting behavior or should we also consider the 'objective probability' of the ceiling's coming down as determined by the engineers? To my mind, only the first has to be taken into account. (ibid., p. 58)

However, despite the decided pre-eminence of the phenomenological perspective, equal attention is paid to physical and social characteristics of the environment through the proposal of psychological ecology.

The originality of the Lewinian position within psychology derives from its ability, on the one hand, to affirm the pre-eminence of perceived reality – that is, of that which he defines as the psychological environment – with respect to the physical-objective environment, and, on the other, to maintain equal interest in the environment and its characteristics (physical and social). Through the proposal of psychological ecology, both the physical and the social environment become factors for explaining the psychological environment.

Within this perspective, Lewin admits his interest in psychological ecology is primarily guided by the aim for socially relevant psychological research, particularly when it involves problems of control of social change, called by Lewin 'planned change' or 'social engineering':

I can see why psychology should be interested even in those areas of the physical and social world which are not part of the life space or which do not affect its boundary zone at present. If one wishes to safeguard a child's education during the next years, if one wishes to predict in what situation an individual will find himself as a result of a certain action, one will have to calculate this future. Obviously, such forecast has to be based partly on statistical considerations about nonpsychological data [. . .]. The essence of explaining or predicting any change in a certain area is the linkage of that change with the conditions of the field at that time. (ibid.)

Through his proposal of psychological ecology, Lewin essentially suggests a form of psychological research able to use and to integrate information of a non-psychological nature for the understanding of psychological phenomena.

In this regard, he further illustrates the characteristics of psychological ecology:

Some problems of the 'life history' of an individual have their places here. The boundary conditions of the life space during long as well as short time-periods depend partly on the action of the individual himself. To this degree they should be linked to the psychological dynamics of the life space. The rest of the calculation has to be done, however, with other than psychological means. (ibid., p. 59)

Lewin often returns to this concept with further clarifications:

The relation between psychological and nonpsychological factors is a basic conceptual and methodological problem in all branches of psychology, from the psychology of perception to the psychology of groups. A proper understanding of this relationship must be achieved before we can answer the many questions raised in efforts to produce an integration of the social sciences. A field-theoretical approach to these problems of 'psychological ecology' suggests some of the ways in which these questions may be answered. (ibid., p. 170)

The 'channel theory' and the psychology of the 'gatekeeper' Lewin's proposal of psychological ecology has been directly applied in various studies; among these, the most emblematic (also according to Lewin) is the one conducted during the Second World War in order to align food habits more closely with the foods available in the United States at that time (Lewin, 1943).

This research has been presented as a paradigmatic example of psychological ecology, having the purpose of singling out the connections between non-psychological and psychological factors in determining food habits. The aim of the research is to find the direction to be taken in order to change these food habits, considered as 'cultural habits' (Lewin, 1951).

Lewin (1943, p. 170) presents it as follows:

> The following discussion of food habits may suffice as an example of a first step in analyzing a field for the purpose of changing cultural habits. This analysis has the purpose of clarifying exactly where and how psychological and nonpsychological problems overlap.

He continues with some considerations which seem expressly formulated for introducing and supporting present-day environmental psychology in its most recent 'contextual' approach (Stokols and Altman, 1987):

> Any type of group life occurs in a setting of certain limitations to what is and what is not possible, what might or might not happen. The nonpsychological factors of climate, of communication, of the law of the country or the organization are a frequent part of these 'outside limitations'. The first analysis of the field is done from the point of view of 'psychological ecology': the psychologist studies 'nonpsychological' data to find out what these data mean for determining the boundary conditions of the life of the individual or group. Only after these data are known can the psychological study itself be begun to investigate the factors which determine the actions of the group or individual in those situations which have been shown to be significant.

In reference to the research aims, Lewin (1943, p. 171) asks himself, 'How should the psychologist proceed to make a contribution towards planned changes?' And he answers himself:

> This question of planned change or of any 'social engineering' is identical with the question: What 'conditions' have to be changed to bring about a given result and how can one change these conditions with the means at hand? (ibid., p. 230)

In this perspective and on the basis of the analyses of cultural habits, in this case consisting of food habits, he arrives at the formulation of 'the channel theory' and 'the psychology of the gatekeeper' (ibid., pp. 174–7).

First, according to this theory, several objective directions, defined as 'channels', exist; the cultural habit under consideration is supported and explicated through these channels. In the case of food habits, two primary

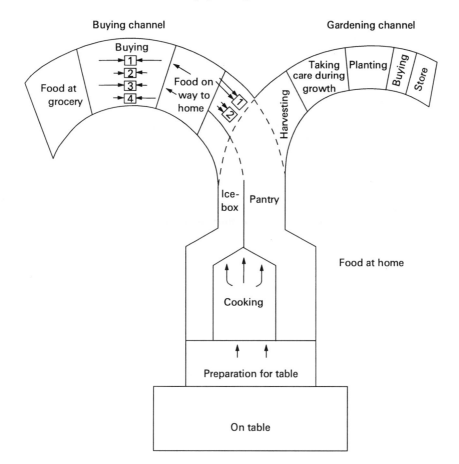

Figure 2.2 *Channels through which food reaches the table (adapted from Lewin, 1951, p. 175)*

channels are specified which food passes through before reaching the table:

(a) the buying channel;
(b) the gardening channel.

For each of these channels, there are other sections which food passes through – coming from outside the house towards the inside – to the kitchen, where the channels unite and the food reaches the table, as illustrated in Figure 2.2.

Second, within these possible channels, there are people, defined as 'gatekeepers', who have the function of controlling access to several passages. 'Entering or not entering a channel and moving from one section of a channel to another is affected by a gatekeeper' (ibid., p. 234).

For example, in the case of buying food, it is generally more usual for the housewife to be in the position of gatekeeper than her husband. At any rate, in this theory, understanding the psychology of the gatekeeper becomes crucial since decisions derive from this which make certain passages through the channel more or less possible.

With regard to food habits, Lewin affirms: 'To understand and influence food habits we have to know in addition to the objective food channels and objective availability, the psychological factors influencing the person who controls the channels' (ibid., p. 177). And he continues:

> The psychology of the gatekeeper includes a great variety of factors which we do not intend to cover fully. The factors might be classified under two headings, one pertaining to the cognitive structure, i.e., the terms in which people think and speak about food; and the other pertaining to their motivation, e.g., the system of values behind their choice of food. (ibid., pp. 177–8)

In any case, it is clear that the systematic analysis of the psychology of the gatekeeper can be carried out only after a preliminary examination of psychological ecology aimed at singling out gatekeepers and relative channels. In this way Lewin synthesizes what he previously presented about the proceeding of psychological ecology investigations:

> Social and economic channels may be distinguished in any type of formalized institution. Within these channels gate sections can be located. Social changes in large measure are produced by changing the constellation of forces within these particular segments of the channel. The analytic task is approached from the point of view of psychological ecology; nonpsychological data are first investigated to determine the boundary conditions for those who are in control of various segments of the channel.
>
> Gate sections are governed either by impartial rules or by 'gatekeepers'. In the latter case an individual or group is 'in power' to make the decision between 'in' or 'out'. Understanding the functioning of the gate becomes equivalent then to understanding the factors which determine the decision of the gatekeepers, and changing the social process means influencing or replacing the gatekeeper. The first diagnostic task in such cases is that of finding the actual gatekeepers. (ibid., p. 185)

Based on this we can say that Lewinian theory seems a mandatory point of reference for e.p. in general and, above all, for its more recent psycho-social developments (Stokols and Altman, 1987).

Not only is the environment, including its physical characteristics, brought to the fore by this theory but, as we have tried to illustrate, in field theory such specific modalities are proposed for considering in psychological terms the physical characteristics of the environment that it is difficult to imagine any development of psychology, in an environmental sense, apart from the Lewinian example.

On the other hand, it must be noted how this example's capacity to influence is evident in various developments of Lewinian theory which also affected subsequent e.p. The main tendencies in this sense can be seen in the United States, first in Roger Barker's school of ecological psychology and, then, in the subsequent theory of Urie Bronfenbrenner (1979) on the ecological approach to human development. Also in this direction are the developments in Europe defined as 'ecopsychology' or 'ecological psychology' by Kaminsky et al. (Kaminsky, 1976; Kaminsky and Fleischer, 1984), Grauman (1974, 1978) and Kruse (1978).

On the one hand, this development of German psychology is explicitly linked to the Lewinian tradition of psychological ecology, as recently illustrated by Fuhrer (1990); on the other, it shows the same orientation as the most recent developments of e.p., as can be seen in these authors' writings, such as the chapter by Kruse and Grauman (1987) on German e.p. in the *Handbook* (Stokols and Altman, 1987).

Roger Barker et al.'s ecological psychology

The Oskaloosa observation station The term 'ecological psychology' refers to a specific line of research carried out in the late 1940s by a group at the University of Kansas, headed by Roger Barker; the latter also chose the term, which he widely discussed and illustrated in various presentations and in one specific volume entitled *Ecological Psychology: Concepts and Methods for Studying the Environment of Human Behavior* (1968).

Barker was a student of Lewin and, thus, trained in the concepts of Lewinian field theory, including those of psychological ecology (Lewin, 1951); overall, these concepts tend to emphasize the role of the environment in determining individual behaviour, assigning it a role equally important to that of personal factors.

These initial experiences with Lewin's group at the University of Iowa, where Barker primarily dedicated himself to the study of infantile frustration in experimental situations, are still today cited by him as crucial experiences at the methodological and theoretical level for the future development of his research (Barker, 1990, pp. 509–10).

But what pushed Barker to embark on the route of ecological psychology was his initial interest in developmental psychology and his great dissatisfaction with the research modalities used at that time (the 1930s and 1940s). According to him, this research was dominated by consolidated laboratory methodology and the psychometry available then, rather than guided by the scientific and social problems of child development.

Therefore, in 1947, following his transfer to the University of Kansas, he and his colleague, Herbert Wright, established the Midwest Psychological Field Station in the small town of Oskaloosa, Kansas (with 715 inhabitants, including 100 children). This was a laboratory or, to use the term he adopted, a 'station' for observing behaviour in the field. Barker and Wright's aim was to understand how the environment of the 'real, daily world' influences the behaviour of children and the people who live with them.

In order to make comparisons, a similar station was established in England soon after, in a small town (Leyburn) in the north of Yorkshire. 'The goals of the Station were to discover and describe the everyday living conditions and behavior of the children of the town and to investigate their interrelations.' This is how Roger Barker (1987, p. 1413) still presents this initiative today, which was a 'revolutionary' undertaking for psychology in the United States at a time when the only pertinent and 'accepted' methodologies were those of laboratory research or the clinical method.

In his studies, Barker has repeatedly claimed his 'break' with traditional psychology; for a long time, he was treated as a 'dissident' or as a 'non-psychologist' by that tradition because of his refusal of the experimental laboratory method and his lack of interest in the variables then considered inseparable from the psychological approach; in particular, personality.

In the 1970s, the American Psychological Association openly rejected ecological psychology, primarily based on its 'overcommitment to personality as an explanation of human behavior', as stated by the APA president of that time, Kenneth Little. Actually, Robert Bechtel (1988, p. 88), who came from the same Kansas group, correctly observes that 'nowhere does Barker repudiate personality, he simply ignores it'.

Barker (1968, p. 16) explains the originality of his perspective of psychological investigation as follows:

> It is not easy, at first, to leave the person out of observations of the environment of molar behavior. Our perceptual apparatus is adjusted by our long training with the idiocentric viewing glasses of individual observations, interviews, and questionnaires to see *persons* whenever we see behavior. But with some effort and experience the extra-individual assemblies of behavior episodes, behavior objects, and space that surround persons can be observed and described. Their nonrandom distribution and bounded character are a crucial aid.

One of the primary points of departure in Barker et al.'s studies is the affirmation of the need for a research methodology in which the psychologist acts not as 'operator', but as simple 'transducer' of the phenomena observed into 'data', in order to produce what Barker calls 'T data', which maintain the property of being linked transitively with the observed phenomena. Barker opposes this modality of approach, essentially based on the unobtrusive observation of behaviours carried out in the context where they naturally occur, to the 'operative' one, in which the psychologist 'dominates the system' observed (Barker, 1965, p. 4) and produces 'O data' – both characteristics of the experimental method. According to Barker:

> T data refer to psychological phenomena which are explicitly excluded when the psychologist functions as operator. [. . .] O data refer to phenomena that psychologists as transducers explicitly exclude, namely, psychological units arranged in accordance with the curiosities of the psychologist. The primary task of the operator is to alter, in ways that are crucial to his interests, phenomena that the psychologist as transducer leaves intact. (ibid.)

On the basis of these points of departure, which primarily propose a new method and criticize obtrusive methods in general and experimental laboratory ones in particular, what Barker defines as ecological psychology developed. Over the years it was enriched with conceptualizations and specific theories (in particular, that of behaviour setting and the theory of undermanning), and today it is still recognized as a specific psychological school.

The first books published concern the results of the initial observations carried out at the Midwest Field Station: *One Boy's Day* (Barker and Wright, 1951) and *Midwest and Its Children* (Barker and Wright, 1955); both are based on meticulous observation of the daily events in the life of the children of the small town of Oskaloosa.

Ecological psychology, proposing naturalistic observation as its exclusive method at a time when today's videotaping techniques were not yet available, required tremendous effort in setting up and carrying out meticulous observation techniques for gathering, through T data, what Barker called the 'stream of behavior'; these data were recorded by means of the technique Barker called 'specimen record', which involved describing what was observed in the most detailed way possible.

Recently, Barker (1990, p. 509) has commented on those first experiments:

> The kits of research methods Herbert [Wright] and I brought from our superior training in the best graduate schools contained no procedure for investigating the everyday lives of children at breakfast, in music class, or at worship service. Nevertheless [. . .] we started with what we had in out kit bags.

It is interesting to note how still today Barker points to Lewin as inspiring the first methodology of the specimen record; he recalls how his colleagues, even during very structured laboratory experiments, were taught to keep a narrative type of detailed record 'without regard for [their] theories' about everything that happened in the subjects' behaviour during the experiment (ibid., p. 510).

Barker also admits the influence of Lewin's lessons (ibid.) in the subsequent methodological step, that is, the identification of so-called 'behavioral episodes'. These were meticulous and detailed methodologies concerning observable behaviour: 'The method for collecting this data was long and tedious and it took teams of trained observers, who had to spell each other every 20 or 30 minutes because of fatigue'; this is how Bechtel (1988, p. 88) describes those first experiences carried out at the Field Station in Kansas.

Today, many years later, Barker (1990, p. 510) still recognizes that 'the development of criteria for the identification and description of episodes in free situations was a major achievement of the Field Station.'

The behaviour setting and the theory of 'undermanning'   After the first works, primarily focused on the detailed reporting of the daily events of individuals in the town, Barker and his co-workers moved on to the definition of more molar units of analysis, above all behaviour setting, which was aimed at singling out units of analysis according to which both individual behaviours and spatio-physical properties seem 'naturally' organized in the environment.

The behaviour settings are considered by Barker (1987, p. 1420) as

> ... ecobehavioral phenomena: they are bounded standing patterns of human and nonhuman activity with integrated systems of forces and controls that maintain their activities at semistable equilibria; the parts and processes of behavior settings have high degrees of internal interdependence in consequence of which they are discrete units – they are entities within the ecological environment.

Thus, the behaviour setting includes a particular pattern of behaviours and certain spatial-temporal characteristics concomitant with these behaviours; it includes the persons behaving within it, but is presented essentially as a supra-individual unit, capable of providing stability and homogeneity to individual behaviours beyond the variety of the individuals participating in the setting. 'When we came to Oskaloosa we found behavior settings (as we later called them) to be basic facts of life for the people of the town' (Barker, 1990, p. 511).

One example of a behaviour setting taken from the observations of Oskaloosa is the Presbyterian church; it includes the patterns of behaviour typical of a church (celebration and participating in religious functions, collection of offerings, singing of psalms, etc.), the physical environment of the church (presence of the pulpit, altar, benches to sit and kneel on, etc.) and the times when the church functions (holidays versus weekdays, daytime hours versus evening/night hours, etc.); other examples of possible behaviour settings include the grocery store, school, beauty shop, service station, Rotary Club, etc.

Barker and Wright also developed a procedure, the 'behavior setting survey', for identifying and describing with precision the variety of settings composing a particular environmental context.

Barker (1968, pp. 16–17), using the example of a school class, lists the distinctive characteristics of the environmental unit that tend to appear clearly during the ecological (that is, naturalistic) observation to single out a specific behavior setting:

> It is a natural phenomenon; it is not created by an experimenter for scientific purposes.
> It has a space-time locus.
> A boundary surrounds a school class meeting.
> The boundary is self-generated; it changes as the class changes in size and in the nature of its activity.
> The class meeting is objective in the sense that it exists independent of anyone's perception of it, *qua* class; it is a preperceptual ecological entity.
> It has two sets of components: (a) behavior (reciting, discussing, sitting) and (b) nonpsychological objects with which behavior is transacted, e.g., chairs, walls, a blackboard, paper, etc.
> The unit, the class meeting is circumjacent to its components; the pupils and equipment are *in* the class.
> The behavior and physical objects that constitute the unit school class meeting

are internally organized and arranged to form a pattern that is by no means random.

The pattern within the boundary of a class meeting is easily discriminated from that outside the boundary.

There is a synomorphic relation between the pattern of the behavior occurring within the class and the pattern of its nonbehavioral components, the behavior objects. The seats face the teacher's desk, and the children face the teacher, for example.

The unity of the class is not due to the similarity of its parts at any moment; for example, speaking occurs in one part and listening in another. The unity is based, rather, upon the interdependence of the parts; events in different parts of a class meeting have a greater effect upon each other than equivalent events beyond its boundary.

The people who inhabit a class are to a considerable degree interchangeable and replaceable. Pupils come and go; even the teacher may be replaced. But the same entity continues as serenely as an old car with new rings and the right front wheel now carried as the spare.

The behavior of this entity cannot, however, be greatly changed without destroying it: there must be teaching, there must be study, there must be recitation.

A pupil has two positions in a class; first, he is a component of the supra-individual unit, and second, he is an individual whose life-space is partly formed within the constraints imposed by the very entity of which he is a part.

The organized and interdependent nature of the various physical and social components of the setting is assured by the existence of the 'setting programme', represented by all of the prescribed sequences, ordered in time, for the activities and exchanges among persons and objects within that setting.

For example, in the case of a library setting, the programme involves modalities for the behaviour of both personnel and users in order for the loan, the reading and returning of books to occur; thus, it will include both the personnel, who have the task of informing the users about how to behave themselves, and the actions of the user. The programme, besides being or becoming known to the participants within the setting, is generally, in part, codified into the library regulations and, in part, continuously reaffirmed by the participants and by the physical features of the setting.

The complete programme is generally known only to the persons in the *leader* position in the setting, in this case the library director. Besides the various components of the behaviour setting, represented by its physical properties, by persons and by the setting programme, there is the 'level of penetration' of the setting by participants, concerning the level of personal responsibility in the setting. As Barker (1968, p. 49) affirms:

Not only do inhabitants enter settings for different amounts of time, but they enter and participate in them in different capacities and with different degrees of involvement and responsibility. One index of the involvement and responsibility of a person in a behavior setting is the depth or centrality of his penetration. Six zones of centrality are defined. The more central the zone, the deeper the penetration and the greater the involvement and responsibility of its occupants.

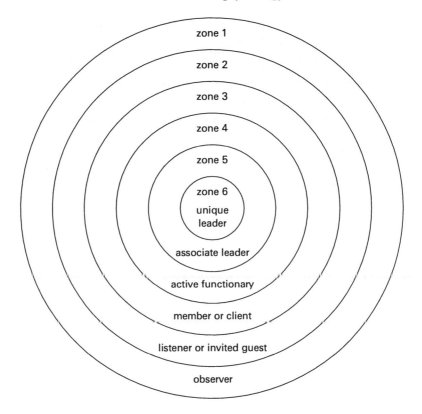

Figure 2.3   *Penetration zone behaviour setting (Barker, 1968, p. 51)*

The six zones initially defined by Barker are outlined in Figure 2.3 with the relative positions of penetration, which go from minimum involvement in the two most peripheral zones of the simple *observer* (1) and *listener or invited guest* (2), to intermediate involvement of the subsequent two zones regarding the *member or client* (3) and the *active functionary* (4), up to the maximum responsibility in the final two zones for the *leader*, in the form of *associate leader* (5) or *unique leader* (6).

In order to underline the fact that the behaviour settings themselves generate pressures of various intensity on the participants for the programme to move ahead, the term 'requests of the habitat to operate' (Barker and Schoggen, 1973) was introduced, corresponding to the various above-mentioned penetration zones. As further support for the supra-individual role assigned by ecological psychology to the behaviour setting, the 'manning theory' of the setting was formulated; it was initially outlined by Barker (1960, 1968; Barker and Gump, 1964) and then completed by Wicker (1969, 1979) and Bechtel (1977).

According to this theory, the various settings are distinguished in relation to the optimal or nonoptimal amount of people who are part of them; settings with less than the optimal amount of occupants are defined as undermanned settings and considered as having specific characteristics compared to those populated by an optimal amount of people.

The theory is primarily based on the study conducted by Barker and Gump (1964) on 'large and small schools'. In this study, systematic differences emerged in a variety of activities and in participant behaviour in which the 'inhabitants' of small schools were more involved than those of large schools.

The authors interpret this result on the basis of the theory of behaviour setting and its programme, which tends to remain unchanged regardless of the number of inhabitants; therefore, they are forced (when they are few in number) into greater activism and involvement in the programme, as well as greater cohesion.

Barker (1968, p. 185) synthesizes the salient aspects of the theory of the effects of the undermanned setting:

> In general terms, undermanned behavior settings in comparison with optimally manned behavior settings impose more and stronger forces on their inhabitants in more varied directions; the forces are, however, more prevailingly directed inward and toward other inhabitants. According to this, undermanned behavior settings have stronger internal interdependence and cohesiveness; they are stronger things vis-à-vis their inhabitants than optimally manned behavior settings.

Essentially, the theory supports the capacity of the size of the setting to influence the type of behaviours and social climate established in it, affirming the superiority of functioning of small settings compared to large or overmanned settings.

Here it is interesting to cite Bechtel's (1988, p. 88) recent judgement of this theory, which he also contributed to:

> Nevertheless, undermanning theory remains an important attempt to explain the impact that small group size seems to have on human behavior. It is an important cornerstone to a situational deterministic viewpoint. But in a society where bigness is always considered superior, the evidence of the superiority of small schools and organizations was not acceptable.

Many of the methods and concepts initially adopted by Barker have been subsequently revised, especially by several of his initial colleagues, such as Wicker (1979, 1987) and Schoggen (1989), as will be illustrated in more detail later (see pp. 161–74 below). Barker (1987) tends to present his work in psychological ecology and his experience with the Oskaloosa observation station (which operated for twenty-five years) as only the beginning of a work still in great part to be developed and 'largely unfinished'.

Actually, the experience of ecological psychology is a mandatory point of reference not only for present-day e.p., but also for any psychological research attempting to work programmatically in 'naturalistic' rather than experimental laboratory situations.

According to various authors, the initial experiences of this school and, in particular, the opening of the field station must be considered as the first *ante litteram* steps of present-day e.p. (Holahan, 1982).

The most recent approach in e.p. – not the initial one, which was often too anchored to the paradigm of the perceptual school – is searching for and emphasizing the direct connection with ecological psychology (Holahan, 1982; Stokols and Altman, 1987).

The recent theoretical approach, defined as 'contextual', is in many ways similar to the type of research proposed by Barker, in which the researcher is a 'transducer' and not an 'operator'. Barker has recently confirmed this distinction between 'discovery research' and 'verification research', the former defined as 'exploring and prospecting a new field of inquiry' (that is, characteristics of ecological psychology), while the latter 'replicates, tests, corrects, refines and elaborates previous developments and discoveries' (Barker, 1987, p. 1414).

The emphasis of Barker's school on the observation of what occurs naturally – that is, not provoked by the experimenter – and of the so-called 'ecological environment' led in certain cases to the common use of the term 'ecological' as a simple synonym of 'naturalistic' (Valsiner and Benigni, 1986). Actually, the ecological environment of ecological psychology is something much more specific than the natural environment; it is the rigidly organized environment of the setting in which observed behaviour is found and explained. Barker (1987, p. 1415) clarifies this: 'Much of the order, stability and predictability of human behavior comes from the ecological environment: from the structured, homeostatic, coercive behavior settings that people inhabit.'

Thus, with ecological psychology we find a further use of the term 'ecological' in psychological research with respect to those we have already touched upon; here the meaning is also different from Lewin's, which Barker's ecological psychology was initially meant to link with.

In spite of Barker's continual reference to Lewin and his school, ecological psychology remained fundamentally different from the perspective which the latter proposed. This was primarily due to the complete absence of the phenomenological-subjective point of view, characteristic of the Lewinian perspective as well as that of Bronfenbrenner (1979), which was also defined as ecological.

The ecological psychology of the Kansas School actually tends to resolve the problematic already formulated by Lewin of the relationship between socio-physical environment and psychological processes, or, as Fuhrer (1990) says, regarding the 'ecological–psychological' gap, in completely objectivist terms. It assumes that the only reality to be investigated is the 'observed' or observable one, thus defined also as the 'pre-perceptual environment' (Barker, 1990, p. 511). This is one of the main limitations which Barker's colleagues, such as Wicker (1987), have noticed and tried to overcome in their most recent revisions of the concept of behaviour setting (treated on pp. 167–70).

Furthermore, it should be noted that the concept of setting, especially if used without the addition of 'behaviour', has become rooted in the psychological tradition, with the aim of identifying the organized socio-physical properties of the context of individual action, and with the capacity to direct the behaviour of the participants within the setting.

Today, this meaning for the term 'setting' occupies a central position in other branches of psychology of rather recent development, such as community psychology (Heller and Monahan, 1977) and organizational psychology (Dunnette, 1977).

The term 'setting' has passed directly from ecological psychology to e.p., often tending to be substituted for the more general term 'environment'. With the use of the concept of 'setting', there is the tendency to foreground the organized nature of both the characteristics of the socio-physical environment and the experience of it for the individual, thus moving in the direction of the still more recent concept of 'place', which present-day e.p. is increasingly directed towards; this will be discussed later (see pp. 161–80).

Urie Bronfenbrenner's ecological approach

Bronfenbrenner's ecological proposal also appears as a direct development of Lewinian theory; it has been centred, not only initially as in the Kansas school, but exclusively on problems of psychological development.

A critical analysis of the research field on human development as regards methods and results and in particular their possibilities of providing indications for the area of social policy are the main starting points of Bronfenbrenner's theoretical work. He then arrives at the proposal of what he defines as 'the ecology of human development' (1977a, 1977b, 1979), which is basically a further articulation of the Lewinian proposal of 'psychological ecology' applied to the problems of child development and social change.

Even though Bronfenbrenner's work is focused on problems of human development, his theoretical proposals go far beyond the limits of the field of developmental psychology. They outline a specific psycho-social framework for the problems of human development, which become relevant even for environmental psychology.

Interest both in the social relevance of developmental psychology research and in Lewin's theoretical perspective led Bronfenbrenner to the consideration of the physical and social environment with adequate conceptual tools. In this regard, he starts from the observation of the way – according to him, 'rudimentary' – psychology takes into consideration the environment and its characteristics, compared to the attention given to the individual and his/her processes:

> What we find in practice, is a marked asymmetry, a hypertrophy of theory and research focusing on the properties of the person and only the most rudimentary conception and characterization of the environment in which the person is found. (Bronfenbrenner, 1979, p. 16)

Bronfenbrenner is also critical of those schools which direct specific attention to the characteristics of the environment in which the psychological phenomena occur, adopting 'naturalistic' observation, that is, the ecological psychology of Kansas and the ethological school. He expresses his main criticism of these two psychological traditions:

> Both groups have adapted to the study of human behavior a model originally developed for the observation of sub-human species. Implicit in this model is a concept of the environment that may be quite adequate for the study of behavior in animals but that is hardly sufficient for the human case. (Bronfenbrenner, 1977b, p. 514)

According to him, the main inadequacies of the implicit concept of environment are the following: 'It is limited to the immediate, concrete setting, containing the living creatures and focuses on observation of the behavior of one or at most two beings at a time, in only one setting' (ibid.).

In contrast to this perspective, Bronfenbrenner holds that

> the understanding of human development demands going beyond the direct observation of behavior on the part of one or two persons in the same place; it requires examination of multiperson systems of interaction not limited to a single setting and must take into account aspects of the environment beyond the immediate situation containing the subject. (ibid., pp. 514–15)

As to method, he proposes 'an expansion and then a convergence of both the naturalistic and the experimental approaches', and 'an expansion and convergence of the theoretical conceptions relative to the environment which underlie them' (ibid., p. 515). Bronfenbrenner's primary aim is to outline a theoretical framework proposing a concept of environment 'considerably broader and more differentiated than that found in psychology in general' (ibid.). Thus, he arrives at the definition of 'ecological environment', conceived 'as a vested arrangement of structures each contained within the next', denominated (beginning from the inside and moving towards the outside) *microsystem, mesosystem, exosystem* and *macrosystem*.

The *microsystem* is defined as that complex of relationships existing between the person and the environment of an immediate setting containing the person:

> A *setting* is defined as a place with particular *physical features* in which the *participants* engage in particular *activities* in particular *roles* for a particular period of *time*. The factors of place, time, physical features, activity, participant, and role constitute the *elements* of a setting. (ibid., p. 514)

The microsystem is represented by the individual's experience of that setting.

It is important to keep in mind that Bronfenbrenner (1979, p. 22) underlines the crucial role of the person's experience of the setting as the element characterizing the microsystem:

A critical term in the definition of the microsystem is *experienced*. The term is used to indicate that the scientifically relevant features of any environment include not only its objective properties but also the way in which these properties are perceived by the persons in the environment.

In support of this perspective, Bronfenbrenner makes explicit reference to the continuity of this theoretical position with the typical tradition of social psychology: Lewin's 'psychological field', Mead's 'role-theory' and Thomas's 'definition of the situation'.

It is also interesting to note that the physical characteristics of the setting are specifically included among the defining elements of the 'microenvironment', also through reference to the concept of place; its use here seems particularly interesting due to recent developments in e.p., which will be discussed later (see pp. 161–74).

The *mesosystem* represents the 'system of the microsystems', because it 'comprises the interrelations between two or more settings, in which the person actively participates' (ibid, p. 25). As an example of the meso-system of a child, Bronfenbrenner cites the relations between house, school and group of peers living in his neighbourhood or, in the case of an adult, the relationship between family, work and social life.

The *exosystem* consists of 'one or more settings that do not involve the person as an active participant, but in which events occur that affect, or are affected by, what happens in the setting containing the person' (ibid.). Again in the case of a child, parents' place of work, class of older sibling, activities of the local school board, etc. are cited as examples of exosystem.

The *macrosystem* 'refers to consistencies in the form and content of lower-order systems (micro-, meso- and exosystem) that exist, or could exist, at the level of subculture or culture as a whole, along with any belief systems or ideology underlying such consistencies' (ibid., p. 26). Bronfenbrenner then illustrates this concept:

Within a given society – say France – one crèche school classroom, park playground, café, or post office looks and functions much like another, but they all differ from their counter-parts in the United States. It is as if in each country the various settings had been constructed from the same set of blueprints. (ibid., p. 68)

Overall, what characterizes Bronfenbrenner's approach to the problem of the individual–environment relationship is the attempt to reformulate the problems of psychological ecology already identified by Lewin into a systemic perspective. He outlines a very articulated framework with respect to both the initial Lewinian proposal and to subsequent attempts by Barker et al.'s school.

Bronfenbrenner points out how his proposal of an 'ecological approach' aims primarily at recovering the systemic, and, thus, interactive and holistic, perspective of naturalistic ecology.

At different times he criticizes psychological research, which he believed is based excessively on the model of the physical sciences – thus mostly assuming models of unidirectional causality – rather than on the biological processes of nature, in which the causality of the processes is always reciprocal and bidirectional: 'Today we all know, as good ecologists, that the processes are bidirectional' (1977a, p. 297).

Within this perspective, Bronfenbrenner's model of ecological environment is primarily meant to outline a framework with systemic characteristics which he believes will provide research with innovative features in terms of formal properties rather than of content, compared to the model traditionally used: 'The distinctive characteristic of the ecological approach is the requirement that the person, the environment and the relations between them be conceptualized in terms of systems and subsystems within the system' (ibid., p. 278). 'In ecological research, the principal effects are likely to be interactions' (1977b, p. 518). 'In contrast to the traditional unidirectional research model typically employed in the laboratory, an ecological experiment must allow for reciprocal processes; that is, not only the effect of A on B, but also the effect of B on A. This is the requirement of reciprocity' (ibid., p. 519). From this it follows that 'environmental structures and the processes taking place within and between them, must be viewed as interdependent and analyzed in systems' terms' (ibid., p. 518).

The type of research which follows these premises has different characteristics from those traditionally found in psychology, especially in its experimental, laboratory approach: 'The primary purpose of the ecological experiment becomes not hypotheses testing but *discovery* – the identification of those systems properties and processes that affect and are affected by, the behavior and the development of the human being' (ibid.).

In proposing this research perspective, Bronfenbrenner highlights another aspect emerging from the systemic approach which has further research potential, that is, that of analysing the so-called 'second-order effects' relative to the phenomena considered. According to Bronfenbrenner, these effects are the typical phenomena generally not taken into consideration by traditional research, which is primarily focused on dyadic systems. On the contrary, the ecological approach points out the existence and importance of these effects.

> The usual paradigm allows only what can be called first-order effects; i.e., the influence of A on B or of B on A. There is neither interest in nor even the possibility of examining how the interaction of A and B might be affected by a third part C [. . .]. This second-order effect appears at successive levels of the system and, each time, opens up new vistas for research. (1977a, p. 279)

Within this theoretical framework, Bronfenbrenner's attention is primarily concentrated on problems, or, better, on the settings or subsystems, relative to child development: the parents–child dyad/triad, home, school, nursery school, etc. The spatio-physical features of the environment generally tend to be considered only indirectly, as the implicit component of the setting under examination; the latter are primarily identified in relation to their importance for child development.

It is important to note that Bronfenbrenner often pays specific attention to the spatio-physical components of settings, with frequent recourse to the concept of place in identifying the sub-systems considered (home, school, nursery school, etc.); furthermore, in some cases, he inquires about their specific effects, such as possible second-order effects, on psychological phenomena.

In this regard, he has considered the results of a well-known group of studies conducted by Glass and Singer in the 1970s to determine the possible effects of very noisy urban environments, with particular reference to the effects on children residing in various areas of Manhattan (Glass and Singer, 1972b).

Since the studies systematically bring to light less auditory discrimination ability in reading tasks in children living on lower floors of buildings in very noisy environments than in those living on the higher floors of the same buildings (thirty-two floors), Bronfenbrenner (1977b, p. 522) argues against the authors' conclusions about the direct influence of environmental noise on childrens' abilities, advancing the hypothesis of the possible influence of second-order effects:

> The real-life setting included other persons besides the children selected as the subjects of the study. Moreover, these other persons – the children's parents and other members of their families – were also exposed to traffic noise and, in all likelihood, affected by it. If so, the possibility remains that the impairment of the children's auditory discrimination and verbal skills might have come about not only as a function of their own difficulties in hearing or sustaining attention in a noisy environment, but also because others around them were similarly affected and engaged less frequently in conversations, in reading aloud, or in correcting their children's verbal utterances. No data are available to demonstrate or disconfirm the existence of such a second-order effect, but relevant information could have readily been obtained if the other participants in the setting had been included in the research design.

Essentially, through his theoretical model, Bronfenbrenner is able to point out, as a very important aspect, the possible effect of the spatio-physical features of the environment on individual behaviour, emphasizing that they constitute second-order as well as first-order effects.

As a matter of fact, when the environmental units considered are not molecular spatio-physical features but complexes of units organized in a molar sense (such as 'places' in the most recent work in e.p.), the possibility that the spatio-physical environmental features affect the individual psychological processes not only directly but also as second-order effects increases; in these cases, the influence of collective processes involving the other participants takes place at the level both of the microsystem and of the broader macrosystem.

The perspective outlined by Bronfenbrenner, even if only indirectly dealing with the spatio-physical aspects of the environment, provides a particularly interesting framework for the psycho-social developments of the most recent work in e.p. (Stokols and Altman, 1987). In particular, his proposal of a systemic ecological approach – and, thus, of research/discovery aimed at identifying the properties of the system rather than at hypotheses testing – forecast the approach of e.p. recently defined by Altman (Altman and Rogoff, 1987) and Stokols (1987) as 'contextual-transactional'. On the contrary, his proposal of approach to the environment by systems and sub-systems moves in the same direction as the more recent place theory, particularly in the work of Russell and Ward, 1982), Rapoport (1990) and Bonnes et al. (1990) on the concept of 'multi-place system' (see 192–7).

PART II

DIRECTIONS OF PRESENT-DAY ENVIRONMENTAL PSYCHOLOGY

3

Characterization of the Field

Emergence of the field and its characteristics

With the preceding we have illustrated both the many socially relevant external forces pushing psychology towards e.p., and the variety of theoretical perspectives within the psychological tradition considering the spatio-physical characteristics of the environment. Keeping both of these aspects in mind, it is not surprising that the emergence of this new area of psychological research has been characterized by remarkable enthusiasm, rapid expansion (especially in the United States) and by great heterogeneity of topics and theoretical perspectives.

At the start, it was difficult to define the field according to unifying theoretical frameworks; the heterogeneity of the field was explicitly affirmed in the early 1970s by various authors (Craik, 1970, 1973; Wohlwill, 1970) who attempted to present e.p. as systematically as possible.

It is also important to note that at the beginning mainly anthological collections (Proshansky et al., 1970; Ittelson, 1973a; Canter and Lee, 1974) were published, rather than basic introductory texts, which only began to appear several years later. The group at the City University of New York (Ittelson et al., 1974) published the first of these texts, followed by others (Heimstra and McFarling, 1974; Bell et al., 1978; Holahan, 1986).

Driven by enthusiasm, the psychologists working in this new area have often been more interested in emphasizing e.p.'s novelty compared to the earlier tradition of psychological research, rather than in reflecting on this tradition to find elements of theoretical continuity.

Therefore, with respect to the psychological tradition, aspects of novelty/diversity have mainly been emphasized, such as:

(a) the programmatic attention to spatio-physical characteristics of the environment where behaviour takes place;

(b)   the peculiarity of the methods adopted;
(c)   the orientation towards problems having clear social relevance;
(d)   the interdisciplinary orientation of research.

Attention to the spatio-physical characteristics of the environment

Attention to the spatio-physical characteristics of the environment is new
for psychology. Besides psychology's general interest in the environment,
which has always existed, attention to its spatio-physical aspects, particularly by the psychology of perception and by social psychology, seems
indirect and non-specific compared to what is being proposed by the
emerging field of e.p. For example, Wohlwill (1970, p. 303) expresses it as
follows:

> When psychologists have talked of environmental influences, they have rarely
> been specific about the meaning for them of the concept of environment. It
> has been used to refer to the most diverse set of conditions of experience [. . .].
> The physical environment that serves as background and context for behavior
> has been of little interest to psychologists; the role of the environment has
> almost invariably referred to social or interpersonal influences, or else to
> effects presumed to be ascribable to the milieu in an altogether unspecified
> sense.

Further on, he concludes: 'To a discipline that has for all too long paid
lip service to the primary importance of environmental variables on
behavior, this [environmental psychology] should represent an exciting
challenge indeed' (ibid., p. 311).

Proshansky expresses himself in a similar vein:

> First and perhaps most important, was its primary concern with the physical
> environment in particular rather than with the human environment in general.
> The use of the term *environment* by social psychologists and all other behavioral
> scientists almost invariably refers to the psychological, social, organizational, or
> cultural systems that characterize human environments. For the environmental
> psychologist, the lens of analysis is focused on the physical systems that by
> definition also characterize these environments [. . .]. For the environmental
> psychologist, there was a shift in the figure–ground relationships in consider-
> ations of the various systems, empirical and abstract, that comprise a person's
> environment. Now it was the physical setting that was moved to the foreground
> to be studied and conceptualized against the background of the far-more-
> frequently-investigated psychological, social, and cultural environments of
> individuals and groups. (Proshansky and O'Hanlon, 1977, p. 103)

Methodological characteristics

Closely linked to this aspect is the necessary diversity of the new field with
regard to the methods of investigation adopted for studying naturalistic
and field situations rather than experimental and laboratory research. This
methodological diversity is seen as more suitable for examining the spatio-
physical aspects of the environment, that is, naturalistic rather than
artificial laboratory situations, such as those taught by the ethological

(Lorenz, 1965; Eibel-Eibesfeldt, 1970) and anthropological traditions (Hall, 1966). Proshansky describes this as follows:

> A move into real-world settings in order to study individuals' reactions to and relationships with their physical settings has carried with it a fundamental constraint insofar as research and analysis are concerned: the integrity of the person–environment events have to be maintained at any cost. These events must be defined, analysed, and observed in the natural, ongoing context in which they occur. What is to be scrupulously avoided, regardless of circumstances, are distortions of these events engendered by the research process itself, extending from such matters as the role of the researcher in the natural setting to attempts to manipulate environmental settings in order to meet the standards of 'scientifically controlled' investigations. To some extent environmental psychologists have received fair warning about the need to maintain the integrity of events that are of interest to them. (Proshansky and O'Hanlon, 1977, p. 116)

Here the opposition of environmental-psychological research to the psychological tradition of laboratory research is underlined. Proshansky often directs critical remarks towards the latter, particularly with regard to its possibilities of providing elements of comprehension regarding natural or 'real-life' situations:

> Although the 'names were the same' the problems and issues they had studied in the laboratory and outside of it under highly controlled conditions held little relationship to the problems and issues that were of concern in the real-life settings. The original real-life issues had been so 'peeled,' 'cleaned up,' and rendered researchable that in the final analysis these problems were no longer recognizable, so that the findings, concepts, and methods of this type of research had no generalizability to nonlaboratory settings. (ibid.)

Social relevance

The social relevance of environmental-psychological research is exalted; emphasis is placed on how it attempts to provide responses to socially relevant problems; these include current environmental problems in general. The perspective of being able 'to enter the real world' through environmental-psychological research is proposed by many psychologists as an attractive opportunity and as a challenge for leaving behind the discomfort that psychological research – and psycho-social research in particular – has often experienced due to the social irrelevance of its work.

Harold Proshansky, for example, has repeatedly stressed this as one of the primary reasons for his enthusiastic adherence to e.p., affirming right from the beginning that he considered his work as a means for 'entering the real world', abandoning the primarily fictional world of irrelevant psychological research. 'Environmental Psychology and the Real World' is the emblematic title of one of his best-known articles on the subject (Proshansky, 1976).

On another occasion, Proshansky and his co-workers observe:

> A physical setting in which the individual's day-to-day existence robbed him of his right to realize his full capacity as a human being because of crowding,

intense noise, physical inconveniences, and still other stresses clearly cast doubt on the value of technological and scientific progress [. . .]. What the 'environmental crisis' in human dignity did, then, was to focus, extend and intensify the interest of a small but increasing number of design professionals and behavioral scientists in the problems of the relationships between human behavior and experience and the nature of physical settings, whether at the level of a school classroom, a city street, an apartment house, or an entire cosmopolitan area [. . .]. Furthermore the emphasis on relevance tended to legitimize for many hesitant and overly cautious behavioral scientists trained in the laboratory tradition of 'pure research', the possibility of studying major social problems in the real-life context in which they occurred and indeed to follow Lewin's (1948) dictum of doing research that was 'theoretically meaningful and socially useful'. The physical settings of modern urban communities – with all the problems that living in these communities entailed – were a conspicuous part of this context. If crowding, urban decay, loss of privacy, and water and air pollution were not relevant, then no other problems could be. (Proshansky and O'Hanlon, 1977, pp. 112–13)

Due to its aim of social relevance, e.p. is often presented as characterized by problem-oriented research and, therefore, as applied research; however, the various authors agree on the impossibility of distinguishing this type of research from the other. Lewin's famous statement on 'theoretically meaningful and socially useful' research is, in any case, considered the only objective worthy of reaching (Altman, 1976, 1988; Proshansky and O'Hanlon 1977; Stokols, 1978).

Interdisciplinary orientation

The other main aspect characterizing the emerging field of e.p., unlike traditional psychological research, is its link with other disciplinary fields also directed towards man–environment problems (geography, architecture, land planning, urban sociology, human ecology, epidemiology/ hygiene, ecology of natural resources); especially, e.p. is seen as part of the wider body of the so-called 'environmental sciences'.

The various authors agree on this point:

> The environment and behavior field is inherently interdisciplinary and encompasses a wide spectrum of scientific and environmental design disciplines. The range of perspectives contributed by different disciplines is occasionally overwhelming and sometimes akin to the Tower of Babel. But this diversity is also valuable. (Altman, 1976, p. 99)

> An e.p. that was focused on the real world and directly concerned with the solution of complex environmental problems must by definition be interdisciplinary in character. (Proshansky, 1987, p. 1474)

> Owing to the complexity of environmental problems and the necessity of approaching them from different perspectives and levels of analysis, contemporary research on environment and behavior is interdisciplinary in scope. Researchers and practitioners in the fields of geography, urban sociology, public health, natural resources management, architecture, organizational behavior, facilities management and urban planning constitute a broad base of professional support for e.p. (Stokols and Altman, 1987, p. 2)

This interdisciplinary perspective is mainly proposed to encourage every possible form of collaboration and exchange between e.p. and other disciplinary sectors involved in the same topics without denying the disciplinary specificity of e.p.; this aspect will be treated in more detail later on.

In this regard, there is a certain divergence in the field of e.p. between environmental psychologists with psychological training (such as Altman, Stokols, Craik, Canter, etc.) and those with non-psychological training (such as Rapoport, Moore, Zube, Golledge, etc.); the latter in particular often show their preference for the term for the field of 'person–environment relationship' instead of environmental psychology; in general, they do not see the need for the disciplinary specificity expressed by the former.

Definition of the field of interest

Considering that the authors initially wanted to emphasize e.p.'s novelty and interdisciplinary approach, it can be noted how the definition of field of interest emerged with some difficulty; at first the authors were often reticent about this definition. Following is an example of how the authors of the first introductory volume on the topic, *Environmental Psychology: Man and His Physical Settings* describe it:

> E.p. can only be understood and defined, however, in the context of the environmental sciences in general: the larger body of study concerned with the consequences of man's manipulation of his environment [. . .] deals with the man-ordered and defined environment; they grow out of pressing social problems; they are multidisciplinary in nature; and they include the study of man as an integral part of every problem. In short, the environmental sciences are concerned with human problems in relation to an environment of which man is both victim and conqueror. (Proshansky et al., 1970, p. 5)

The same authors go on to state that at the moment it is not possible to adequately define e.p., and they propose a completely operational definition, 'environmental psychology is what environmental psychologists do' (ibid., p. 5).

It is interesting to note that the same difficulty in defining e.p. is found almost ten years later in one of the first introductory textbooks in the field (Bell et al., 1978). Here the authors specifically state that 'if given a choice' they would again adopt Proshansky et al.'s (1970) definition of e.p., and only if forced to define e.p. in less than twenty-five words would they 'hazard the following definition, with all its potential shortcomings: environmental psychology is the study of the interrelations between behavior and the built or natural environment' (Bell et al., 1978, p. 6).

Despite the initial difficulty of the City University group to provide a clear definition of e.p., several years later these authors agreed on the type of definition which had been proposed in the meantime by others: it

Table 3.1　*Area of interest of e.p. in relation to the*
characteristics of the environment considered

	Degree of human influence	
	Minimum (natural environment)	Maximum (built environment)
Small scale	Ex.: tree	Room
Large scale	Ex.: park	City

Source: Adapted from Craik, 1970

qualifies the new area of research mainly in terms of its attention to the physical aspects of the environment: 'We will consider environmental psychology as a discipline that is concerned with the relationship between human behavior and man's physical environment' (Heimstra and McFarling, 1974, p. 5); environmental psychology is defined as the study of man in his physical setting in Kantowitz, (1977); 'Environmental psychology is defined as an attempt to establish an empirical and theoretical relationship between behavior and experience of the person and his built environment' (Ittelson et al., 1974, p. 303).

It is interesting to note how e.p.'s primary attention to the spatio-physical aspects of the environment caused the new area of studies to be not only initially defined but also articulated in relation to the characteristics of the physical environment; the distinction between physical-built and physical-natural environment is the one we find most used besides that between 'large-scale environments' and 'small-scale environments'.

The schema for the field proposed by Craik (1970) in one of the first introductory articles (see Table 3.1) illustrates this. Here he proposes distinguishing the environment according to two main criteria: first on the basis of the dimension represented by 'the degree of human influence present', with the two poles of the natural environment (with minimum level of human influence) and the built environment (with maximum level of human influence); second on the basis of the 'scale dimension', with the two poles of small and large scale; this is defined according to the possibility/impossibility of the individual's direct perception through a 'simple glance' at the environment in question.

According to this schema, the variety of the field of e.p. is outlined depending on the characteristics of the spatio-physical environment considered.

Besides these initial attempts to define the field of e.p. mainly according to the characteristics of the spatio-physical environment, other proposals have been made to define the field more as a function of the type of psychological processes studied. On the one hand, the distinctions appearing most often deal with the prevalent modalities for considering the causal relationship between environment and individual (Wohlwill, 1970): environment as cause or rather as result of the psychological phenomena/processes studied. On the other hand, the peculiarity of the psychological phenomena or processes deriving from that relationship is considered.

These kinds of definitions aim at emphasizing the disciplinary peculiarity of the field, above all characterized by the consideration of psychological processes dealing with the socio-physical individual–environment interface, that is, the individual in interaction/transaction with the environment:

(a) phenomena/processes of manifested behaviours (Bonnes, 1979a) or physical-behavioural ones (Stokols, 1978; Holahan, 1986), represented primarily by 'spatial behaviour' (territoriality, privacy) and by 'environmental stress';

(b) phenomena/processes of implicit behaviours (Bonnes, 1979a) or cognitive-symbolic ones (Stokols, 1978), represented by the various psychological processes/phenomena which can also be regrouped under the broad heading of 'environmental perception/representation': environmental cognition/knowledge, environmental affect, environmental attitudes, environmental assessment and environmental personality (see Chapter 4).

The schema proposed by Stokols in his review article in 1978 is interesting in this regard; both of these perspectives are utilized to outline the entire field of studies (Table 3.2).

The proposal to assume this theoretical framework is advanced by Stokol together with the need for e.p. to adopt the transactional perspective as the more suitable one for facing the problems of the individual–environment relationship. This perspective, which we will return to in more detail (see Chapter 5), is primarily aimed at affirming:

(a) the continuous exchange and reciprocity which characterizes the relationship of the individual with his/her environment;

(b) the primarily active and intentional role – that is, planned and directed by goals – of the individual towards the environment.

The concept of 'environmental optimization' is proposed by the author as a substitute for 'environmental adaptation'; with this term he points out the active and intentional (and not mainly 'reactive') orientation which the individual has with the characteristics of the environment:

> A distinction can be drawn between adaptation and optimization. Adaptation refers to people's attempts (behavioral, cognitive, physiological) to cope with existing environmental conditions. Optimization involves a more planful and cyclical process whereby individuals not only adapt to the existing situation, but also opt to maintain or modify their milieu in accord with specified goals. Optimization subsumes adaptation but places an equal emphasis on man's reciprocal control over the environment. (Stokols, 1978, p. 258)

The author observed that 'although environmental optimization is never realized in its ideal form, the concept is heuristically useful in emphasizing

Table 3.2   *Area of interest of e.p. in relation to the modality of person–environment transactions and to the consequent psycho-environmental phenomena/processes considered*

		Form of transaction	
		Cognitive	Behavioural
		Interpretive	*Operative*
	Active	Cognitive representation of the spatial environment	Experimental analysis of ecologically relevant behaviour
		Personality and the environment	Human spatial behaviour
Phase of transaction		*Evaluative*	*Responsive*
	Reactive	Environmental attitudes	Impact of the physical environment
		Environmental assessment	Ecological psychology

Source: Stokols, 1978, p. 259

the goal-directed and cyclical nature of the human/environment trans-actions and in suggesting certain processes by which these transactions occur' (ibid).

On the basis of these premises, Stokols outlines a double articulation for framing the variety of research in e.p. according to the 'form' or the 'phase' of the individual–environment transactive process considered (see Table 3.2). On one side, he distinguishes the tendency of research to focus on the modality – more cognitive (or symbolic) or, rather, behavioural (or physical) – of the 'form' of the transaction considered; on the other side, he distinguishes the tendency to consider the modality – more active or rather reactive – of the 'phase' of the transactive process considered. Combining these two aspects, it becomes possible to specify four other modalities with which the individual carries on transactions with the environment; these also involve the various psycho-environmental processes in different ways:

(a)   *interpretive*, for the cognitive-active transactive modality;
(b)   *evaluative*, for the cognitive-reactive transactive modality;
(c)   *operative*, for the behavioural-active transactive modality;
(d)   *responsive*, for the behavioral-reactive transactive modality.

Thus, it becomes possible to place most of the research domain of e.p. according to each different modality, providing a comprehensive picture of the field, as illustrated in the schema of Table 3.2.

Stokols's proposal seems particularly interesting also because, in the same article, he specifies two other very crucial aspects for defining the new area of e.p.

1   He defines e.p. with reference to the broader corpus of the so-called 'human–environment' relationship studies where, according to the programmatic interdisciplinary aims of the field, the convergence of studies from various disciplines can be seen, that is, not only from psychology but also from sociology, anthropology, economics, geography, architecture, etc.

Due to repeated statements about the necessity for pluridisciplinary and interdisciplinary approaches to the field by both psychologists and non-psychologists, Stokols (1978, p. 255) is particularly concerned with defining the specific role of psychology as the primary disciplinary area for approaching human–environment problems, with reference to possible and desired contributions from other disciplinary areas:

> The research concerns and strategies subsumed under the rubric of 'environmental psychology' can perhaps be best represented as parts of an emerging interdisciplinary field of environment and behavior, or 'human–environment relations'. This field encompasses several diverse perspectives on environment and behavior such as human ecology, environmental and urban sociology, architecture, planning, natural resources management, and behavioral geography. While closely related to these areas, environmental psychology diverges from them by placing relatively greater emphasis on basic psychological processes (e.g. cognition, development, personality, learning) and on individual and group (vs societal) levels of analysis.

Thus, the specific unit of analysis of every disciplinary area is indirectly proposed with reference to psychology, which, however, is set apart due to its specific attention to basic psychological processes.

2   From many points of view Stokols's article represents an important step in the development of e.p. in a psycho-social sense. In fact, here he introduces the concept of 'socio-physical environment' – no longer only 'physical environment' – for outlining e.p.'s field of interest: 'Environmental psychology pertains to the interface between human behavior and sociophysical environment' (Stokols, 1978, p. 253).

This definition has been completely assumed by the subsequent literature, as confirmed in the recent *Handbook* (Stokols, and Altman, 1987). The necessity for e.p. to take into consideration the physical environment within a molar perspective – which also considers the social aspects of it – rather than in a physico-molecular way is stressed by the main authors. This will be discussed in greater detail later.

Both of Stokols's perspectives have been reaffirmed and further reinforced in the publication of the *Handbook* (1987), where the following definition is proposed for the field: 'environmental psychology, i.e., the study of behavior and human well-being in relation to the socio-physical environment' (ibid., p. 1).

With the proposal of this definition, the authors tend not only to confirm what Stokols and others had previously emphasized regarding the primarily psycho-social nature of the field, but they also indirectly indicate a further dimension of interest of the field, that is, the problem of 'human well-being'.

The proposal of the latter as objective of the field underlines both the research aim and also its possible involvement in socio-environmental change and intervention; this points to the possible practical involvement of e.p. also in environmental organization and management. Several authors (Holahan and Wandersman, 1987; Saegert, 1987) are particularly interested in this aspect and they have speculated about the implications that a psycho-environmental 'practice', directed not only towards study but also towards social change, would have for perspectives of analysis and reference paradigms.

In any case, besides the possibility for e.p.'s involvement in both research and psycho-environmental intervention-change, another aspect must be emphasized regarding the definition of the field; this aspect is linked both to this type of consideration and to the assumption of the already mentioned transactional-contextual theoretical perspective, which will be specifically discussed later (see Chapter 5).

At this point, the modalities for considering the environment and its characteristics emerge as dynamic rather than static, as primarily made up of 'processes' not of simple 'objects' or 'characteristics'. Thus, analogous to the way psychological processes are assumed as units of analysis for the person, the importance of assuming a dynamic perspective of the environment and its characteristics must also be stressed; here the analysis should also be oriented in terms of processes rather than environmental characteristics. We believe that the most appropriate definition for the field of e.p. is: the area of psychology which is concerned with the relationships between psychological processes and processes of the socio-physical environment.

The spatio-physical environment in present-day environmental psychology: identifying the paradigm

Considering the variety of theoretical perspectives in psychology on the problem of the relationship of the individual with the spatio-physical characteristics of the environment, the initial psycho-environmental research has been characterized by diversity and heterogeneity.

Particularly crucial for this new area of psychological studies have been the modalities for conceptualizing and dealing with the spatio-physical environment; essentially this has involved defining the research paradigm (Kuhn, 1962), that is, defining the 'often implicit assumptions underlying a theory or model suitable for influencing the researcher's concrete way of proceeding and his view of reality' (de Grada and Mannetti, 1988, p. 10; see also pp. 149–52 below).

Beyond the heterogeneity of topics and theoretical perspectives, it is possible to show how the modalities used by e.p. for approaching the relationship between psychological processes and spatio-physical aspects of the environment can be primarily traced back to the main double theoretical perspective existing in this respect in the psychological tradition, that is, the psychology of perception, on the one hand, and social psychology, on the other.

Actually, the initial proposals of the principal founders of e.p. (Craik, 1970; Proshansky et al., 1970; Altman, 1973; Ittelson, 1973a, 1973b; Stokols, 1978) leave no doubts about the choice of the psycho-social paradigm rather than the physico-perceptual one; this emerges clearly in their various theoretical works. However, in this regard, a tendency towards divergence can often be perceived between their professed theoretical aims – overall, definitely oriented towards the molar position of social psychology – and the parallel modality of doing empirical research – often anchored instead to the physico-molecular viewpoint of the tradition of the psychology of perception.

The aim of the placement of the emerging field of e.p. within the tradition of social psychology is manifest in the expressed intention of many of the authors/founders to consider the physical environment from within a molar, non-molecular perspective, as well as to consider the close connection between the physical and social aspects of the environment under examination.

The first steps made by e.p. at the beginning of the 1970s, with the initial articles and introductory volumes, were invariably accompanied by this type of theoretical introduction. Kenneth Craik, in his first introductory article (1970, p. 15), affirms that the physical environment, object of the emerging field of e.p., is not the environment as defined by the physicists, but the 'environment *qua* molar'.

> Psychologists have made use of variables that physicists have provided, for example, temperature, luminance, chromaticity, and amplitude, but have not attempted to explore the physical variables that geographers and environmental designers provide, or that might be developed through collaboration with these environmental experts. The feasibility of an environmental psychology rests upon confidence that an adequate taxonomy of dimensions, and eventually a system of metrics, can be developed for the ordinary physical environment.
>
> A pathway into a wilderness track, a dilapidated tenement house, the interior of a department store, the Great Plains of western Kansas during a drought – these environments surely possess descriptive and identifying properties beyond those offered by the physicist.

He continues, referring to Tolman's distinction:

> In this sense, approaching the environment at its ordinary, everyday level raises issues similar to those encountered by Edward C. Tolman when, in 1932, he introduced the concepts of behavior *qua* molar, and behavior *qua* molecular [. . .]. By 'the *molecular* definition of behavior', Tolman meant behavior 'in terms of its strict underlying physical and physiological details, i.e., in terms of receptor-process, conductor-process, and effector-process per se'. By the *molar*

definition of behavior, he referred to 'behavior, as such', which is 'more than and different from the sum of its physiological parts'. (ibid.)

Craik then proposes along with Tolman that:

> 'Just as "behavior-acts" can be interpreted through the "underlying molecular facts of physics and physiology", environmental entities can be considered in terms of the underlying facts of physics and chemistry, yet both phenomena possess, "as molar wholes", certain emergent properties of their own' (Tolman, 1932, p. 7). Just as 'it is these, the molar properties of behavior-acts, which are of prime interest to psychologists', so also are the molar properties of the physical environment of interest to us as environmental psychologists.
>
> The term 'molar', which Tolman used in a metaphorical sense regarding behavior, can be used in a strict sense regarding the physical environment. Now that Tolman's campaign to consider behavior *qua* molar, after three decades, has met with general success, the time has come to consider the physical setting of molar behavior: the environment *qua* molar. (ibid.)

The same approach advanced by Craik has also been repeatedly proposed by the exponents of the founding group at the City University of New York; they have affirmed the necessity for a perspective that is both molar – in this case through the concept of 'total environment' – and specifically psycho-social:

> The environment is experienced as a unitary field. Although we perceive the environment as discrete stimuli – sight, sound, taste, smell, touch – the total constellation of stimuli determines how we respond to it. It is the complexity that constitutes the physical setting in which men live and interact over extended periods of time that must be considered in assessing the influence of environment on human behavior. (Ittelson et al., 1974, p. 12)

Further, the same authors note that

> there is no physical environment that is not embedded in and inextricably related to a social system. We cannot respond to an environment independently of our role as social beings. Even a solitary person reacts to his setting on the basis of his isolation. The nature of an environment will affect the functioning of groups whether this environment be a city or a school-room.

Proshansky expresses the following:

> For the environmental psychologist, however, the physical environment of interest goes well beyond the stimuli and patterns of stimuli of interest to experimental and human-factor psychologists. Indeed he rejects these conceptions of the physical environment because they represent analytical abstractions of this environment rather than a realistic description of it as it relates to the actual behavior and experience of the individual. The physical environments to be observed and studied are all those places and spaces that provide the locus and definition of the varied multiple of human activities that characterize day-to-day existence. And these spaces and places are in turn defined by the social realities. (Proshansky and O'Hanlon, 1977, p. 103)

And Stokols specifies:

> First, in contrast to most subareas of psychology, environmental psychology (and in particular, ecological psychology) brings an ecological perspective to the study of environment and behavior. Accordingly, the environment is construed

in multidimensional, molar terms, and the focus of analysis generally is on the interrelations among people and their sociophysical milieu rather than on the linkages between discrete stimuli and behavior responses.

However, in this regard Stokols (1978, p. 254) has to immediately admit that

> ... much of the research in this field has attempted to isolate physical dimensions (e.g., noise, temperature, space) of the broader milieu in order to assess their specific effects on behavior.

This admission shows what we previously noted about the initial tendency in the field towards divergence between theoretical aims with a psycho-social orientation and research practice with a molecular orientation in the two directions, that is, physicalistic and individualistic.

On the other hand, the need to assume the psycho-social perspective for this new area of psychological research was affirmed by Stokols in the same article; here the environment, object of e.p., is no longer defined as 'physical environment' but as 'socio-physical environment'.

Also, in examining the characteristics of the then emerging field of e.p., Altman (1976) has indicated the presence of 'a global, molar perspective' in first place and 'the psycho-social orientation in second place'.

With regard to the first aspect, he emphasizes the coincidence of that perspective with the systemic approach, providing already at that time several interesting insights; he would develop them more fully later on (see pp. 152–61) in relation to the perspective he initially defined as 'ecological-socio-systemic' (1973) and, then, 'transactional-contextual' (Altman and Rogoff, 1987). According to Altman (1976, p. 98):

> Environmental research views phenomena as complex, patterned and often not amenable to a strictly analytic approach, as represented in the terms 'systems', 'patterns', 'networks' and 'Gestalten'. For example, an implicit principle is that one is usually dealing with people–environment units in which it is difficult to tease apart components. Also, the assumption is made of complex cause–effect relationships between environment and behavior, not unidirectional links between variables.

With regard to the second aspect, Altman has strongly supported both the importance of the psycho-social perspective in e.p. and social psychology's interest in the development of this type of study. In 1976 this stimulated a lively debate in the *Personality and Social Psychology Bulletin* with other authoritative researchers, such as Proshansky, Epstein and Stokols (Altman, 1976).

At the same time, he has emphasized how 'it should be noted however that a social and interpersonal perspective on environmental phenomena is only just beginning. Whether social psychology will actually have a substantial impact on future environmental research and practice remains to be seen. I am optimistic that this might be the case' (ibid., p. 99).

Certainly, Altman is one of the founders of environmental psychology who has been most involved in that direction, working both theoretically, through his proposal of a 'transactional-contextual approach', and empirically. He has managed to arrive at a general redefinition, in psycho-social terms, of the various lines of research concerning several psycho-environmental processes of spatial behaviour (privacy, territoriality, personal space; see Chapter 4), showing the transactional character of the persons–places relationship (Oxley et al., 1986) in various studies conducted using non-intrusive methods (photographic documents, participant observation, etc.).

In the following chapters we will present the major topics of study occupying present-day e.p.; we will attempt to show the progressive emergence and consolidation of the psycho-social perspectives within them. In Chapter 4, we will first show the growing importance of the so-called 'internal mediator processes' by examining the relationship between physical-environmental aspects and behaviour (for example, in spatial behaviour, in crowding, in the reaction to stress factors, etc.). These processes are essentially represented by the symbolic processes of interpretation and attribution of meanings – understood as integrated processes of both cognitive and affective aspects – which have always been at the core of social psychology.

Then, in Chapter 5, we will examine several specific key concepts of present-day e.p. which seem to have the greatest possibility for development in psycho-social terms, such as the concept of 'person–environment transaction' and that of the concept of 'place' according to the most recent formulations (Canter, 1977, 1986; Stokols, 1981; Altman, 1986), as well as new constructs with a clear psycho-social orientation, such as 'place identity' (Proshansky, 1978) and 'social representation of place'.

4

Main Research Topics

The dynamic of internal and external factors contributing to the emergence of psychology's specific interest in the 'environment' can be seen more relevantly in the empirical research carried on by environmental psychologists in various socio-cultural contexts. The main implications related to this dynamic are revealed as differentiated attention to various topics constituting the overall field of interest as well as different modalities for formulating more general questions about the relations between people and their environments. The remarkable variety and the number of contributions produced has outlined a field of competence which, as already shown, allows for a formal definition based on very broad criteria, too general to have a unifying function.

It has often been noted critically that this generality is a consequence of the heterogeneity of approaches underlying most of the studies conducted. In effect, the purpose of restoring that 'specificity of place' (Russell and Ward, 1982) to behaviour and human action, considered as neglected or treated inadequately by the psychological tradition, has been the clearest shared goal in this new field of research. However, many diversified strategies have been adopted for reaching the objective, and many differences are found at the various levels of analysis.

Considering the theoretical-methodological level as the one where the most evident lacks of coherence are found, the major differences derive both from the plurality of ways for conceptualizing the relation between persons (behaviour) and environment and from the degree of sensitivity to pluridisciplinary collaboration demonstrated by environmental-psychological research in following its basic objectives.

With regard to the first issue, we are faced with the co-presence of frameworks which, as expressions of different epistemological premises, propose diversified causal interpretations of the relation which connects person and environment; that is, in explaining behaviour they define differently the role to assign to the person's characteristics and to those of the environment (Altman and Rogoff, 1987). In this respect, the predominant position attributes to the environment the deterministic role of 'independent variable', that is, of a variable which linearly produces effects on the outcome of behaviours (responses) through its objective properties (stimulations).

However, other tendencies have intervened in opposition to or at least as mediated versions of the one just described. Two other main positions need to be mentioned here: in one case attention is shifted from environment to individual psychological experience; in the other, interactions between persons and environments are emphasized. According to the first position, persons 'interpret' the environment and every aspect of the relationships they establish with it is explained by specific individual characteristics. On the contrary, the second position considers these relationships as the outcome of processes in which the characteristics of persons and of the environment interact to give life to a continuous dynamic of reciprocal influences.

With regard to the disciplinary definition, e.p.'s area of competencies has been outlined by the simultaneous reference to a particular 'object' of study (psychological processes in relation to the environment) and to a more general 'perspective' of analysis (aimed at studying individuals' problems in the environment). This contingency involves the multiple presence of coordinates which define the spaces frequented by the research with different modalities: on the one hand, the more classical psychological one, which takes the environment into specific consideration (Russell and Ward, 1982); on the other, the broader space of the environmental sciences, which attempts a pluridisciplinary integration of knowledge regarding the multiform relations linking individuals to the environment (Stokols, 1978; Saegert and Winkel, 1990).

Expression of the different degree of complexity attributed to these relations, the frequenting of one or the other of these spaces, is reflected primarily in the adoption of at least two main and distinct approaches to specific problems. The first approach is oriented towards the recurring manifestations of human functioning with respect to the environment and is focused on the individual, his/her behaviours and/or knowledge and evaluations of the environment. The second, more interested in the interconnections between the individual as 'agent-actor in a context' and the respective environment, also pays particular attention to situational and socio-cultural variables (Altman, 1976; Bonnes, 1977, 1978; Secchiaroli, 1979a; Stokols, 1981, 1987; Altman and Rogoff, 1987).

The theoretical-methodological differences noted above are obviously associated with others regarding the various levels of conceptualization implied in every research activity: from the most general and abstract concerning the relation which links individuals and the environment to that concerning the empirical definition of the variables selected for this purpose (Bonnes, 1979a).

In order to reconstruct a synthetic map of the territory frequented by environmental psychologists, two types of closely linked questions must be answered: one concerns the main topics they are interested in and are currently working on in their research; and the other concerns the prevalent modalities or procedures for carrying out these activities.

The relationship between thematic areas and conceptual frameworks guiding research has assumed increasing importance in the current internal debate in e.p. According to periodical reviews in the *Annual Review of*

Psychology (Craik, 1973; Stokols, 1978; Russell and Ward, 1982; Holahan, 1986; Saegert and Winkel, 1990) and the recent *Handbook of Environmental Psychology* (Stokols and Altman, 1987), the issues being debated are now more a sign of positive development than a limitation of the open perspective of this field of investigation.

The most adequate way of clarifying the attention psychologists dedicate to the physical environment and its properties through research with respect to 'human behaviour and experience' (Holahan, 1986) is perhaps to return to the main questions they have posed in this regard.

According to various systematic reviews of the above-mentioned literature, the presence of at least two general questions traces a preliminary differentiation of research objectives. The first of these concerns behaviours people exhibit in relation to the characteristics of the environment, and the second, the ways in which they arrive at 'knowing' and 'evaluating' it. The two thematic areas outlined by these interrogatives reflect the implications linking environmental-psychological research both with other domains (external) of environmental research and with orientations of more general psychological research.

In attempting to respond to the first question, e.p. has a predominantly practical objective: to identify components, properties or overall dispositions of the physical environment which impede and/or facilitate people's behaviours and actions. This objective, which refers more directly to problems of adequacy of the 'built' environment with respect to its functions, intersects with the current needs of disciplines such as architecture and planning. The task initially assumed by British architectural psychology is certainly the most significant proof of this position (see Chapter 1).

In order to find indications about the modalities people follow to arrive at knowing the environment and/or interpreting its physical properties in evaluative terms, research has been primarily oriented towards investigating the outcomes of the psychological processes which mediate the person–environment relationship; that is, to clarify the role people play in defining the characteristics of the environment they are interacting with. In this sense, the objectives are not exclusively linked to the built environment, but are open to the consideration of the 'natural' environment. They are more clearly placed on a parallel with those of the ecological sciences, particularly with behavioural geography, which considers the component of 'environmental perception' as a constituting aspect in the physical-geographical definition of the environment that individuals are a part of.

However, it is evident that investigating human functioning with respect to the environment, focusing on 'processes of knowledge' and relative outcomes rather than on manifest behaviours, is an alternative which finds its most consistent support in the psychological disciplines.

Besides this primary differentiation of research into broad areas of content, another emerges in the literature regarding the ways empirical analysis is carried out in both of the thematic areas just described.

As we have pointed out in the preceding chapters, this second differentiation can be traced back to the prevalence of an analytical or 'molecular' approach, alongside one which tends to be more 'molar' (Craik, 1970) or 'total' (Ittelson et al., 1974). In the first approach the specific relations which link particular properties of the environment to equally partial aspects of individual functioning are focused on molecular or 'elementary' units of analysis. In the second, the many factors involved in the definition of the relations which connect persons to environments are emphasized. As a consequence, research is oriented towards analysing these relations in a more integrated (not fragmented) way (molar or 'complex' unit of analysis). In this case, both Barker's 'ecological' demands and the more general contextual-interactive perspective proposed by Lewinian psychology seem to be acquired.

An example of the unit of analysis adopted in the first approach can be found in research on physical-environmental factors such as noise, temperature and light. Here, what is usually focused on are the links emerging between the 'stimulus properties' of these factors (modalities and degrees to which they are manifest) and individuals' specific 'responses' to them. This is true even if, when speaking of responses, reference is made not only to behavioural manifestations, such as the performance of particular tasks or aggressivity expressed towards others, but also to the outcome of psychological processes such as perception, formation and/or change of attitudes and evaluation.

In studies following the second approach, adopting more complex units of analysis, there are those concerned with people's uses of physical space (spatial behaviour), and primarily those concerned with knowledge-evaluations (or representations) people structure with respect to their daily life environments, such as homes or residential areas in the city.

In the first example, the spatial dimension is not uniquely assumed as a variable which localizes and physically defines the opportunities and ways of locomotion and activities in the environment, but primarily as the means (of communication) used by people in interactive processes with the (social) environment they are a part of; for example, to express their degree of accessibility to (or nearness to/farness from) others by means of collectively shared models of behaviour.

It appears evident that this approach implies the consideration of socio-cultural data apart from those regarding the more strictly physical properties of space; these data permit an adequate reconstruction of the environmental and situational contexts where the behaviours analysed take on specific meaning.

With regard to the second example, the significance this topic has with respect to the perspective of inquiry we are considering has already been noted. In fact, we refer to that specific research topic which, following its initiation with studies of 'environmental perception and cognition', has emphasized the cognitive-evaluative function accomplished by the processes involved; this is true particularly with regard to environmental settings which, like the city, present such complex characteristics that they require the activation of (cognitive) strategies which facilitate an effective organization of behaviours.

Apart from the general theoretical issues which have been repeatedly discussed and more thoroughly investigated (see Chapter 2), attention must be turned towards the specific tendency to assume cognition (or, better, cognitive representation) as a significant indicator of the type and quality of the complex relationship individuals establish, maintain and/or change with their life environments or, in other words, with the many dimensions contributing in each case towards characterizing the specificity of this relationship (Stokols, 1981; Bonnes and Secchiaroli, 1986). It was through this particular definition of environmental cognition that the need for research to assume more complex units of analysis was recognized, that is, to consider the manifold nature of the two variables involved in the relation being studied.

In this perspective, the environment not only constitutes a source of stimulations or sensory information, whose saliency derives from the intrinsic properties of its physical components (for example, architectural, spatial, functional structures), but also includes factors of symbolic prominence, of norms and/or opportunities for action and systems of social relations. These factors become constitutive properties of the environment primarily through shared attributions of meaning, constructed through social interaction and communication.

Similarly, in this case, people are no longer considered as 'thinking machines' responding uniquely to the laws of mental functioning, or as pure 'subjectivity', singular interpreters of the external world. As Ittelson (1973a, 1973b) has pointed out, it is really difficult to imagine persons as simple spectators inside processes which bring them to know and evaluate environments which they experience daily through action; that is, to consider the processes of human knowledge as completely separate from the system of goals which guide behaviours.

It would be equally reductive to neglect that persons (and their models of action), as components of a social as well as a physical context, are differentiated not only in terms of individual characteristics but also in relation to their position in the social space.

By means of a more detailed analysis (which will be proposed subsequently), the novelty of such a theoretical-methodological perspective for the overall area of environmental-psychological research will be more evident. In any case, two main characteristics must be pointed out in this regard: a definition of environment in which the physical dimension is considered as strictly correlated to the social one; and a research approach which, starting from the placement of persons in a position of active exchange with this environment, meets the essential prerequisites for a contextual analysis of human—environment relations.

Besides reflecting the increasingly desired direction for developments in e.p. (Bonnes and Secchiaroli, 1986; Altman and Rogoff, 1987; Stokols,

1987), these characteristics outline applications substantially analogous to those which direct a great deal of current European social psychology.

The following illustration of the main areas of research has been organized on the basis of the types of general questions e.p. intends to respond to: in the first part, studies investigating the relations between physical properties of the environment and individuals' behaviour will be considered; in the second, studies specifically interested in the psychological processes involved in these relations will be described.

In agreement with the foregoing, both of these sections will present examples which are also differentiated with respect to the type of unit of analysis adopted.

The spatio-physical dimension of behaviour

The studies concerned with relations between persons and the environment, focusing on behaviours exhibited by the former and the properties which can be objectively shown of the latter, can be considered as the most immediate and direct expression of the programmatic intentions e.p. referred to in outlining its specificity and novelty with respect to the tradition of psychological research.

Asking how people act as a function of the physical characteristics of the environment is not, however, a completely unexplored area in psychological studies. Although in episodic terms, or, better, in the absence of formally expressed objectives, the psycho-social literature offers some representative examples in this direction.

The first, in chronological order, now a classic, dates back to the 1930s and is found in the programme of experimental research carried out by Elton Mayo (1933) in a large industrial concern. Proposing to analyse the relations between physical properties of the work environment and levels of productivity, these studies focused on the lighting factor. The hypothesis predicted that by varying the degree and quality of lighting in the environment, correlated variations in the workers' productivity levels would be found. By now it is also well-known that the results obtained in a series of experimental conditions created for this purpose did not confirm the hypotheses. Several of these experiments showed a tendency towards stability in certain productivity standards, regardless of the change (either positive or negative) in the lighting conditions. Besides the physical lighting factor, factors of a different nature emerge to explain these results, in particular those defined as 'human factors', concerning the types of relations established between the subjects during the experiments and/or already existing in the work environment when the research was carried out. With respect to work productivity, the subjects' behaviour in this situation responded to a shared norm, or was an expression of the existence of confronting groups, identifying themselves as opposing the firm's direction. In the explanation of the behaviours studied, a social dimension of reality was shown to be in clear competition with a more truly physical one.

A second example can be found in the studies conducted in the 1950s by Leon Festinger et al. (1950) in an urban residential environment. In this case, the hypothesis predicts significant connections between different models of social interaction practised by residents and the position of their homes in the environmental space of the area studied. One of the results the authors particularly point out is the role assumed by the proximity factor and by the sharing of routes in which the residential space is organized. These conditions emerge in particular as facilitating the structuring of meaningful relations between inhabitants.

The questions faced by Festinger and Mayo highlight two main areas of study comprising the environmental research sector we are now considering: the area that assumes the overall 'spatial dimension' of the environment as its main object of interest and the one that focuses attention on more specific physical properties or particular types of stimulations coming from the environment (above all, noise).

The broad and systematic interest shown in these two directions has been expressed in the development of inquiries which have enriched the repertoire of topics e.p. has faced and have demonstrated the need to overcome the general hypothesis which predicts linear relations between physical-environmental characteristics and behavioural outcomes.

In this sense, the importance assumed by studies on the spatial dimension derives more from the attention dedicated to ways people manage and use physical-environmental space ('spatial behaviour') than from specific interest in the linear determinations produced by the objective organization of the latter on behaviour.

Analogously, the most interesting development of the study of the ways in which more specific environmental stimulations ('ambient-environment' features) can reflect negatively on behaviour has been the emphasis on the role of cognitive 'mediations' people can activate in this regard. That is, when attention is shifted from more direct and objectified 'disturbing effects' of these stimulations to considering them as potential stress factors.

Behaviour as response to the physical characteristics of the environment

Many studies have proposed to determine which spatio-physical properties most facilitate several forms of behaviour or, vice versa, impede the performance of specific activities. The research sector most involved with this question is particularly representative of one of the purposes initially emphasized by e.p. in characterizing itself as oriented towards concrete problems.

In this case, importance has been assumed by studies on the ways people react or respond to specific dispositions/organizations of physical space, and the literature shows how this sector tends more than others to hypothesize and test solutions whose outcomes are meant to assume a primarily operative valency. They are often proposed as contributions which directly meet the basic needs of planning and building environments for human use: to identify the physical characteristics environmental space must have in order to be adequate for the functions it is meant to carry out, or, more particularly, to facilitate the behaviours and actions of respective users.

The built environment for residential purposes is certainly the subject most studied. Particular attention has been dedicated to those types of residences in which – as in the case of university dormitories and, above all, psychiatric wards – many people must share a physical space designed to fulfil the essential functions of everyday life. With its primarily psychosocial interests, this research begins from the general hypothesis that the manipulation of the environment and physical space constitutes an effective means for influencing occupants' relational behaviours.

The most representative contributions can be found primarily in studies of the psychiatric ward environment. As previously mentioned, e.p. faced one of its greatest challenges in this particular area: to find ways in which spatio-physical disposition can contribute to a more effective accomplishment of the goals/functions of that environment.

Moving in this direction, researchers' attention has been primarily focused on the therapeutic purpose of the psychiatric institution and the major question concerns the spatio-physical organization for encouraging contacts and interpersonal relations between patients, which, in this case, assume a primarily therapeutic valency.

Scarcity or lack of interaction between patients, or between patients and the health personnel and external visitors, emerges as the central theme, recurring in almost all research on the psychiatric environment; just as often, the verification of operative hypotheses for the solution of the problem constitutes the integrating part of the programming and execution of these studies by means of direct experimentation of dispositions and alternative organizations of physical spaces.

The technique of 'behavioural mapping' has been used before and after comparisons in renovation and physical refurbishment. This technique, also widely used in other areas of research, involves a systematic observation procedure at time intervals and classification (both qualitative and quantitative) of behaviours exhibited by individual subjects in the spaces of the physical environment considered. The version that Ittelson et al. (1970) developed by studying psychiatric patients distinguishes three specific types of behaviour, defined as 'social', 'isolated-active' and 'isolated-passive'. The three different categories describe:

(a)   communicative-interactive behaviours with others (from conversation to play and to coordinated actions);
(b)   behaviours that do not imply relationships with others but are carried

out through any form of activity (such as reading, individual pastimes, personal hygiene);

(c) behaviours which, besides emerging through isolation, do not imply any type of activity (lying on a bed without sleeping, sitting in silence, wandering aimlessly).

The examples provided in the literature with regard to the hypothesis of intervention on the physical environment propose situations in which the manipulation of the spatial organization may concern both the disposition of furniture and furnishings in individual rooms (Sommer and Ross, 1958; Holahan, 1972; Holahan and Wandersman, 1987) and the creation *ex novo* of larger areas; this may involve, for example, night zones, structured in spaces which, even though designed for a limited number of persons, are arranged so as not to prevent reciprocal access and communication (Holahan and Saegert, 1973).

With regard to results, on the one hand, the research published on this topic tends to show the primarily quantitative increases in interpersonal behaviours exhibited by patients following interventions; on the other, it focuses on more general indications, proposing psychological evaluations in the direction of planning problems regarding the relationship between physical spaces and behaviour.

Faced with the objective of establishing and maintaining a positive social climate, this research points out how the disposition of environmental space must first offer users opportunities both for individual privacy and for contacts and social interaction (Ittelson et al., 1970).

As well as in studies on the psychiatric environment, this general indication has also been empirically supported in research conducted on other types of environments, such as university dormitories in the United States. Comparing students with the same length of annual residence in dormitories with different physical dispositions of residential space, Baum and Valins (1977) hypothesized and experimentally verified different tendencies towards forms of 'social' behaviour in the two cases considered.

The authors find greater sociability between subjects in dormitories with space organized in many small rooms than in those living in dormitories with only a few very large rooms and, thus, continuously open to contact between the various occupants.

Beyond the undisputed procedural-technical rigour (above all, experimental) involved in obtaining results, studies like this one are particularly important due to the growing critical debate that has developed around them in theoretical-methodological terms. In fact, the limitations deriving from their strictly physicalist and behaviourist perspective are evident.

With regard to this, Ittelson et al. (1970) point out how, in trying to identify only the direct connections between spatio-physical characteristics ('stimulus situations') and interpersonal behaviours (responses), one, *a priori*, renounces the opportunity – extremely relevant from a psychological point of view – of determining the role played by people in the dynamic of this relationship. Commenting on the results of their research in psychiatric environments, these authors also call attention to the behavioural differences between two groups of patients: the first group, in a structure with individual rooms, shows a very broad range of inter-personal behaviours compared with the second, in a structure with many people in a few rooms. They go beyond just noting these objective results, and they look for an adequate, primarily psychological interpretation, through a hypothesis which places particular emphasis on the 'perceptive' dimension.

If they only needed to go back to the spatio-physical disposition in order to explain these differences in behaviour, the authors believe their research results would show an opposite trend to what was obtained empirically. The spaces housing more people should constitute stimulus situations with greater probability of social interaction.

Therefore, a more plausible explanation of these differences takes into consideration the different limitations individuals perceive in the two cases considered with regard to the opportunity/freedom of being able to choose between forms of personal-private and/or interpersonal-public behaviour. In the case in question, the authors conclude that the greater number of interactions found in the first spatial structure (single rooms) is primarily linked to the perception of a greater number of alternatives compared to what is allowed in the second spatial structure (multiple rooms).

In contrasting the reductive simplification that a rigidly physicalist approach can lead to, this type of interpretation shifts attention to persons and to the processes through which they actively evaluate the whole environment. This hypothesis assigns a central position to a cognitive need, considered typically human, to have guaranteed that 'freedom of choice' which can be exercised only in the presence of a variety of alternatives. In this perspective, the spatio-physical disposition of the environment facilitates interpersonal behaviours if and to the degree it allows for the perception of alternative opportunities and, thus, personal control of choices.

In contrast with the more deterministic and elementaristic approach dominant in this type of research, the preceding interpretation outlines a person–physical environment relationship in which the person plays an active, not only reactive, role. The environment becomes relevant with respect to behaviour because of its overall spatial characteristics rather than because of those regarding its single component parts.

In this view, the attention dedicated to human behaviour is exclusively centred on cognitive needs for personal control and, thus, on the dynamics of psychological processes primarily regarding the individual dimension.

Since a different perspective is introduced, the hypothesis of 'personal control' contributes towards creating new areas for research. In fact, this hypothesis allows for the interpretation of many forms of environmental behaviour.

As will also be seen further on in this review, the function of theoretical-methodological reference, which has frequently been assigned to this hypothesis, reflects the persistence of a primarily individualistic orientation in various research topics. More generally, it indicates e.p.'s uncertainty and difficulty in moving towards its declared intention of confronting concrete problems using a more clearly psycho-social perspective.

Spatial behaviour

Although keeping the spatial dimension of the physical environment as its centre of interest, research on human spatial behaviour has moved towards objectives – and used approaches – often very different from those characterizing the above-described area of inquiry.

In fact, in research on 'spatial behaviour' the objective arrangement of space is considered not only as the possible antecedent of environmental behaviour but also as an expression of the uses people make of the space. In this case, rather than focusing on responses associated with specific spatial organizations, attention is turned towards the complex functions spatial behaviours can have in the relationship between persons and environments.

Rather than investigating the observable outcomes of these behaviours, this area of research proposes clarifying the meanings they can take on, primarily in the dynamics of social relationships.

Actually, studies on spatial behaviour have their roots both in ethology, traditionally interested in animal behaviour in physical-geographical space, and in anthropology, concerned with the discovery of the cultural meanings the various ways of using environmental space can take on, particularly in exchange-communication systems regulating the functioning of specific social contexts.

The fact that the developments in this area of environmental-psychological research have assigned a central position to several relevant questions is probably also due to the many propositions advanced by these disciplines. Questions are first posed concerning the functions that the spatial dimension can carry out in defining positions of relational proximity/distance between persons and the types of messages that are sent into the surrounding social environment through the definition of the geographical boundaries of space.

Although classified in three distinct categories, that is, 'personal space', 'territoriality' and 'privacy' (Holahan, 1986), much of the research on human spatial behaviour can easily be traced back to the common perspective of considering the implications existing between the physical components of space and the interpersonal-social dimension of behaviour.

An illustration of these three areas shows how these types of implications have too often been associated with the psychological function of 'control' or personal 'defence', and how this has limited potential research developments in the areas of personal space and territoriality. This concerns the limitations which, besides showing the need for more coherent theoretical references, have provided an incentive for reflection, leading to the outlining of new research perspectives.

The indications emerging from the study of privacy are particularly significant. Theoretical proposals have been developed which, on one side, are more adequate for the complexity of relations which may link space and behaviour; on the other side, they seem particularly promising with respect to the purpose of unifying references to serve as a guide for the entire area of research concerning human spatial behaviour.

Personal space   A first characterization that human behaviour can assume with respect to the spatial dimension of the environment is, therefore, what environmental psychologists have identified by centring attention on the space immediately surrounding the person. This is the area which, according to Sommer, has 'invisible boundaries surrounding a person's body, into which intruders may not come' (1969, p. 26). This area he defines as 'personal space' (Sommer, 1959).

The term 'personal space' has been adopted to indicate the specific domain of research which includes a vast number of contributions and is specifically involved in studying the modalities of behaviour people adopt for defining the boundaries of the spatial area maintained in contacts with others, regulating the 'distance' which separates them.

In its initial empirical applications, the concept of personal space primarily reflected the ethological approach, inherited from comparative research on animal and human behaviour. Starting with Sommer's studies, emphasis was placed on the defensive function carried out by mechanisms for regulating distance, but most of all on the idea that the spatial area defining this distance tends to be maintained by the person, almost indicating a sort of fixed 'territory'. On the one hand, these premises tend to outline a primarily reactive concept of use and management of space and, on the other, they contrast with the frequent variability the functioning of human spatial mechanisms can assume in relation to various types of environmental settings and situational and relational factors.

Analysing patterns of spatial behaviour, these studies show that people tend to maintain greater distance both when the physical space of the environment is very tight (Davies and Swaffer, 1971) and when individuals interact within 'competitive', rather than 'cooperative', relational contexts (Sommer, 1969; Cook, 1970).

These simple indications also call attention to the primary function of interpersonal regulation, always accomplished by distance, starting from the fact that it is possible to define the existence of a personal space only in the presence of an interaction between at least two persons. In fact, the developments that this area of environmental-psychological research have registered over time are primarily linked to the centrality recognized in this type of function.

As already noted, this area has traditionally attracted the attention of more than one discipline and, thus, it provides many descriptions. Cultural anthropology has offered the most effective contributions, both in terms of systematic thought and empirical research. In this regard it is mandatory to cite Hall's (1959, 1963, 1966) classical works. Interested in studying the functions and meanings of the space people interpose between themselves 'in conducting everyday transactions', Hall explicitly uses the term 'interpersonal distance' and considers the spatial dimension of these behaviours as a primarily 'communicative' phenomenon. In fact, distance gives information both to participants and to an external observer of the qualitative characteristics of an ongoing interaction (Hall, 1959). It delineates a phenomenon which, involving the cognitive as well as the behavioural component, also implies an active position for the individual. For this reason, and similar to what has been outlined by studies on non-verbal communication, patterns of behaviour relative to the maintenance of personal space are open to an analysis of necessarily more dynamic hypotheses. Argyle and Dean's (1965) proposals are an example of this. According to them, the use of space in regulating interpersonal distance serves the purpose of balancing the contrasting desires of entering into contact with/avoiding the other person.

Within this perspective, individuals' use of space is at the centre of attention and, as Gifford (1987) has pointed out, space itself assumes the double meaning of indicator and of constitutive component of interpersonal relations.

Synthesizing his elaborations on this topic through the concept of 'prossemic', Hall (1963) has pointed out many aspects which are also relevant in a psychological perspective of analysis. In fact, considering the need to link this specific category of spatial behaviour with the organization of physical-environmental space, he has traced a differentiation between three types/degrees of this organization: the stable one, found in the setting of built environments, such as cities, buildings, houses and rooms; the semi-stable one, constituted by mobile objects, such as furnishings; and the informal one, outlined by the distances individuals maintain in their encounters with others.

However, in Hall's (1966) perspective, this differentiation does not become a premise which limits the analysis to the objective aspect of the spatial dimension. Hall considers the study of both how persons use that space and how they perceive it as equally central. His research and thinking are primarily concerned with 'informal organization'. Because of his interest in the role played by cultural factors, Hall considers the various modalities of space management emerging from cross-cultural comparisons as different strategies that can be used to perform analogous functions. On the basis of these premises, he outlines a typology of 'zones or spaces of interpersonal distance' which considers the expression of different categories or 'phases' to which human relations can be traced: 'intimate', 'personal', 'social' and 'public' (Hall, 1966).

Also including a quantitative-metric definition of distances, this typology risks re-introducing a rather static view of the problem. And perhaps it is not just chance that critical positions have emerged in e.p. in this regard. Several authors have called attention in particular to the property of continuum which must be attributed to interpersonal distance (Aiello, 1980).

Although Hall's proposal has been criticized, several important reviews have clearly pointed out its utility/validity. In fact, it seems to offer several indications which have not been thoroughly explored by environmental-psychological research, such as the role of cognitive processes in the definition of personal space (Evans and Howard, 1973; Gifford and Price, 1979).

With regard to empirical research, the interest that environmental psychologists have dedicated to the relationship between personal space and the built environment has been primarily guided by the purpose of identifying the optimal dispositions for furnishings in that type of environment; that is, to verify which objective dispositions constitute the most adequate solutions for facilitating the maintenance of personal space and/or for predisposing the possibility of regulating the interpersonal distance between the respective users. The study of many public environments, such as libraries, airport waiting rooms, schools, offices and restaurants, has been carried out. Particular attention was initially dedicated to psychiatric hospitals, as mentioned above. The studies conducted in this area by Osmond (1957) have offered several methodological reference points which have been used in research on other types of environments.

Osmond was mainly interested in the identification of the characteristics of the built environment that favour or inhibit social interaction. He coined the terms 'sociopetal/sociofugal' to distinguish environments in which the physical disposition of the functional furnishings (for example, the placement of seats) provides or does not provide individuals with opportunities for interpersonal contact (sitting in front of someone or, vice versa, sitting behind someone).

The connotation (positive/negative) assigned by Osmond to the two terms derives from the therapeutic function that social interaction assumes for psychiatric patients. When the same distinguishing terms are adopted for investigating the issue of personal space, they lose the positive/negative connotation and become a descriptive reference. From a functionalist perspective, Gifford (1987) points out that physical dispositions cannot be considered positive or negative in themselves, but only in relation to models of behaviour that may be more or less appropriate to the specific environmental contexts under investigation. In this sense, the spatio-physical characteristics which guarantee individuals the possibility of easily balancing (increasing/decreasing) their distance from others become the main research issue.

However, this perspective seems extremely complex; above all it remains anchored to a primarily deterministic view, or, when it emphasizes physical-environmental variables, it seems to neglect others (both personal and situational-social) which are equally relevant to the problem.

Since the beginning of the 1970s, several authors have been pointing out the need to conduct studies that compare the influence of the principal variables in play by means of 'multivariate analysis' to reveal their interrelations (Evans and Howard, 1973).

However, more recent reviews show that the empirical results regarding the variations in interpersonal distance have been primarily obtained by considering single variables such as personality traits, sex, age and status. In particular, these results point out people's tendencies to enlarge their personal space, that is, to increase the importance of interpersonal distance, both with increase in age, in degree of personal 'coldness' and in situations of unequal social status.

With respect to gender, males are more inclined to maintain wide personal space, primarily in interactions with persons of the same sex (Lott and Sommer, 1967; Gifford, 1982); on the contrary, the distance tends to decrease when the interaction involves persons of the other sex, to become lower than that maintained in interactions between females (Kuethe and Weingartner, 1964).

These findings call attention to the interconnections which must first be hypothesized between the interpersonal and social dimensions of human behaviour. In fact, as Altman (1975) notes, the relations found between personal space and gender seem to reflect differences linked more to the different socialization of the two sexes than to characteristics of a biological nature. Therefore, it is reasonable to expect that different tendencies may be found in different socio-cultural contexts. The indications provided by anthropological research are particularly important in this regard, not only because they document the existence of differences but also because they draw attention to the need to investigate first of all the world of ideas, beliefs and meanings that underly human spatial behaviour.

In order to bridge the gap that has been underlined by many authors in this area of research, it is important to move towards the study of the specific meanings (cognitive-symbolic) which guide persons in the use of space.

Following one of the most useful indications of both anthropological research and the most recent orientations of psycho-social research, attention should be focused on the socially shared aspects of these meanings, rather than orienting analyses towards the discovery of inter-individual differences.

Territoriality   Obviously it is not possible to study the spatial dimension of human behaviour without considering where it is precisely located in the physical-geographical environment. In fact, one of the primary directions followed by psychological research is that concerning the complex spatial unit called 'territory'.

This term has many implications, both in its current use in everyday speech and in conceptualizations formulated for research purposes. The first implication concerns the specificity (types and degrees) of links established between persons and the different parts of environmental space. In this sense, the central role played by the physical-geographical dimension in the definition of territoriality cannot be separated from that of the meanings which environmental spaces can variously assume for individuals' behaviours.

Only recently has a specific consideration of this type of implication emerged in the literature. In fact, since the beginning the majority of studies have started from rather reductive definitions of 'territory' and 'territoriality'.

According to one of the most representative definitions, proposed by Sommer, the term 'territory' indicates 'a geographical area that is personalized or marked in some way and that is defended from encroachment' (1969, p. 33). What is central in this definition, as in numerous others found in the literature (Brown, 1987), is the concept of defensive demarcation, which is also emphasized in the definition of 'personal space'. This is the same concept that the biological sciences have traditionally linked to the control of resources for survival and have referred to for interpreting territorial behaviour in animals.

In fact, most of the environmental-psychological research has stressed the 'adaptive' function of human territoriality (Craik, 1973, 1977) and has focused on models of spatial behaviour people use to maintain control of their territory and/or defend it from intrusions and violations.

Anthropological research has also moved in the same direction. In studying territoriality in a hunter-gatherer society, researchers have interpreted it as historical evidence of the biological bases of human territorial behaviour. However, if it is true that the biologists were the first to abandon a similar interpretation, it is also true that anthropologists have always more clearly emphasized the social, cultural and religious meanings involved in the notion of territory and in human analysis of territorial behaviours (Tuan, 1977; Blundell, 1983).

In psychological research it has often been pointed out that, in spite of its heuristic function, a solely adaptive-defensive interpretation of territoriality is rather reductive and, in any case, is an inadequate framework for analysis (Stokols, 1978; Russell and Ward, 1982). Regardless of this, attention has been primarily dedicated to the study of physical markers which can be used in different ways (and show effectiveness) for defining territorial spaces.

As Pastalan (1970, p. 10) pointed out, even starting from a definition of territory as 'delimited space that a person or group uses and defends as exclusive preserve', the sole consideration of the forms of behaviour exhibited by individuals in the study of human territoriality is extremely limiting. In fact, this definition explicitly involves the processes of 'psychological identification with a place, symbolized by attitudes of possessiveness and arrangements of objects in the area' (ibid., p. 11). Following this premise, a more profitable analysis of territoriality is proposed as the study of the ways in which places and things become part of both the identity of persons and the social processes they more or less directly participate in.

In the more recent literature this perspective – defined by several authors as 'social' (for example, Brown, 1987) – seems to compete with the biological tradition. Interest in the study of the relations between territoriality and characteristics of the social context is more and more evident, as well as in the discovery of the functions territoriality can perform in defining the personal and social identity of those who manage it (for example, through the personalization of space). However, the change in perspective marked by these new directions has only begun in this area of research. This is true not only because of the consistent number of studies which continue to approach territoriality in terms of intrusion/violation, but also because of the prevailing reference to hypotheses which place physical signs of territorial demarcation and patterns of behaviour in a cause–effect relationship.

This tendency emerges primarily in the area of research concerned with 'crime in the territory'; and 'vandalism', in particular, constitutes the most representative example of territoriality intended as exclusive expression of a space to defend. The general hypothesis which guides a great deal of this research emphasizes the spatio-physical characteristics through which residential territories are marked, defined and controlled by the occupants. According to what Oscar Newman (1972) defines as the theory of 'defensible space', the decrease in acts of vandalism and/or violation of territory (and the simultaneous increase in the residents' sense of safety) is hypothesized in strict correlation both with the presence of real and/or symbolic 'barriers' which delimit the territories and with the opportunities occupants have to observe the 'suspect activities' occurring in them, thanks to the physical arrangement of the built environment.

In a critical review, Taylor et al. (1980) point out that in this type of research the attention initially dedicated to the relationship between markers and behaviours in violation of the territory has been progressively shifted, on the one hand, towards, the 'sense of territoriality' persons tend to cognitively associate with the physical disposition of residential environments and, on the other, towards the different degrees of homogeneity they perceive with respect to the network of relationships defining the environments in a social sense. In fact, several studies have shown that the physical markers of a territory are not sufficient for explaining either the frequency of acts of vandalism or violation of the territory, or the level of resident safety.

Based on direct findings and on accounts of the local police in Baltimore, Maryland, Taylor et al. (1984) reached the conclusion that the main factors associated with a greater sense of safety among the residents of the urban neighbourhoods considered consisted in a clearer cognitive representation of the environment in terms of territory, and in a growing perception of the homogeneity of the relative population. Thus, the role that these factors seem to play is comparatively more relevant than the presence of those physical markers which, according to Newman, should render the space more defensible.

A study by Brown and Altman (1983) in this same direction considers barriers – material or symbolic – for delimiting inhabited spaces as messages that communicate and/or induce perceptions of a 'strong sense of territoriality'. The authors find that in these cases homes tend to be the object of invasions, violations and thefts less frequently than cases in which the home territory is not marked in any way. On the other hand, it has been determined that individuals with a clearer perception of the environment in terms of territoriality are also those who tend to think less apprehensively about the possibility of criminal phenomena (Normoyle and Lavrakas, 1984).

The importance for research of the issue concerning 'physical markers of territorial space' can also be deduced from the presence of other studies, not directly connected with problems of invasion/violation. Many studies have investigated the differences territorial behaviours can assume in relation to variables such as culture, gender and composition of social groups occupying a certain space.

In particular, the role played by culture with regard to the ways people manifest the need for territorial spaces and the models of behaviour they adopt for defining and regulating them emerges clearly from these studies. Several cross-cultural comparisons have been made through the study of territoriality in spatial areas such as beaches where people coming from many countries gather. Observing groups of French and Germans, Smith (1983) has found that, in this type of situation, the Germans show a much more striking sense of their own territory than the French. Much more frequently than the French, the Germans tend to define their own territorial space using signs (such as sand-castles) which have the precise function of indicating certain areas of the beach as 'reserved'.

Another study compares the ways Greeks and Americans show their sense of territoriality (Worchel and Lollis, 1982). In this case, the authors use the expedient of disposing a trash bag in three different spots on the space adjacent to the dwellings: in the front courtyard, on the sides of the house, on the sidewalk in front of the house. Their aim was to assess how quickly the two groups removed the bag. The Americans removed the trash more quickly than the Greeks when the bag was placed in the last two areas. The authors point out how eloquent this result is as an indicator of two different cultural modalities for thinking about dwelling territory, that is, much more restricted and limited to the immediate adjacency for the Greeks than for the Americans.

With regard to gender, many studies have shown the male tendency to define their own territoriality through much larger spaces than females (Mercer and Benjamin, 1980). Studies of the domestic environment have shown how gender differences also tend to be specified qualitatively depending on the various parts of the dwelling space. In a study conducted on Israeli families (Sebba and Churchman, 1983) it has been shown that in spite of the idea that husband and wife share the house as a common territorial unit, women tend to identify the kitchen as their own territorial space. These and numerous other studies confirm the close interconnection between human territoriality and socio-cultural factors.

Identification with a space-territory clearly involves different processes from those regarding the claim to and/or defence of the territory. At any rate, the 'control' that people exercise or tend to exercise over the territory, primarily in a psychological sense, seems to be a basic question in both cases. This is also the reason why various authors have pointed out the central role played by territoriality in the more general identity formation processes.

According to this perspective, what seems crucial for psychological research is not so much the investigation of patterns of territorial behaviour as the exploration of the complex links which connect persons and territories in both the cognitive and emotional senses.

In spite of the lack of empirical studies, the literature offers many systematic reflections on this issue. Useful points of departure have been proposed primarily by researchers inspired by the European tradition of Bachelard (1969), which have focused attention on territoriality as a process of 'appropriation of space' (Barbey, 1976; Korosec-Serfaty, 1985); that is, a process in which the attachment individuals establish with the environment is defined and characterized by the activity they carry out in the space.

Apart from the European tradition, Altman's (1975) proposal is especially significant in this regard. Pointing out the need to differentiate the various types of territories in terms of their structural characteristics, he developed a descriptive schema of classification, not based exclusively on physical criteria but, rather, on the most general consideration of human territorial behaviour as behaviour towards 'meaningful objects'; that is, towards objects people develop an attachment to because of the symbolic-evocative function they perform both in relation to particular individual biographies and to the most shared socio-cultural frame of reference (Csikszentmihalyi and Rochberg-Halton, 1981). In fact, Altman specifies three different types of territories, according both to the 'psychological centrality' an 'organized space (or territory)' holds for occupants and to the duration of the occupation.

A first type of territory (for example, a house), which has relevant importance in the life space of persons and is occupied by them for long periods of time is defined as *primary*. Opposite to this is *public* territory, which can be represented by the space of a seat on a bus or at a reading table in a library. In this case, besides less psychological centrality and shorter duration of occupation, the connotation of public is also derived from the characteristic of a space which is open to access by a large number of people. Referring to the environment of private clubs as a prototypical example, Altman identifies an intermediate type of territory, which he defines as *secondary*. In fact, secondary territories are characterized both by less psychological centrality for users (compared with primary territories) and by more limited accessibility (compared with public ones). Moreover, the duration of stay in these does not depend so much on individuals as on the community which has control over these territories through possession.

Beyond the presence of markers indicating claim to or defence of the space, many of the territories that can be defined as primary are recognizable by the various modalities adopted by occupants to personalize them. The home, defined by several as the 'sacred symbol of the self' (for example, Cooper, 1972), represents the type of territory which has received increasing interest. Many of the authors who have studied this subject start from the premise that the personalization of domestic spaces constitutes a true mirror of the occupants' personal and social identity. Various studies have shown the relations between styles of personalization of internal spaces, culture and inhabitants' social status. More recently, attention has been centred on furnishing styles. Various researches have studied modalities of organizing and furnishing the domestic interior, with particular reference to the most 'public' room of the home, that is, the living-room or drawing-room, according to the different terminology preferences, which may vary as a function of the different socio-cultural positions of the inhabitants (Giuliani, 1987). Complex psycho-social aspects are considered as connected with the ways inhabitants arrange this particular room because of the 'mediating' role it performs with respect to the home in general, as well as functions of communication, presentation of the self and one's social position in front of possible visitors who will be received there.

A large comparative study was carried out in Europe on the domestic interiors of three large cities, Rome, Paris and Lundt (Sweden), using observation by means of photographs and systematic analysis of furnishing (Bernard and Bonnes, 1985). This study showed interesting similarities and differences between the various countries with regard to both the modalities of furnishing the room (in terms of structure, organization and animation of the space; Bonnes and Giuliani, 1987) and the role played in this respect by socio-demographic and socio-professional characteristics of the inhabitants (Bernard et al., 1987).

The studies carried out by Altman et al. on the home (Altman and Chemers, 1980; Altman and Gauvain, 1981; Gauvain et al., 1983) further specified the general hypothesis that inspired a large part of this research. The main suggestion advanced by the authors has been to point out the co-presence of at least two relevant aspects in the personalization of dwelling spaces: one aspect, represented by indicators such as design and decorations, ways of access, internal spaces and objects, reflects the distinctive quality of the residents; and the other, constituted by physical characteristics of construction, more clearly shows the social links persons maintain with their own community and culture.

As a result of the most recent developments on the topic of human territoriality, the overall perspectives of the investigation have broadened. Emphasis on the relations which link the spatial dimension to processes of definition and maintenance of identity (personal and social) has, in fact, found a major response in the growing attention dedicated by research to cognitive, affective and socio-cultural components which contribute towards specifying the relationship between persons and the spatial dimension of the environment.

The idea that it is not enough to define territoriality only in physical terms is prevalent among researchers because, even when there are no boundaries, territoriality is never only an abstract concept but is something operating primarily in the area of social interaction. As Altman (1975) pointed out, even 'territorial behaviour' must be considered more properly as a 'mechanism' which regulates the borders of the self/other through the process of personalization or demarcation of places or objects possessed by a person or a group. In any case, this concerns a mechanism which, useful for describing the more general process underlying the relationship between persons and environmental space, is clearly expressed through outcomes which are differentiated as a function of the diversity of situations and socio-cultural contexts in which it operates.

Privacy The main issues e.p. has faced in studies on personal space and territoriality have been synthesized into the concept of privacy.

According to Altman, this concept designates the 'selective control of access to the self or to one's group' (1975, p. 18) that individuals tend to practise with respect to the surrounding environment (primarily, social).

Since it implies processes of a communicative nature, privacy can be approached using many strategies. The studies on spatial behaviours people adopt to regulate interpersonal distance (personal space), or delimit/demarcate physical-environmental space (territoriality) are the most significant examples of these strategies.

In spite of the centrality occupied by the idea of privacy in the Anglo-Saxon cultural tradition, a common use of the same term tends to emphasize conditions of closure towards others; in any case, it indicates the desire to keep information regarding one's private life reserved. Excluding the innovations introduced into the area by Altman's theories, empirical research is largely characterized by this tendency.

As Russell and Ward (1982) point out, the many meanings attributed to privacy in the literature are associated with concepts of solitude, anonymity, intimacy, secrecy and reserve. As a consequence, the major interest of empirical research has been to study and measure the more strictly motivational and evaluative aspects (needs, expectations, values) individuals variously associate with privacy.

Confirmation of a similar trend is found in the studies concerned with privacy in work environments and in institutional/public environments where – in the case of hospitals and residences for the aged, and especially prisons – privacy becomes a problem.

In the first case, particular attention has been devoted to the office environment, in order to check the adequacy of the physical setting with respect to the occupants' needs (Becker, 1981; Wineman, 1982a).

Even though specific work tasks are more or less consistent with privacy, and office workers consider privacy in various ways, the studies in question tend to show the high degree of consensus usually found in evaluating the importance of privacy. Some studies have attempted to verify this tendency by analysing the degree of satisfaction expressed by groups or categories of office workers after their offices, previously structured on the basis of wall separations, are transformed into open spaces (Sundstrom et al., 1982). In this case, the dissatisfaction which emerges is mostly linked to increasing visibility and the reduction of the possibility of communicating without being heard by everyone.

The same type of problem has also been studied in the school environment in a more indirect way. Some studies have focused on the relations emerging between degree of teacher satisfaction in their work with the class and different types of physical classroom structures (Ahrentzen and Evans, 1984). The results show that increasing definition of the classroom by means of walls tends to be associated with a higher degree of satisfaction. However, studies like this one primarily show how the definition of privacy may correspond to a situation in which opportunities for distraction are reduced.

With regard to institutional environments, the main research perspectives are oriented towards finding more suitable environmental solutions for satisfying the privacy needs shown in the various categories of persons using them. Particularly representative of this perspective is a very large investigation conducted in the United States in fifty-three different residences for the aged (Howell, 1980). The aim was to study privacy and the behaviour patterns of the residents connected with the configuration of the physical structure of the environments. By means of interviews and observations of the spatial disposition of these environments before and after the arrangement introduced by the residents, the author focused on a series of operative indications aimed at optimizing levels of privacy in this type of environment.

Except for these and a few other examples, attention to analyses directly centred on relations between the physical environment and privacy are very rare. As some authors have pointed out (for example, Archea, 1977), in spite of the more or less implicit presupposition that the physical disposition may constitute, support and/or impede the practice of privacy, the spatial dimension does not seem to be included in any of the theoretical guidelines offered in the literature on this topic.

More than representing a gap to fill, this tendency appears increasingly as a consequence of the deep reflection developing simultaneously around the concept of privacy. It was motivated in particular by the need, emphasized by many authors (Stokols, 1978; Russell and Ward, 1982; Holahan, 1986), to introduce greater theoretical coherence into the sector.

With regard to problems deriving from imprecise definitions, Kelvin (1973) has for some time been calling attention to the difference between privacy and 'isolation': the latter concerns a lack of social relations as an imposed condition, while the former is the consequence of choice. Through this distinction, the author proposes a definition of privacy in terms of perception of the limitations of others' power over oneself, primarily emphasizing the cognitive component implied in the concept. Moving from a similar level of abstraction, Altman identifies privacy with the 'mechanisms that regulate access to the self' (1975, p. 18).

Even in the diversity of the underlying perspectives, these definitions call attention to psychological processes the concept of privacy tends to imply. In this sense, they very clearly show the versatile function the construct of privacy can perform in the analysis of many aspects of the complex relationship between individuals and environment. In effect, the construct has received attention more as a general theoretical reference than as a subject of empirical research.

Recognition of the importance of Altman's contribution in this regard is almost unanimous in the most recent literature. Interested in discovering the modalities people use to regulate their relations with the social world – or render themselves psychologically more or less accessible to others – he has developed a broad and systematic reflection on privacy, starting from an integrated view of the various aspects of human spatial behaviour. According to Altman (1975), the ways in which people define and manage environmental space can be considered as messages through which, analogously to what occurs with verbal and non-verbal instruments, they communicate their 'openness/closedness' towards others.

Drawing upon the findings that emerged from his studies on the inhabited environment (Altman and Gauvain, 1981), Altman further emphasizes how the uses of this specific environmental space reveal the accomplishment of this regulative function, making possible the control of privacy.

Underlying these findings, both personal space and territorial behaviours are assumed by Altman to be mechanisms used by individuals primarily to regulate privacy, that is, to maintain their openness/closedness towards others at optimal levels. Within this perspective, the author assigns to the notion of privacy the unifying theoretical function of a concept which bridges the more specific notions of personal space and territoriality.

However, the regulations Altman speaks of in referring to privacy are not related to psychological processes that exclusively involve the individual dimension; the interweaving of messages of personal identity and of social belonging, which, according to the author, are expressed by the various characteristics of inhabited environments, indicates that these regulations involve processes typical of social interaction. More than once, the author underlines that, similar to every phenomenon connected with social interaction, so is the regulation of privacy extremely dynamic; above all in the sense that it is not easy to define it once and for all (stability) because it is primarily correlated with contexts and situations (change).

By integrating these various reflections, Altman outlined a new theory of privacy through which he first reformulated the concept of openness/ closedness. Rather than designating a pre-established continuum along which the different possible degrees of privacy are defined, this concept indicates a polarization of the two conditions which, always co-present, together dialectically contribute towards defining the specific positions assumed by individuals.

In this perspective the regulative function of privacy, although remaining central, is also redefined. It is no longer only a 'mechanism' which guarantees the attainment of an ideal state of openness/closedness towards others, but rather a process; its dynamics and outcomes are strictly correlated with the specificity of the 'contexts and social circumstances' (Altman and Gauvain, 1981; Altman and Rogoff, 1987).

Behaviours, disturbing environmental features, environmental stress

The physical dimension of the environment is certainly not only definable in terms of organized spaces and objects or things variously placed in them. It is also definable through characteristics and particular properties – such as those manifesting in the form of light, acoustic and thermal stimulations – more directly involving our sensory activities and, thus, contributing towards specifying the quality of the environments in which we live and perform our daily activities.

The interest of e.p. in this subject is only an expression of the more general question regarding the physical factors that can interfere with processes of adaptation to the environment.

Studies have been conducted on the limits of tolerance directly manifested by people concerning different degrees and qualities of stimulations produced by these properties. More specific attention has been devoted to the disturbing effects they involve for carrying out tasks that imply various types of activities (from physio-motoric to more mental ones), including those involving interaction with other individuals.

Moving in this double direction, empirical research has favoured laboratory experimentation and has encouraged the tendency to treat the properties in question as variables which, stimulating the organism, produce such direct and specific effects that they can be just as easily isolated and measured. Even though they focus on several basic indications, useful as general reference points for a more systematic study of the problem, the results of these studies point out the limits of the approach, primarily in terms of the emergence of a double order of tendencies: on the one hand, the non-generalizability of the connections emerging between specific physical stimulations (for example, the objective intensity of noise) and the outcome of complex activities (for example, the level of performance shown in learning tasks); on the other, the different consequences these stimulations involve, depending on whether immediate reactions are considered or the experience people make of them, coping with them continuously for long periods of time.

As will be seen in more detail, research has assumed the concept of stress as its central reference point and has defined the disturbing environmental properties as variables which can act as stressors. According to this perspective, the problematic aspects of the relation between physical-environmental features and individuals' responses are definable in terms of more complex conditions of discomfort (psychophysical); this is due less to the direct and immediate effect of specific physical properties of the environment than to the consequences of repeatedly activated strategies, at the psychological level, to cope with and/or neutralize the disturbance/threat component which the various properties may involve.

Synthesized in the concept of 'environmental stress', this discomfort actually touches the more general problem of 'costs' the daily life environment may at times require of individuals – and not only through its particular physical properties, but also through its complex rules of functioning.

Light, noise, temperature

Empirical studies of people's limits of tolerance of sensory stimulations from the physical environment have favoured visual (light and colour), thermal (extreme temperatures) and above all acoustic (noise) ones. More recently, air quality (atmospheric pollution) has also became part of this area of inquiry. Primarily based on laboratory experiments, these studies have measured limits, both on the basis of qualitative parameters regarding several elementary functions of the human organism and on the basis of specific physiological reactions.

Studies have been conducted in order to discover how lighting conditions influence visual functions. Attention has been particularly devoted to finding out which tasks (more or less complex) of discrimination and recognition of details are most affected by a change (increase/decrease) in degree of light. The quantitative levels at which light facilitates (in terms of speed and accuracy) the fulfilment of these tasks (Bennet, 1977) have also been investigated.

Analogously, research has been interested in colour, with particular reference to chromatic matches which generate contrast and may, thus, constitute disturbing factors for effective visual functioning. With regard to temperature, various studies have been conducted to determine the quantitative range (minimum/maximum) for defining thermal conditions as comfortable.

Certainly the richest topic in this area of research is noise. The possibility of rather accurate measurement of the main characteristics manifesting this stimulation (intensity, frequency and periodicity) is associated with the increasing importance its presence has assumed in most daily life environments. The limits of human tolerance of noise were first studied through the reactions that various degrees of intensity of noise produce on the functioning of several physiological processes. Positive correlations were found between increasing intensity of noise and alterations in normal values of blood pressure and breathing rhythms (Kryter, 1970; Glass and Singer, 1972a, 1972b; Jonsson and Hansson, 1977).

The findings provided by this type of research correspond in only a general way to the objectives e.p. posed from the beginning. As Holahan (1982) and others underlined, these objectives were very functionally oriented. In fact, the major aim was the identification of the ways these specific physical properties affect the fulfilment of equally specific activities people carry out in many environments. Experimental research developed in this direction particularly when it proposed identifying the specific stimulations which generate disturbing effects on specific task performance. This aim is similar to the research goals in areas such as human engineering and ergonomics, particularly in the 1950s and 1960s. This type of research is linked to the designing of man–machine systems, functionally effective for the work-production aims of large-scale industry. That is the reason why it has emphasized the consideration of human factors in the construction of machines destined to be substituted for a person's manual performance, even if he/she still has the task of ensuring their functioning.

Broadbent's (1971, 1978) and Glass et al.'s (1969, 1973) reviews, among others, have shown how noise produced in the laboratory does not constitute the systematic origin of relevant negative effects on performance in the solution of various types of problems assigned to experimental subjects. Corcoran (1962) and Warner (1969) have pointed out that in some circumstances carrying out activities is actually facilitated by certain noise levels, that is, it may stimulate subjects to remain alert and attentive. Other authors (Cohen and Weinstein, 1981), on the contrary, call attention to the great simplicity of the tasks assigned in these cases in terms of the psycho-motoric and mental abilities they require. In fact, studies conducted in a wide variety of experimental situations demonstrate that the degree of complexity of the task together with the characteristics (quantitative and qualitative) of the noise administered and duration of exposure constitute the main variables which most significantly contribute to the growing negativity of the emerging effects. In these cases, the complexity of the tasks is mainly defined in terms of either levels of implicit attention-concentration (Broadbent, 1958, 1971) or quantity of information to be taken into consideration simultaneously (Glass and Singer, 1972a); the more marked these characteristics, the more disturbing the effects of noise.

With regard to the qualitative characteristics of noise, it has been shown that the most negative effects are manifest in the presence of an intermittent noise rather than a continuous one, especially if the intermittence is marked by irregular intervals (Broadbent, 1957; Theologus et al., 1974). The negative effects of noise have also emerged strictly in correlation with an increase in exposure time (Hartley and Adams, 1974). In several studies it has also been found that long exposure may produce negative effects which surface even after abandonment of an environmental situation with a high noise level (Glass et al., 1969; Sherrod et al., 1977).

Research on the disturbing effects of noise has been carried out in real situations as well as in laboratory ones. One of the most representative contributions is certainly that of Cohen et al. (1973) on several residential buildings in New York City which are particularly exposed to traffic noise. In fact, these buildings are located in the immediate vicinity of several important interhighway connections. The authors proposed studying the type of correlation existing between the noise and the reading ability of children living in these buildings.

The structure of the buildings considered (thirty-two floors) provided differentiated residential conditions with respect to noise intensity (tested through special measurements). Noise was higher on the lower floors, adjacent to the traffic, and much lower on the upper floors.

The research hypothesis predicted that, given its unpredictability, the traffic noise would be negatively correlated with the reading ability of the children living in the building. Before beginning, the fifty-five school-age children participating in the study were administered a hearing test to determine their degree of auditory discrimination.

The results confirmed the hypothesis, showing that the subjects most exposed to the noise not only demonstrated more evident lacks in reading ability but also had a greater deficit in auditory ability. The authors interpreted the first result as the postponed effect of prolonged exposure to noise, since the levels of performance in reading also tended to be lower in relation to the length of the children's residence in the buildings.

To explain these results, the authors considered that auditory capacity was also correlated negatively with noise. The concomitance of these two tendencies led them to focus on the effort sustained over time by the most exposed subjects in adapting to the noise in their environment. The hypothesis was that this effort should be primarily linked to the need for learning to ignore acoustic recall. Similar learning inevitably involves signals linked to verbal language, and the subjects in question would find themselves in an unfavourable position for developing the basic abilities of auditory discrimination for learning to read.

In terms of content, the results of this study confirm the general hypothesis that prolonged exposure to noise and the processes regulating adaptation to it can generate consequences for both physical health and cognitive functioning.

The study is also rather significant because of the methodological suggestions it provides: this is particularly true with respect to the articulation of routes to follow when the effects of a specific property of the physical environment have to be accounted for.

Other examples of research confirm this opportunity, even if they involve analyses concerned with the disturbing effects of noise as variables that can affect the degree of individuals' satisfaction/dissatisfaction towards their own life environment.

The results of a study conducted on residential environments in two Italian cities, Rome and Milan (Bonnes, 1979b), are particularly interesting in this regard. In this case the aim was to check the degree of satisfaction/ dissatisfaction with the residence and the disturbing effects of environmental noise. A comparative analysis was made between equal samples of subjects residing in apartments built with and without acoustic insulation (insulated and non-insulated dwellings).

In both cities the samples included residents in apartments exposed to different degrees of objective noise (classified as high, medium and low). The research hypothesis predicted that the increase in degree of noise would correlate with increasing levels of dissatisfaction, mainly among residents in non-acoustically insulated dwellings. The results of the study, carried out with 500 subjects, showed the opposite. The occupants of the insulated dwellings manifested dissatisfaction significantly more consistently with conditions of increasing noise.

When the level of environmental noise was equal, the disturbing effect reported by insulated buildings was greater than that of non-insulated dwellings. This result seems unexplainable when noise is considered as the only objective variable producing disturbing effects.

In fact, a more thorough analysis of the data shows the central role played by a psychological variable, that is, 'expectations', and the different position assumed in this respect by insulated and non-insulated dwellers. Knowing about the building's acoustic insulation at the time of purchasing the apartment probably contributes to increasing the level of expectations with regard to silence, reducing tolerance for noise.

Among the general indications provided by these types of studies, at least two are particularly relevant. The first consists in the evident mediating function that psychological processes (cognitive-evaluative) fulfil in defining the disturbing effects of specific properties of the physical environment. The other derives from the fact that, unlike what happens in laboratory situations, in most real situations it is particularly problematic and limiting to isolate specific effects, explaining them as the consequence of the equally specific property considered. In effect, studies on individuals' satisfaction/dissatisfaction with their own residential environment has often confirmed the multidimensional nature of processes involved in the evaluation. Many and various are the environmental characteristics (physical, social, functional) that people tend to assume simultaneously as reference points for defining the degrees of their satisfaction/dissatisfaction. Moreover, the outcomes of the evaluation tend to be established as the result of a complex interaction between personal variables and characteristics of the broader environmental context (Bonnes et al., 1991a).

Environmental stress

The study of the disturbing factors in various environmental contexts confronted environmental-psychological research with the need to enlarge its horizons, especially in terms of not limiting analysis to only the direct and immediate effects found in specific behaviours and activities. The fact that the relationship between individuals and environments usually has continuity extending over time has called attention to the cumulated effects that can derive from the presence of these disturbing factors.

In this respect, the concept of stress has been particularly useful and revealing in a theoretical-methodological sense. Broadly outlining 'every situation in which the environmental demands on individuals exceed their ability to respond' (Evans, 1982, p. 1), this concept offered to environmental-psychological research a potentially unifying frame of reference for the analysis of many non-optimal conditions in which individual–physical environment interactions take place.

In spite of the remarkable familiarity assumed by the term 'stress' in everyday language, the psychologists concerned with environmental stress have not neglected the preliminary need for an accurate conceptual definition (Cofer and Appley, 1964; Appley and Turnbull, 1967; McGrath, 1970). In effect, as Gary Evans (1982), among others, pointed out, research on stress refers primarily to two main models. The first, in chronological order, is the one developed in the area of biomedical studies and focuses on the reactions of the organism and its physiological processes, which are activated through interaction with the external environment and/or by its demands (Selye, 1956). The second accentuates the psychological processes that mediate the relationship between individuals and the environment. Specific reference is made to the cognitive processes through which people 'interpret' the environment and evaluate the 'threat' of its characteristics (Lazarus, 1966).

As shown in the literature (Evans, 1982; Evans and Cohen, 1987) the two perspectives have never been completely integrated, and the physiological model has been the most influential in the whole research domain.

According to the tradition started by Cannon (1932), this model centres attention on the autonomous emergency response system and on the functions it is meant to perform for the organism in confronting or, vice versa, avoiding damaging stimulations and/or adverse situations considered as threats for its internal equilibrium. In this perspective, the functioning of the organism is entrusted to those homeostatic regulation mechanisms which tend to maintain the fluctuations (or changes in the state of equilibrium) induced by the external environment, within certain limits. Thus, the responses that are produced to the disturbing agents, called stressors, primarily carry out the function of re-establishing lost equilibriums. Within this dynamic, stress figures as a consequence of the solicitations the mechanisms of homeostatic regulation are repeatedly subjected to.

With the transposition of a similar model from the physiological domain into that of the more general relationships linking individuals with their environments, the defensive position assigned to individuals with respect to the properties threatening the maintenance of the most balanced levels of adaptation which they tend towards is emphasized.

It is primarily in this perspective that a type of environmental context, such as the urban one, has often been assumed by environmental-psychological research as an emblematic situation for describing the origins of stress. In particular, emphasis has been placed on the persistence and continuity with which equilibrium must be maintained, because of the multiform and equally continuous solicitation by external environmental factors. As Selye (1956), among others, has pointed out, every defensive position which does not consist in the escape from the field necessitates the use of adequate strategies and, thus, of investments of psychological as well as physical energy.

In this sense, the effects of environmental stress become costs individuals find themselves sustaining in facing properties and/or unfavourable conditions in the surrounding environment, and which primarily involve their physical health and psychological well-being. When the hypothesis of a direct connection between disturbing properties and immediate effects on individuals' behaviour is reorganized in this way, the central research problem is to pinpoint the most adequate modalities for determining the extent and nature of these costs.

A relevant direction of research in this context is dedicated to inter-individual differences, that is, to the ways different people react to factors of environmental stress. Under the same conditions, these differences refer to the saliency and significance assumed by the implied factors in individual perceptions.

Especially starting with Lazarus's (1966) proposals, the concept of environmental stress has been increasingly used within the more general hypothesis of a cognitive mediation intervening to specify the relationship between disturbing factors and behavioural responses. According to this author, the objective conditions of the environment contribute towards producing stressing effects to the degree to which they influence the processes of perception/evaluation simultaneously put into action by individuals with regard both to environmental properties and to the personal resources necessary for coping with them.

The close connection noted between environmental factors and psycho-logical processes governing individual functioning constitutes a new possibility for defining the disturbing stimulation, no longer exclusively entrusted to physicalist criteria. As Holahan (1982) reminds us, in this sense noise becomes 'a sound the listener does not want to listen to', and not just an acoustic stimulus that surpasses a certain intensity, measured in decibels.

In more general terms, a consistent premise is outlined for taking into consideration the psychological nature of the costs that environmental stress in itself implies and for a more specific analysis of the consequences persons are faced with in adapting themselves to stressing environmental conditions.

Various authors have defined the cumulated costs deriving from this adaptation in terms of cognitive fatigue (Glass and Singer, 1972b; S. Cohen, 1978, 1980). Calling attention to the results of several studies, these authors point out the active effort always involved in the task of coping with unfavourable environmental conditions. Also, once again regarding the study of the effects of noise, these studies (Glass et al., 1969, 1971, 1977; Glass and Singer, 1972a) assume paradigmatic value regarding the problem of environmental stress, conceived as a problem of psychological costs, especially since they suggest interpretive hypotheses for explaining many environmental properties that may become disturbing.

Authors such as Glass and Singer (1972a, 1972b) began these studies to determine the different effects produced respectively by exposure to periodic noise (which manifests at regular intervals) and to 'aperiodic' noise (which manifests at random intervals). They started from the general hypothesis that when people have to adapt to stressing environmental conditions, the costs of the investment of psychic energy are relatively higher if there is no possibility of predicting/controlling the onset of the disturbing stimulation.

In experiments it has been found that, while no differences emerge between the two conditions (periodic-predictable/aperiodic-unpredictable noise) with regard to the modalities of immediate adaptation to noise stimulations, the subjects who undergo the unpredictable condition experience negative effects following their exposure to noise more than do the others. The negative effects specifically involve a decrease in degree of personal tolerance to frustration and in effectiveness in performing specific cognitive tasks (problem-solving) in a subsequent phase of the experiment.

The authors interpret these results as confirmation of the primary role carried out by processes of cognitive mediation in defining the stressing effects of unfavourable environmental conditions. The results especially support the hypothesis that the nature and degree of these effects are closely linked to opportunities for 'personal control' to be exerted at the onset of disturbing stimulations.

These authors find a more precise confirmation of this hypothesis in another study comparing two groups of subjects. One of the two groups was given the possibility (in fact not true) of interrupting the emission of noise by pressing a buzzer. Just the presence of this virtual possibility brought about differences in the quality of performances the subjects in the two groups were subsequently asked to make. The degree of efficiency demonstrated was less negative in the subjects with the presumed noise control compared to that shown in the other group (Glass and Singer, 1972a).

It is obvious that this type of personal control is bound to function as a defence from stress as long as the subjects can continue believing in the possibility of interrupting the disturbing stimulation. However, it has been shown that control itself can also produce positive experimental effects when the subjects know they can exercise it in an indirect way, that is, in this case, when they were informed that if noise levels were too high, they could signal and the experimenter would intervene.

Accentuating the role carried out by individual cognitive mediation in defining stress and its negative effects, Cohen (1978, 1980) proposed an alternative hypothesis to the above-described one. After defining the environment as the context from which individuals select the information necessary for organizing their behaviour and actions, Cohen moved in a direction opposite to that predominantly followed in experimental research on this topic. He started by considering people's expectations, the first of which is receiving adequate information from the environment for effective accomplishment of their behaviours or actions.

Within this premise, the disturbing properties of the environment are considered as an 'information overload' people have to cope with and, therefore, the reason for a surplus of cognitive work compared to that otherwise necessary and/or expected: the more unpredictable the ways these properties are manifest, the more attention and elaboration ability is required by the information coming from them. Since they are advanced in a context perceived as threatening, similar requests may assume dimensions surpassing the individual's capacity to face the impact.

Cognitive fatigue, also referred to in other hypotheses for describing environmental stress and its effects, is conceptualized in this case as a consequence of an information overload the environment relays repeatedly over time.

The expectation underlying behaviours oriented towards aims is perhaps the variable which has come to assume the greatest importance in the psychological conceptualization of environmental stress. Various authors have proposed the definition of this concept in terms of the incongruence between aims (and/or needs) and opportunities offered by the environment. In this case, the stressing effects of specific environmental conditions are evaluated as a function of the degree of inadequacy perceived with regard to objectives and aims relevant for individuals (Michelson, 1970; Stokols, 1979; Caplan, 1982).

Faced with the many ways of defining stress, a unique dominant tendency seems to mark the study of environmental stress as regards contents. Besides the focus on physical properties such as noise, atmospheric pollution and density, considered as the main environmental conditions acting as stressors, this domain of study assumes the urban environment as its main context of reference. The consistency with which residents may find themselves cumulating the disturbing effects of the above-mentioned properties over time has led various authors to recognize a paradigmatic example in the urban environment of the conditions causing cognitive fatigue and, thus, producing stress. Some of these authors have indicated life in the city as one of the specific situations giving rise to attitudes of forced resignation, that is, the type of attitude that leads people to consider any action as inadequate or ineffective for neutralizing the negative aspects of the surrounding environmental conditions. Seligman (1973, 1974, 1975) used the term of 'learned helplessness' to describe this psychological condition. Individuals can acquire it through the development of beliefs and/or expectations that the course of undesirable phenomena is completely out of their control. Interpreted as the cumulated effect of extended exposure to stressing environmental conditions, a similar position has also been described by others as responsible for a more general weakening of the individual's ability to cope with environmental demands.

With regard to empirical studies, increasing interest in the features of the physical environment of the city (such as noise, atmospheric pollution and density-concentration), defined as urban stressors (S. Cohen et al., 1979), consists first of all in a more systematic attention to the subjective evaluations people make of them. As to the negative effects these properties can produce, particular attention has also been given to some manifestations of interpersonal behaviour such as aggressivity and the tendency to avoid others.

Research on aggressivity has been primarily carried out by means of large-scale opinion polls, aimed at determining the degree of annoyance people perceive/declare. Studies conducted in various countries have shown a consistent tendency among people living in urban areas to indicate traffic noise as one of the most disturbing factors. As Cohen and Weinstein (1981) have pointed out, the studies in question indicate that adaptation to this type of noise seems rather difficult to pursue, especially with regard to residential environments. From the comparisons that several of these studies have made between short- and long-term residents in the same residential environment, no significant evaluation differences emerge: in both cases noise emerges as one of the most disturbing factors.

With respect to atmospheric pollution, since awareness of this environmental property usually only occurs in the presence of very consistent signals (for example, obscured visibility, unpleasant odours), the studies only indicate the high inter-individual variability in awareness of it. In a review, Barker (1976) pointed out how, in the majority of cases, the differences found are the consequence of induced evaluations (primarily through information from mass media) rather than of direct personal experience.

Degree of 'density', in both a spatio-physical and social (population) sense, is one of the features which, together with traffic noise, has great importance in the evaluations people make about the quality of their life environment. High concentrations of people and things tend to be among the primary disturbing factors characterizing the urban socio-physical environment. Also in this case, the remarkable variability with which individuals evaluate this feature shows the limitations of hypotheses predicting a direct correlation between the objective conditions shown by the environment and the manifestation of stressing effects in individuals.

Reflecting the need for an approach more psychologically oriented towards environmental stress, these studies on density/crowding emphasize the mediating role that must be assigned to perception/evaluation. As Baum and Paulus (1987) have pointed out, this is confirmed by the fact that the recent literature uses two distinct conceptual constructs: density and crowding. The first construct designates the objective feature of the spatio-physical restrictions, and the second indicates the outcome of individual perceptions of these restrictions.

In agreement with the premises, many studies have been concerned with inter-individual differences in the perception of crowding as the basis for the prediction of stressing effects. More recently, other studies have been directed towards verifying the indirect influence that extra-individual variables can have on perceptions.

In a series of studies on the modalities and content used by residents in an urban area to define their own neighbourhood as satisfying/dis-satisfying, Bonnes et al. (1990) confirmed both the importance that residents attribute to the social density factor as a criterion for evaluating environmental quality and the consistent inter-individual variability with which density is perceived in terms of crowding. Through further analyses of these data (Bonnes et al., 1991a), it also emerged that these differences are not correlated with the actual degree of density in the various areas of the neighbourhood where the sub-groups of the subjects analysed reside. The variable primarily correlated with the diversity of perceptions/ evaluations was, instead, constituted by socio-economic level, that is, when it was lower, the perception of density in terms of crowding was accentuated.

These tendencies emerged in relation to different lifestyles of the various categories of subjects considered: at lower socio-economic levels they were marked by frequenting of and uses mostly circumscribed by the neigh-bourhood territorial area; at higher ones, there was more consistent gravitation into extra-neighbourhood areas (with particular reference to the centre) (Bonnes et al., 1990). These results essentially show that individual perceptions are linked to various behavioural opportunities for avoiding a potentially stressing factor and that some of these behavioural options are associated with belonging to one social group rather than another.

The connection between urban stress and modalities of interpersonal behaviours has also been studied in relation to the specific factor of density/crowding. Living in the city there are often many situations that imply high concentration of a spatial and/or social nature: from those relative to building density and the great numbers of vehicles on the streets, to those regarding the co-presence of high numbers of people in the same physical space. Research has addressed these situations in particular, and many studies have focused on the stressing effects deriving from prolonged exposure to them.

The study of interpersonal behaviours in experimental situations with different concentrations of subjects in the same physical space has been carried out primarily with children. In particular, it has been shown that the increase in the number of subjects present tends to be associated with a significant increase in aggressive behaviours (Ginsburg et al., 1977).

In adults, these behaviours have been analysed comparing males and females. Various studies have found a great tendency in males towards aggressive behaviours in conditions of increasing density (Stokols et al., 1973, 1978; Saegert et al., 1975). Other modalities of interpersonal behaviour have also been correlated with conditions of high density, particularly those expressing a tendency towards withdrawal or a decrease in helping behaviour. In this respect subjects exposed to environments with high social density have been found to be less talkative and less group-oriented (Sundstrom, 1975; Baum and Koman, 1976).

Less univocal tendencies have emerged from attempts to explain episodes of lack in helping behaviour towards persons in need. Several studies have concluded that it is not so much the social density variable that accounts for this type of behaviour, as the overall characteristics of the situations which are created in these cases (Holahan, 1977; House and Wolf, 1978).

Some authors have emphasized the hypothesis that helping behaviour is above all controlled by individual cognitive factors. Zajonc (1980) has particularly stressed the process of evaluation activated in these circumstances concerning both the number of persons and their characteristics. This would be the way by which individuals find out who can provide better help among the present persons.

Perhaps more clearly than any other area of investigation, the studies concerning environmental stress summarize the characteristics that have marked the most significant developments of environmental-psychological research as a whole. Accepting the psychological definition of stress as an alternative to a strictly physiological-reactive view, the research on environmental stress has, in effect, assumed the centrality that this psychological model attributes to cognitive mediations in specifying the relations that link properties of the physical environment and people's responses. In a more general sense, it emphasizes a more interactive frame of reference, in which individuals are put in an active position towards the environment and behaviours are more appropriately defined in terms of activities guided by goals.

In agreement with the remarks of various authors, it appears that different theoretical-methodological problems remain open within this specific area of investigation. Following Stokols (1978), it is evident that the unifying potential of the psychological concept of stress has only in part been taken advantage of at the level of empirical studies. In fact, the persistent tendency characterizing these studies involves the isolation of various properties and/or single environmental stressors and the fragmentation of complex areas of effect (and/or aspects of behaviour) associated with them.

Also, according to what other authors have pointed out (Magnusson, 1981; Lazarus et al., 1985), the effectiveness of the psychological model of stress as a conceptual framework for research should first consist in the opportunity it offers for overcoming the distinction between environmental (objective) and personal (subjective) components. In other words, a consistent reference to the psychological model of stress would allow for a dynamic description of the complex interplay which both of these components can initiate in different situations.

According to these considerations, a definition of stress has recently been proposed as a 'complex rubric reflecting a dynamic, recursive relationship between environmental demands, individual and social resources to cope with these demands and the individual's appraisal of that relationship' (Evans and Cohen, 1987, p. 573). This proposal, again emphasizing the hypothesis of cognitive mediation, seems to summarize the main conceptual reference points as they have been defined in the overall area of studies on environmental stress (Stokols, 1979; Baum et al., 1982; Evans, 1982). Although in this case an evaluative process is referred to which has as its object the perceived relations between demands and resources rather than simple stimulus properties, it is the isolated individual, with his/her personal needs/aims, who continues to be assigned the primary position of arbiter.

Processes of environmental evaluation and knowledge

The very large, rich and diverse literature concerned with environmental evaluation and knowledge can be considered as the most significant expression of e.p.'s growing interest in the analysis of the role people play in the qualitative definition of the environments they interact with.

Focusing on the internal processes of human functioning, this domain of research is moving towards general objectives which find support in some of the most consolidated theoretical paradigms in the psychological tradition. That is why environmental evaluation and knowledge also emerges as the topic that more adequately shows the specific contribution a psychological perspective can bring to the investigation of an issue constituting a pluridisciplinary object of interest. Following the premises of personality psychology, the individual differences in 'dispositions towards the environment' and its qualities have been studied as variables which allow for predicting the models of behaviour persons will adopt towards various types of environments. However, with regard to the specific evaluative and cognitive dimensions of behaviours, attention has been focused on the study of emotional and perceptual-cognitive components.

As Craik (1977) and others have pointed out, this way of proceeding provides an opportunity for introducing greater theoretical coherence into environmental-psychological research, particularly when it confronts the complex question of environmental knowledge. In fact, in studying this theme reference is made to the theoretical frameworks proposed by the cognitive approach in psychology.

Through this approach, one of the most consistent theoretical alternatives to behaviourism has been outlined and, with it, the possibility of overcoming both an exclusively physicalist view of the environment and a deterministic explanation of the relationship between the environment and human behaviour. This very promising perspective for the development of environmental-psychological research has not impeded the specific topic we are now concerned with from re-proposing several of the limitations revealed by the cognitive approach in its various applications in the psychological disciplines.

As will be illustrated in more detail in the following sections, this especially regards the prevailing tendency to treat the emotional-evaluative and cognitive dimensions separately, and to analyse the outcomes of processes linked to these dimensions in exclusively individualistic terms.

The broad and systematic considerations on environmental cognition show the awareness that has been reached in this respect, and they focus on the problems that must be resolved in order to surpass these limits. An increasing emphasis has been put both on components of meaning, which are considered to be inevitably involved in relations between persons and environment, and on the active-constructive role which individuals play in processes of environmental knowledge and evaluation.

Besides responding to the primary need for an effective orientation in physical space, environmental knowledge has increasingly been considered and analysed as the terminus of routes that 'concrete' persons (in that they are part of a socio-physical context) follow in structuring the reference points – in a symbolic, functional and evaluative sense (Stokols, 1978, 1981) – necessary for adapting to the environment or at least becoming familiar with it. According to this perspective, environmental evaluation and knowledge processes are meant to carry out the complex function of transforming the environment into more specific 'places' (Canter, 1977, 1983).

With a research topic defined by these characteristics, the need emerges, on the one hand, to look at both behaviour and the environment from a molar perspective (Craik, 1970), and, on the other, to compare the study of the relations between them using a contextual approach (Stokols, 1987; Altman and Rogoff, 1987).

Looking at the remarkable quantity of theoretical contributions that fall into this large and complex thematic area, there are many confirmations of the growing importance which this perspective has assumed over time.

However, this tendency figures more as a programmatic proposal for future research than as an effective criterion for grouping existing empirical studies.

The coordinates that emerge as more adequate for this purpose are constituted by two of the principal ways research has faced the study of both environmental evaluation and knowledge. One is more clearly oriented towards showing people's psychological responses to the environment and its features; the other is more interested in considering and describing the processes involved in structuring evaluations and knowledge.

The first modality comprises the study of personal dispositions and attitudes, as well as cognitive mapping. In these cases the aim consists in checking, respectively, the evaluative responses individuals give to environmental qualities and the cognitive responses they structure concerning the spatial organization of the environment.

The second modality comprises the study of the ways individuals arrive at (symbolically) representing the molar (or socio-physical) environment as well as the contents of that environment.

Environmental evaluation

The two main areas of investigation concerning the modalities and content through which persons evaluate the environment and its characteristics have been indicated in the literature with the terms 'personality and environment' and 'environmental attitudes'. Alongside these, the more specific area, concerned with evaluation, has been defined in terms of 'perceived environmental qualities'.

With regard to studies on personality and environment, the outcomes of evaluations have been mostly considered as the expression of personal dispositions possessed by individuals and kept stable over time. According to the most classical tradition of psychological research on 'personality traits', these dispositions have been assumed as variables that allow the prediction and explanation of environmental behaviours. Analogously with several specific developments reported in personality studies, this area of environmental-psychological research has recently emphasized the processes through which individuals conceptualize the environment (studies on 'cognitive complexity'), starting from the supposition that these processes are anchored to systems of expectations and goals ('personal projects') through which individuals confront the environment. Within this perspective, the emphasis initially given to traits and their stability has been shifted to the consideration of the role played by more complex – but at the same time specific – situations in which behaviours are performed.

The study of environmental attitudes, together with attitudes concerning the modalities for evaluating 'environmental qualities', constitutes the area of research most directly involved with the issue of satisfaction/dissatisfaction with the characteristics of various types of environments.

With regard to attitudes, specific attention has been given to the importance of the positions that individuals take concerning the most current and relevant problems and risks, such as pollution and environmental deterioration. As will be seen in the concluding section of this chapter, the evaluation of environmental qualities has been studied according to two main perspectives: in one case centred on the objective properties of various types of environments, and, in the other, focused on persons and the ways they perceive these properties.

Personality and environment   Initiating the research domain concerned with 'individual dispositions' towards the environment, e.p. turned again to one of the most representative topics in the psychological tradition: personality, considered as a series of internal factors that account for the specific ways each individual establishes relationships with the external world. Starting in the early 1960s, the activity carried out by the Institute of Personality Assessment and Research (IPAR) in Berkeley, California, showed the clear continuity that this domain of studies has maintained with the classical paradigm of evaluation-measurement of personality 'traits'.

As explicitly pointed out in Craik's first publications on the subject (1966, 1968, 1970), the study of dispositions towards the physical environment posed as its primary objective the development of technical procedures for the measurement of individual differences, assuming as a reference point environmental topics considered particularly significant and, where possible, suggested by experts in the area (such as naturalists and operators of the built environment).

The more general hypothesis underlying this perspective is that by knowing specific individual dispositions regarding a vast repertoire of these topics, predictions can be made on an individual's environmental behaviour.

The primarily psychometric approach of this research has been characterized from the start by the construction of questionnaires – for example, the one developed by Little (1968, 1972a, 1972b) for discriminating individuals oriented towards 'persons'/'things' – and above all scales for measuring dispositions towards specific aspects of living in the environment. A series of scales initially developed by the IPAR group at Berkeley was particularly representative of this. An example is the scale on dispositions towards 'pastoralism' and 'urbanism' (tendency to value nature and open spaces, or the cultural stimulations and social relations of city life) and towards 'environmental adaptation' (preference for preserving the environment, rather than its exploitation as a function of changing human needs). Through progressive validations and statistical elaborations, these scales and others were subsequently integrated into the more complex 'Environmental Response Inventory' (McKechnie, 1974, 1977, 1978), including 184 items relative to both the natural and built environment.

In this same direction, other authors have proposed inventories of 'environmental personality', focusing attention on a series of traits. An example of this is Sonnenfeld (1969), who articulated his 'Environmental Personality Inventory' around four main concepts: environmental density, defined according to the importance and complexity of the environmental aspects relevant to the person; environmental mobility, regarding both the degree of interest in the discovery of new and distant environments and evaluations of the risks involved; environmental control, corresponding to individual placement with respect to the opposing beliefs of controlling/ being controlled by the environment; environmental risk-taking, defined according to evaluations regarding the risk/non-risk of specific activities in the environment.

The rich literature, accumulated in only a few years, includes not only ambitious and complex inventories, but also simpler instruments, focused on specific aspects, such as Kaplan's (1977) 'Environmental Preference Questionnaire' and Weinstein's (1978) 'Noise Sensitivity Scale'. Following the empirical approach of personalogical studies, for at least a decade research has continued to be intensely involved in the construction of these instruments, starting from presuppositions of the stability of the different traits focused on and (conceptualized) and of the inter-individual differences. Thus, in speaking of environmental dispositions, reference is made to evaluate positions or to preferences of individuals with regard to environmental topics, but primarily to positions destined to remain stable over time.

The literature clearly shows how the objective of verifying the validity of these premises was for a long time the most relevant one. As well as the considerable theoretical effort (Little, 1987), attention was also focused on studies aimed at confirming the results obtained through testing, in particular on comparisons between environmental behaviours and attitudes shown by individuals, and predictions from outcomes of these tests.

Some of Little's (1976) studies asked residents in an area of Berkeley to describe the distinctive characteristics of three local shopping centres. The subjects' positions on the 'orientation vs persons/things' continuum was already known through their responses to the questionnaire. The investigation was aimed at delineating the different quality of the descriptions hypothesized by starting from the subjects' different orientations. The results confirmed the predictions: broader descriptions were provided by those classified as not having a specific orientation than by the others. These descriptions also showed a more accentuated tendency to note physical aspects among subjects 'oriented towards things'.

Gifford (1980) used a similar procedure with respect to the application of the 'Environmental Inventory Response'. In this case, the questions concerned the modalities and criteria that subjects with different dispositions towards the environment would use to evaluate different typologies of buildings, presented through a series of slides. Besides a comparison between individual scores on personality tests and on building evaluations, the author also proposed pursuing results which were in some way generalizable. Positive correlations between the disposition towards 'pastoralism' and the tendency to prefer images of buildings in which people are not visible emerged from the results as well as between the disposition towards 'environmental adaptation' and the preference for newer and larger buildings.

As Little (1987, p. 232) has pointed out, considering the most recent developments in these studies, the 'search for the basic anatomy of the dispositions toward the physical environment' has shown that the investigation of the 'deeper structure of acts, through the filter of orthodox trait measurement simultaneously blurred the primary subject of investigation', that is, the impact of the environment on personality, especially with respect to the aspects of meaning that the molar structure of the environment provides to persons' behaviours/actions.

The changes which occurred in the more general orientations of the psychological disciplines have certainly contributed towards correcting the image of an individual made passive with regard to the environment by his/her personal-stable dispositions. One need only think of the new accent placed on the active role of the mind in processes of knowledge by the cognitive approach. This was already emphasized in Kelly's (1955) hypothesis on the individual cognitive abilities for producing relevant 'personal constructs' for the individual experience. Projected onto the more specific topic of the relationships between personality and environment, a similar hypothesis led Friedman (1974) to develop procedures for analysis and measurement of the 'cognitive complexity' individuals manifest in conceptualizing 'things' populating the environment. But this hypothesis also stimulated broader reflections and led to an emphasis on the primary importance to be attributed to 'personal projects' (Little, 1987) in view of a more appropriate understanding of both individual personalities and the types of relationships individuals have with the socio-physical components of the environment they live in. Starting from Kelly's hypothesis, Little has stressed the concept of 'project' in order to call attention to the opportunity to consider 'personal constructs' as strictly linked to the 'interrelated sequences of actions oriented toward goals'.

Other equally relevant theoretical considerations made possible a critical re-examination of the strictly personalogical approach to the individual–environment relationship. As Little (1987) has pointed out, beginning with the perspective outlined by Brunswik's (1943, 1957) theory of perception, the entire area of psychological research had to look at behaviour from a perspective less anchored to the general laws of intra-individual functioning and more attentive to the processes contextually involving persons and their environment.

In studies on personality, a paradigmatic example of this approach can be found in the most radical theoretical proposal advanced by Mischel (1968). This author has conceptualized personality by clearly shifting attention from individual stability (traditionally attributed to internal traits) to 'situational' (context) factors. He considers the situation as responsible for the control of human behaviours and, consequently, for their change.

Besides re-proposing the perennial controversy over the importance to be given to internal/external factors in explaining variations and differences in and between individual behaviours, Mischel's proposal on personality probably constitutes another of the premises in the psychological disciplines favouring an interactive (besides a contextual) view or conceptualizing the more general relationship between environment and behaviour.

The study of the relationships between personality and environment has been outlined since the beginning as a work programme aimed at constructing a bridge between the individual and the physical components of his/her life contexts, between psychological and environmental disciplines. Perhaps because of its emblematic position, this study figures as an equally emblematic synthesis of the crucial main problems e.p. is also faced with in more specific and circumscribed areas.

Environmental attitudes Another route followed by environmental-psychological research in studying evaluative responses to various properties and/or components of the physical environment is the one articulated around attitudes. Also interested in the processes underlying individual behaviour, this route is an alternative to the one which focuses on the concept of personality and on its component traits.

Traditionally considered as an individual, acquired disposition to act with regard to specific objects, persons and/or situations in the outside world, 'attitude' is a concept used by social psychologists to account for variations in individual behaviour in similar circumstances, that is, to compensate for the evident shortcomings in analysis which only connects behaviour to stable dispositions, independent from the specificity of the situations the individual may find him/herself acting in and from the objectives the action may be aimed towards.

When concerned with 'environmental attitudes', the research focuses attention on the affective-evaluative and cognitive-informative content of the positions persons express towards aspects or specific properties of the physical environment. As Stokols (1978) pointed out, in this case the main objective consists in showing 'tendencies to respond favorably/ unfavorably' to the environmental characteristics considered.

Another aspect also characterizing this study is its quantitative approach and the extensive use of measurement instruments, such as 'attitude scales'. Empirically speaking, this approach follows two main directions: the first considers attitudes as expressions of individual satisfaction/ dissatisfaction towards the environment, and it primarily emphasizes the evaluative component; the second tends to approach them as positions with respect to several important environmental problems (such as pollution, limited resources and environmental risk), and pays particular attention to the informative component (Stokols, 1978).

Attitudes and environmental satisfaction. In this case, the purpose is to study the evaluations people express about the various properties of the environmental settings in which their daily life takes place, especially with reference to residential and/or urban settings. In this type of research, the evaluations constitute the premise for comparative analyses aimed, on one side, towards grasping the importance of various properties or components in defining the degree of environmental satisfaction/dissatisfaction; and, on the other, for verifying the influence that can be exercised on these evaluative hierarchies by socio-demographic variables (such as sex or age) and/or by some other variables that contribute towards specifying the more complex relationship between persons and the environment (for example, socio-economic level, working or not, length of environmental residence).

Among the many studies following this approach, a significant example can be found in a complex study conducted on a sample of inhabitants in Rome (Secchiaroli and Bonnes, 1983; Bonnes and Secchiaroli, 1986; Bonnes et al., 1987b). Apart from other findings, which will be discussed in more detail later in this volume, the study also proposed to discover analogies and differences in evaluative attitudes expressed by residents about the various parts of the city (one's own urban neighbourhood, city centre and periphery). A double order of comparisons was made. The first regarded the degree to which the various properties or components competed in specifying the satisfaction/dissatisfaction expressed about each of the three urban places; the second regarded the relative position assumed by each of these properties in the evaluation of the more complex urban environment.

A questionnaire was prepared to identify attitudes, and a list of bipolar adjectives, taken from the 'Scales of the Affective Quantities Attributed to Places' (Russell and Pratt, 1980), was also used. From the data analyses, developed in both of the above-described directions, positive attitudes emerged towards the centre and the residential neighbourhood (mostly defined as 'pleasant' and 'stimulating'), and clearly negative ones emerged toward the periphery (connoted as 'monotonous' and 'depressing'). Results regarding the hierarchies of aspects and components referred to by these attitudes also reveal the different roles played by most of them in evaluations of the neighbourhood and the centre. With regard to the centre, the positive evaluation is clearly anchored to physical-architectural characteristics, and for the neighbourhood socio-relational qualities of the environmental context prevail (types of persons and interpersonal relationships). Different reference points also emerge with regard to the negative evaluations: in the case of the neighbourhood, primarily functional types of components (linked in particular to environmental mobility, such as streets and traffic) are involved, and for the centre, 'excesses of stimulation' – although their connotation is more ambivalent than clearly negative.

The emergence of correlations between these results and the different ways various categories of persons actualize their 'use relationship' with the urban environment and its parts highlighted the opportunity for further investigation, starting from the hypothesis of a link between attitudes and actions, between environmental evaluation and the aims which guide actions. With regard to the neighbourhood, as the part of the urban environment having the greatest 'psychological centrality' in the representations of the subjects interviewed, an analysis was carried out comparing the above-described attitudes with the expectations the subjects expressed when envisioning an 'ideal neighbourhood' in which to live (Ardone et al., 1987). In agreement with what Stokols (1981) suggests, in this way environmental evaluation is redefined as a function of the 'congruence' people perceive between their own needs and aims and the opportunities offered by the environment, rather than as a response linearly attributed to the objective properties of the latter.

Together with the most significant outcomes of these investigations, the theoretical implications will be discussed in Chapter 5. Here some results seem worthy of further discussion concerning the attitudes expressed by residents about their neighbourhood. They consist in two main tendencies regarding:

(a)   the central position assumed by some particular environmental characteristics in determining the degree of positive connotation of the attitudes;
(b)   the connections linking the evaluations with length of residence and time spent in the neighbourhood every day.

Since the availability of public green areas emerged as a particular relevant environmental component in the residents' preliminary description of their neighbourhood, an attempt has been made to identify its specific effect on degrees of overall satisfaction expressed regarding the neighbourhood environment.

The central role of this component in environmental evaluation is confirmed by the results of a factorial analysis. In fact, the availability of green areas reveals its simultaneous association with two factors: the first regards the evaluation of the general availability of space; the second, instead, the evaluation of availability/functioning of services (such as schools and public transportation) (Bonnes et al., 1988a, 1988b). The temporal dimension of residential experience in the neighbourhood is also correlated with the differentiation of environmental attitudes: a less negative evaluation of factors of 'environmental density' (in the spatial and human sense) tends to be associated with an increase in length of residence in the neighbourhood; a less negative evaluation of several functional components (above all, specialized structures of commercial distribution) tends to be associated with an increase in time spent daily in the neighbourhood (Bonnes et al., 1988a).

These findings seem particularly interesting for the methodological problem regarding the study of environmental attitudes.

A first suggestion in this respect derives from the many relations emerging between the various environmental components that constitute the object of evaluation. As a somewhat systematic tendency, this result calls attention to the importance of studying environmental attitudes from a molar perspective. In other words, when, as in this case, the object of satisfaction/dissatisfaction is constituted by the everyday environment in which individuals live, a perspective seems needed which (a) does not limit *a priori* the analysis to only physical components, but also includes social ones; and (b) does not proceed in a fragmented way, isolating the single components.

Another suggestion derives from the evident complexity of evaluative processes in which persons are involved. In particular, the results stress the opportunity of proceeding by considering the relation that links attitudes and perceptions of environmental conditions as congruent/incongruent with respect to the aims of the action. Since actions and aims can be difficult to pursue, apart from the contexts of social relationships, this consideration should not be taken as a premise for an individualistic approach to the study of environmental attitudes. Actually, attitudes represent a component of human functioning which, when marking 'differentiations' (individual), also outlines areas of possible 'sharing' (social).

Attitudes towards environmental problems. The increasing interest of environmental psychologists in the study of attitudes towards some environmental problems is linked to the growing objective relevance that these problems have assumed (and also thanks to environmentalist movements). Specific problems include the intensive exploitation of resources, the various forms of environmental pollution, and risks that some systems of energy production (primarily nuclear) can involve for people's health and well-being.

Empirically speaking, research has been primarily oriented towards the study of ways in which people perceive and evaluate these problems. Particular attention has been devoted to the types of information individuals have about specific problems, since information is their means of reference for structuring attitudes.

As Stokols (1978) reminds us, e.p. has also proposed verifying the coherence between attitudes and behaviours people tend to adopt in view of an improvement in environmental conditions.

The quantitative approach, also adopted in this case, gives the development of measurement scales top priority. Developed in the 1970s and 1980s, many instruments are now available: some are directly aimed at scaling evaluative positions towards various environmental problems (Lounsbury and Tornatzky, 1977); others at measuring the consistency and the knowledge individuals have about the environment (Maloney et al., 1975); and still others at discriminating orientations towards behaviours and actions considered 'ecologically responsible' (Antil and Bennet, 1979).

Various authors have investigated the methodological aspects connected with these instruments, primarily through comparisons between the results obtained using different scales. From several of these verifications (Van Liere and Dunlap, 1981), a tendency towards coherence emerges between the outcomes of measurements regarding attitudes towards pollution, the use of resources and environmental regulation. However, in some cases the correlation is less univocal between the positions expressed by persons in terms of attitudes and orientations of environmental behaviours/actions.

These are the cases which call attention to the well-known debate in psycho-social research concerning the concept of attitude and the hypothesis that assumes it as the psychological structure for predicting and explaining individual behaviour.

As already mentioned, due to its involvement in applied research, the study of environmental attitudes also includes the formulation of predictions about behaviours. The literature shows the prevalent tendency to primarily focus on the degree and quality of information/knowledge people have about various environmental problems. That is the starting point from which investigations are made to point out the connections between information, people's evaluative positions towards specific environmental problems and readiness of behaviours for safeguarding and improving environmental conditions.

Investigating the problem of atmospheric pollution, a very large opinion poll carried out in the early 1970s in various European countries (Great Britain, Hungary and Yugoslavia) has shown, for example, that the majority of subjects questioned ignored both the possible causes and the possible effects on health of agents producing this type of pollution (Kromm et al., 1973). As an extreme case, this example shows how the assumption of 'non-ecologically responsible behaviours' by these persons, together with their neutral or indifferent attitudes towards the problem, are associated with a lack of information/knowledge.

According to what has been specifically demonstrated in several studies, there is a higher probability that persons assume responsible behaviours when they are informed about the consequences of pollution (Heberlein and Black, 1976, 1981).

Other examples of this type of study regard the analysis of the relations between the specificity of evaluative positions on particular environmental problems and people's more general orientations, for example, political ones.

Several studies have pointed out that besides being younger and primarily female (Cornwell, 1982; Van Liere and Dunlap, 1981), those who express more negative attitudes about nuclear energy also tend to have less conservative political attitudes and to emphasize the social, rather than personal, nature of the risks involved in the use of certain technological innovations (Craik et al., 1982).

Past (Three Mile Island, USA, 1979) and more recent events (Chernobyl, USSR, 1986) which brought the problem of safety in producing and using nuclear energy to the centre of public attention encouraged various researchers to begin systematic and continuous monitoring of attitudes towards this problem by reaching vast strata of the populations in various countries.

The social relevance which this problem assumed following the incident at Chernobyl was discussed by the *Journal of Environmental Psychology*. Recently, the journal published a monograph (10, 1990) containing a series of studies on attitudes towards nuclear energy, conducted after May 1986 on very large population samples in various countries of Western Europe and Australia. Aimed at studying reactions, this research proposed revealing the consequences produced by the incident at Chernobyl on attitudes towards nuclear energy and its uses.

The most shared hypothesis links the attitude towards nuclear energy with the 'perception of risk' about its consequences (Van der Plight and Midden, 1990). According to this hypothesis, anti-nuclear attitudes are considered the consequence of the high risk individuals perceive connected with the production and use of this energy. A large part of the research conducted on the topic has focused attention on these perceptions and has considered these major incidents as an opportunity for testing this type of hypothesis more specifically.

With regard to Chernobyl, the data gathered in September 1986 on several groups selected from the Swedish population (Drottz-Sjoberg and Sjoberg, 1990) confirm that the predominance of negative attitudes towards nuclear energy is strictly correlated with perception of the risk of radiation, that is, this perception is more accentuated when the persons interviewed live in regions more exposed to fall-out from the explosion.

Although considering the perception of risk as an antecedent of the diffused opposition to nuclear energy, the hypothesis of this research is formulated above all with reference to the role played by mass media in directing public opinion. What is emphasized in particular is the condition of uncertainty created as a result of the abundant – but also contradictory – information diffused both on the general characteristics of nuclear energy and on the specific predictions/evaluations of risk linked to the incident.

In analyses of uncertain situations, the literature concerning stress has pointed out that they may be associated with specific response strategies. Janis and Mann (1977) have distinguished the 'defensive avoidance' strategy from that of 'hypervigilance'. Referred to conditions of informative uncertainty, the first of these strategies indicates a tendency to avoid information on the problem, to delegate the responsibility to others (politicians, experts) for its solution and to be selective about information (preference for what supports one's own point of view). The second strategy consists in a tendency to be open to any type of information, without discriminating its relevance or reliability.

In agreement with this perspective, one of the large-scale opinion polls conducted in West Germany (starting in November 1986 and subsequently in May 1987 and 1988), revealed that individuals' predominant response to the incident at Chernobyl was expressed in terms of uncertainty about its effects on health. This uncertainty created a problem regarding appropriate alimentary behaviour but, above all, it paralleled the various sources at the time of the incident (Peters et al., 1990). In an even more striking way, the results of a questionnaire administered to 840 subjects (in Australia, Britain, France, West Germany and Holland) in June 1986 showed that those who considered themselves interested in and informed about the topic of nuclear energy not only were those most upset by the news from Chernobyl, but were also the least inclined to adopt avoidance strategies. On the contrary, much more marked among these subjects was the tendency towards self-trust and showing accentuated 'vigilance' (Eiser et al., 1990).

The longitudinal perspective adopted by these studies permitted investigation of the important issue of stability/change of attitudes over time. The data collected in West Germany primarily show a tendency towards stability in the way interviewees evaluate the relevant dangers caused by the incident, but also a corresponding decrease in degree of opposition to future use of nuclear energy (Peters et al., 1990). These results in some way contradict the hypothesized connection between negative attitudes towards nuclear power and high risk perception.

But the most interesting results on the stability/change of these attitudes comes from the five studies carried out subsequently (from December 1986 to October 1988) on Dutch subjects (Midden and Verplanken, 1990). In this case, important specifications emerge from a series of cross-comparisons.

From a first comparison between pro and con attitudes towards nuclear energy, it emerged that the 'pro' tend to be less stable than the 'con'; those who show more favourable attitudes also show greater ambivalence in the way they perceive the relationship between 'risk' and 'advantages' in the use of nuclear energy. This is true even if the ambivalent perception of this relationship is strictly correlated with stability of attitudes, independent of their connotation (pro or con).

Making a more detailed quantitative analysis of the changes in attitude registered during the time separating the five studies, the authors compared the individual scale positions with those relative to the means of the entire sample. The outcome of this comparison shows that the average attitude tends to be more stable over time with respect to the (more changeable) trajectories of single individual attitudes.

As a final, interesting result, the authors of this study point out that even when a change of position occurs towards nuclear energy, it tends to involve specific beliefs held by persons rather than their overall attitude.

A more general consideration deriving from these findings concerns the questions to be answered by the psychological research on environmental problems. In this respect, the purpose of discovering what people know about the main environmental problems, and how they perceive and evaluate them, probably assumes a priority compared with the aim of making predictions about behaviour. And what makes the study of attitudes particularly useful in this sense is that the orientations of very large population samples can be known and introduced into circuits of social communication.

The attention that has been dedicated to the topic of stability and/or change of attitudes is perhaps the issue which most stimulates theoretical-methodological reflections because of the complex dynamics involved in the types of attitudes analysed. In spite of their predominantly descriptive nature, the specific results described here offer at least two types of indications. The first consists in the different openness to change respectively manifested by the pro and con positions to nuclear energy, and in the equally different degree of involvement of single components with respect to the overall structure of the attitude analysed. The second calls attention to the role played by perception/evaluation of the relationship between risks and advantages both on the tendency to hold the attitude stable and on the importance assumed by information as the possible generator of uncertainty. These indications confirm the complexity of the psychological processes involved in the assumption of an evaluative position regarding a problematic issue, and they call attention to the need for more thorough analyses of these processes.

The classical modality for studying attitudes, however, indispensable for an exact reconstruction of the characteristics a specific environmental problem assumes for the individual, seems to require the complementary use of further conceptual instruments. In fact, the main question to be answered concerns both the understanding of dynamics the processes in question respond to and the discovery of the way the evaluative component of attitudes is connected to the implicit cognitive representation of the object/problem evaluated.

Among the many issues that have animated the more general critical debate around the study of attitudes in social psychology in the past, these questions have recently been noted again, particularly in Europe.

As Jaspars and Fraser (1984, p. 151) point out, 'to obtain a better understanding [. . .] it is necessary to go beyond the responses that subjects make in many investigations on attitudes' and to take into consideration the role played by the social dimension in the characterization of the processes in question. In particular, attention should be oriented towards the degree to which implicit cognitive representations of the attitude's objects are shared between individuals belonging to the same social group.

In the light of this perspective, the objective of identifying the relations between attitudes and belief systems people structure regarding objects of evaluation appears as the most relevant indication for the research. According to the theory of 'social representations' (Moscovici, 1963, 1973, 1976, 1984a), these belief systems are socially construed, maintained and/

or changed and can be considered as the matrices for defining the relevance and meanings of the various components of the environment people interact with,

The evaluation of environmental qualities   It has already been mentioned that from the beginning interest in the qualitative characteristics of the environment has delineated the more specific, but also complex, objectives for ascertaining the various environmental aspects/qualities correlating with the satisfaction and well-being of respective users. Moving towards a similar programmatic objective, the rich domain of research which has studied the topic of environmental evaluation has always affirmed that its peculiarity consists in its concern with 'perceived quality' (Craik and Zube, 1976).

This general premise brought research to focus more on final outcomes than on the modalities people follow in evaluating the various characteristics of the environment they interact with. A further conceptual distinction was emphasized between 'preference' and 'evaluation', which involved the establishment of two different areas of inquiry. In fact, the study of 'environmental appraisal' is connected with the systems of personal preferences with respect to environments, 'environmental assessment' is concerned both with the objective evaluation of 'qualitative standards' of the various types of environments (Craik, 1971; Craik and Zube, 1976) and with the judgements people make about them.

A first substantial difference is that the studies regarding appraisal are clearly centred on the person and those concerned with environmental assessment show an almost exclusive interest in the environment and its properties, starting from the presupposition that the quality of the latter can be measured, although always as a function of the fundamental need for the well-being of environmental users.

What primarily marks the assessment approach is its predominant attention to the applied dimension of environmental psychology research.

As Zube et al. (1982) have pointed out, a large part of the research on assessment concerning the quality of the natural environment was activated in the United States as a response to the practical needs of management and environmental planning, particularly as a consequence of legislative norms on 'environmental impact'. In fact, the identification of a qualitative standard for environments consists in the empirical construction of parameters which primarily environmental operators refer to for obtaining indications as to the types of impact that can be linked to specific environmental properties and/or their changes and for making suggestions about the planning of interventions on the natural and/or built environment.

With regard to methodology, the approach followed by these studies initially used psychometric measurement systems. According to what is now considered a tradition inaugurated by Craik (1971), and similar to what psychological research had been doing for a long time in measuring people's qualities or characteristics, these systems were used to measure qualities of 'places'.

Craik has identified five main types of environmental characteristics that have measurable qualities: physio-spatial properties; the types and quantity of artefacts present in the environment (from room furnishings to machines in an industrial environment); the typical traits of various types of environments (from those concerning the panoramic dimension of natural landscapes to those regarding office or home environments); the functional aspects of various environmental settings (with respect to the individual's usual behaviours in them); and the institutional aspects of the social climate (with particular reference to hospital environments: see Moos, 1973).

The empirical works on this subject have assumed the physical and social dimensions of the environment as their main reference points. With respect to the former, research has been conducted on the definition of office quality (Acking and Kuller, 1973; Hershberger and Cass, 1974), water, air and noise (Cermak and Cornillion, 1976; Craik and Zube, 1976; Carp and Carp, 1982). With regard to the social dimension, interest has been primarily directed towards the study of the 'interpersonal climate' in organizations or institutional environments (Insel and Moos, 1974; James and Jones, 1974; Gavin and Howe, 1975; Moos, 1975).

Some studies have approached the environment as unities of physical and social resources. In this case, attention has been focused on the quality of housing and of the neighbourhood (Onibokun, 1974; Marans, 1976; Smith, 1976) and on residential care facilities (Moos and Lemke, 1984).

Another popular topic regards predictions about the impact both technological and social interventions on the environment can generate within specific communities (Wolf, 1974, 1975).

In any case, the most relevant characteristic of this approach to the study of environmental qualities seems to be its particular methodological option tending towards objectification. In fact, due to its increasing diffusion, this approach can be considered as an alternative to more classical studies which from one side consider the outcomes of evaluations as a product of personal dispositions (or 'preferences') and from the other side focus on the evaluative connotation (positive/negative) as an expression of attitudes towards various components and/or environmental properties.

As evidenced in the literature, the dominant trend in the research in assessment of environmental qualities consists in the development of measurement procedures and techniques (Craik, 1971; Craik and Zube, 1976; Craik and Feimer, 1987). Representative examples include the investigation carried out by Craik (1983) to find procedures for the assessment of qualities of natural landscapes, and the equally complex procedure formulated by Moos and Lemke (1984) regarding the hospital environment (that is, the 'Multiphasic Environmental Assessment Procedure).

Apart from the unequal possibility for different environmental characteristics to be subjected to technical-instrumental quality measurement, one of the major methodological problems this area of research has had to face consists in the inevitable use of procedures based on researchers' observations. In effect, in constructing qualitative standards to be proposed as reference criteria, almost exclusive recourse has been made to this procedure, although observation has been primarily entrusted to experts such as architects and planners or, at any rate, to persons who have non-episodic relations with the environments studied.

Specifications have been advanced from many sides concerning the fact that the 'assessment' of environmental qualities should be considered as an operation completely distinct from that involved in 'preference' judgements. As Gifford (1987) points out, an observer can assess the architecture of a certain city, defining it as high quality, but prefer the architectural style of another.

Unlike 'evaluation' studies, which focus on the 'perceived quality' of the direct users of the environment (individual and/or group-social categories), for research aimed at finding criteria/standards to be assumed as basic references for environmental assessments, the existence of an agreement between the various judges involved in the operation becomes crucially important.

With respect to this problem, research has used the most elementary statistical procedures to check the significance of differences. And 'indices of perceived environmental quality' (Craik and Zube, 1976) have been established on the basis of these results.

However, some theoretical questions remain unanswered regarding the 'mediated' nature of the perceptions referred to in this case and the implicit idea of experts as representatives with respect to very large, composite populations. This constitutes one of the more general problems faced by e.p. in many areas.

Only in the last decade have studies on the assessment of environmental qualities reported more interesting developments (Holahan, 1986). One of the most significant aspects involves the overcoming of the initial project to construct indices of perceived environmental quality, with validity generalizable to vast typologies of environmental situations. Craik (1981) has pointed out that these indices can be effective for research only if they are defined with respect to the specificity of various environmental contexts. As a consequence, the units of analysis focused on have been the various places people interact with directly; they also became the primary sources for identifying environmental aspects and/or components which, perceived as relevant, are destined to form the basic reference for constructing instruments for data collection on environmental qualities.

Besides this change, which seems to be an almost inevitable correction of the simplistic initial position, another has to be mentioned in this area. It consists in the growing interest in the use of newer technologies. In this regard, we need only mention the simulation procedures that characterized the activity of the Berkeley Environmental Simulation Laboratory in California. Here, complex computer-controlled electric-electronic devices have been used for reproducing scale models of various types of environments in the laboratory, which can be modified in terms of composition and other characteristics (Craik and Feimer, 1987).

The divergence which has always marked the developments of this research sector on both the applied and theoretical side is rather evident.

In spite of growing interest in less objectivistic approaches, studies on environmental qualities still seem to be more interested in the development of instruments and empirical procedures for providing responses to concrete questions than in systematic reflection on the complex psychological factors involved in evaluative processes of environmental qualities. This shortcoming has been repeatedly pointed out in the literature (Stokols, 1978; Holahan, 1986) and indicates the need for an approach that confronts the two main components in a more integrated way: the environment or, better, places with their properties/qualities, and the people who actively interact with them by acting, knowing and referring to specific belief/preference systems.

Moving in the direction of evaluation studies, and with attention on the cognitive dimension of human environmental behaviours, several authors have shown particular sensitivity towards this type of problem. The proposals of Kaplan and Kaplan (1982) are among the most significant. These authors formulated a conceptualization of the processes involved in the definition of environmental preferences which considers both the peculiarities of the environmental setting and the active role played by the person-observer.

Starting from the consideration of preferences as the outcome of processes of adaptation continually pursued by the human species with respect to the environment, the Kaplans first stress the function of cognitive processes. They recognize their central role in determining what people do in 'giving sense' to the environment and in 'involving themselves' in it; that is, in pursuing the satisfaction of some needs of the human species considered fundamental by the authors.

In agreement with these premises, a preeminent interest is oriented towards the characteristics of processes common to all individuals when they interact with the environment (that is, apart from the consideration of every possible element of difference, personal and/or social). Meanwhile the role attributed to the environment is not at all secondary. In fact, the authors point out that the individual's preferences are, in turn, associated with those environmental qualities which 'offer a promise of being involving and making sense' (Kaplan and Kaplan, 1982, p. 80).

In this regard, they emphasize environmental qualities, such as *coherence* (as responsible for the ease with which a scene can, for example, be cognitively organized); *complexity* (as the ability of the environmental setting to keep the person active); *legibility* (or clarity of the physical disposition which renders the environment easily and effectively explorable); *mystery* (as a property which encourages discovery and greater interaction with the environment).

The guidelines coming from psychological theories are evident, even though they concern the processes of perception rather than those of cognition, particularly in the case of Gibson's 'ecological theory of perception' (see Chapter 2). Here, for example, the concept of 'affordance' is directly adopted to emphasize the 'immediate knowability' of the four environmental qualities described. However, the position of Stephen and Rachel Kaplan presents an important difference. They explicitly speak of 'cognitive affordance' to point out that, in order to be activated and to produce results, the (cognitive) process in question requires information from the environment.

Another and more specific topic which has assumed a central position in the domain of environmental evaluation studies is that of the affective component of evaluation. Already in the reflections of researchers interested in perception, for example, Ittelson (1973b), mention is made of the fact that 'the first level of response to the environment is affective. The direct emotional impact of the situation [. . .] in general governs the directions taken by subsequent relations with the environment' (p. 16).

The importance which even common sense usually recognizes in this component for describing and explaining human behaviour towards the environment points to the need for a systematic analysis of the role it plays in processes of evaluation. However, unlike common sense, this should not imply an exclusive identification of the emotional-affective dimension with 'subjectivity', nor should it mean adopting hypotheses which attribute every possible explanation of the relations linking persons with their environment to that dimension. Instead, a more accurate understanding of the connection between the affective and cognitive dimensions is needed, as components always involved in processes of environmental evaluation.

In this regard, the literature offers more general considerations than specific, empirical works, and analyses are developed which alternatively emphasize one or the other of these components. In connection with this tendency, the relationship between the affective and cognitive dimensions has emerged as one of the most debated issues in e.p. And this is not only true with reference to processes of evaluation, but also in relation to the need for deeper understanding of the complex relations linking these processes to a person's behaviour and actions in the environment.

The main frameworks for the analysis and interpretation of environmental evaluation are also representative of the positions respectively centred on the emotional-affective component and on the cognitive component of the processes involved.

One of the first studies concerned with the affective component was that of Mehrabian and Russell (1974, 1975). Approaching the topic in terms of 'emotional responses' to the environment (as expression of degree of 'pleasure', 'arousal' and 'dominance'), these authors emphasize the mediating role played by this component between the molar environment and both personality and behaviour. Their hypothesis predicts that the levels of these responses are simultaneously influenced by environmental variables (whether they are physical properties and/or information) and by individual personality characteristics, and that responses originating in this way in turn influence some behavioural schemata (such as the general tendency 'to approach' or, on the contrary, 'to avoid' certain environments) or the more specific schemata concerning work performance and non-verbal communication.

Empirical verifications of this hypothesis were made in a series of studies (Mehrabian, 1977, 1978; Russell and Mehrabian, 1978) which presented verbal descriptions of environments to subjects whose personality tendencies were already known; the subjects were asked to indicate how they would act in these environments.

Also based on the criticisms underlying limits of validity in the use of purely verbal procedures (Daniel and Ittelson, 1981), Russell et al. (Russell and Pratt, 1980; Russell and Ward, 1981; Russell and Lanius, 1984) investigated the conceptual structure of descriptions given by persons in defining the affective qualities of environments. In this case, the issue of affective qualities has been redefined in terms of 'attributed qualities'.

Assuming the affective component as 'emotion expressed through language', these studies show that the conceptual structure in which the meaning of the terms commonly used by persons for describing the 'emotional qualities of places' can be empirically found in the orthogonal space defined by two main bipolar dimensions, respectively defined as pleasant/unpleasant and arousing/sleepy.

After emphasizing the distinction between 'the emotional and the cognitive component [. . .] underlying the meaning of the affective terms', these authors hold that the two dimensions resulting from their research (pleasant and arousing) are probably the only ones that denote an 'internal emotional state *per se*', above all in the sense that, unlike those of a cognitive nature, they do not reflect 'beliefs about antecedents, consequences and such similar properties of the emotional state' (Russell and Pratt, 1980, p. 313). These specifications are not aimed at confirming a dichotomous view of processes that control the evaluation of or, better 'attributions of meaning' to the environment. In fact, on the one hand, the authors point out that the way individuals respond emotionally to the environment 'depends on how it [the environment] is perceived and known' (ibid.); on the other, they question the possibilities of tracing a distinction between the emotional and cognitive dimensions which underlie the meaning of the terms expressing affective connotations (Russell et al., 1981). Data from the study of the 'similarities' individuals perceive between different environments show that evaluations of the characteristics referred to by persons for tracing analogies and differences between a number of environments and the perceptual, cognitive and affective aspects are strictly correlated.

As Gifford (1987) points out, the interest of these authors has increasingly shifted from the affective responses to the environment, to 'cognitions' expressed by the same responses. In any case, calling attention to verbal language in the expression of evaluations constitutes a methodological contribution which has become central to e.p.

Among the studies interested in filling the lack of research on this topic, those produced by several Italian researchers must be mentioned (Mainardi Peron, 1985; Mainardi Peron et al., 1985, 1988; Baroni and Mainardi Peron, 1987, 1991). Specifically interested in language as an instrument for expression of 'environmental knowledge', the authors point out how, in real-life situations, people 'learn' about places not only through direct contact, but also through speaking about them: describing them, making comments, giving information to others, expressing their feelings about them. They consider this a good reason for systematically studying the types of advantages and problems linked to the use of verbal accounts in environmental-psychological research.

Unlike Russell et al.'s (1981) approach in research on the structures underlying the attribution of affective qualities, the interest of these authors in learning and communication of environmental knowledge is more clearly oriented towards a dynamic perspective. In referring to the results of their experimental research, they recently pointed out how the use of verbal accounts is a particularly appropriate way 'to bring light to processes, rather than to the results of environmental knowledge' (Baroni and Mainardi Peron, 1991, p. 13).

As already mentioned, similar to the perspective favouring the affective component, the study of evaluation in terms of 'environmental preferences' has also been approached from a cognitive viewpoint.

Perhaps the most representative example is that of Stephen Kaplan (1982, 1983). According to this author, people's environmental preferences must be considered as a matter of 'decision-making' and 'choice', with respect to which the cognitive processes of categorization and inference play a primary role in the structuring of affectively connoted evaluations. Adopting the well-known concept of 'plan' (Miller et al., 1960), Kaplan connects this moment of decision/choice to actions people propose carrying out in the environment and to the alternatives they perceive as possible. In this perspective, the evaluation of environmental qualities tends to be exclusively considered as the outcome of a cognitive 'control' on the environment and/or of a selection of relevant information it provides with respect to the aims of action (Kaplan, 1983).

Since it was primarily approached through the more classical framework adopted by psychology for describing the basic processes of human functioning, the study of environmental evaluation treated the affective and cognitive dimensions separately. This mode of procedure has often risked re-proposing the misleading perspective in which the two dimensions are positioned antagonistically with respect to the influence they can produce on the outcomes of the evaluation as well as on behaviour towards the environment, respectively.

In any case, the fact of having assumed them as relevant topics of study has facilitated an approach, on the one hand, more molar, more attentive to gathering their overall characteristics, rather than centred on single response traits; on the other hand, oriented towards considering the involvement of these dimensions in processes of environmental evaluation in a more integrated way.

The suggestions which have emerged in this area of e.p. are, in any case, connected with the parallel conceptualization of the environment in terms of 'place'. Starting from the indications provided by Canter (1977; see Chapter 5 below) and developed by many other authors (Stokols, 1978; Russell and Ward, 1982; Bonnes and Secchiaroli, 1986), the concept of place outlines a complex unit of analysis that emerges from the interaction between three main components of a specific human–environmental setting; these include its physical attributes, the activities persons carry out there and the cognitive representations individuals make of both of the preceding components.

When emphasis is on the interplay linking behaviours oriented by goals ('actions') and cognitive representations, this concept includes the process of evaluation. In this case, what is specifically recognized is the fact that, in identifying the places that allow for the satisfaction of one's needs and/ or the achievement of goals in an undifferentiated environment, the individual moves in a direction in which the motivational dimension (relevance of goals) intersects with the perceptual-cognitive one (representation of the environment and the opportunities perceived in it).

Following Canter (1983), the evaluation becomes an expression of the degree to which places facilitate the achievement of relevant objectives of action for the individual. Among these objectives, Canter first indicates those regarding 'spatial access', 'convenience', 'comfort', 'safety and the practice of social interaction'.

Unlike the emphasis that Stephen Kaplan (1982, 1983) also places on goals of action as a central reference point for the analysis of environmental evaluation, in this case the evaluation not only consists in the 'cognitive control' of information/opportunities offered by the environment, but also includes the possible degrees of motivational saliency assumed by various goals.

As will be seen in Chapter 5, the concept of place also constitutes a useful reference point for the study of the ways complex ties between persons and environments are created and develop, as well as of the factors that contribute to specifying the quality and intensity of these links.

The first steps made by the concept of place towards the main factors involved in environmental evaluation emphasize the need in e.p. for a more integrated and systematic theory of the processes of environmental evaluation. In this regard, Canter's (1983) suggestions must be mentioned first, particularly his proposal of a 'purposive' and 'multivariate' model of the 'experience of places' (p. 666).

This proposal is articulated around the premise that 'evaluations are directed toward goals'; it emphasizes the 'multimodal' nature 'of the experience of places', or the fact that 'the interactions of the individual within a place are always correlated with a certain number of objectives . . . thus they have referents . . . which are social and physical' (ibid., p. 664–5).

As already mentioned, Canter identifies social referents primarily with the practice of social interaction, and physical referents with spatial accessibility and with functional structures responding to needs for use and comfort.

Within this perspective, his model constitutes a methodological proposal for resolving some important questions generally neglected by environmental-psychological research. The first is that concerning the classification of this triple series of referents. According to Canter, they are always co-present in a place and strictly intercorrelated and must be considered as 'important and distinct aspects of the experience of place' (ibid., p. 666). Canter also emphasizes the different degree of relative importance that each aspect forming the various categories of referents can have for the goals structuring the personal experience of places. This emphasis leads him to specify a 'hierarchy of places', based not directly on environmental properties and on their reciprocal relations, but on the level of interaction a place implies for an individual. One of the main references relative to the hierarchy/evaluation is, therefore, identified in the 'different ranges over which an individual interacts with a place' (ibid., p. 669).

On the methodological side, the references which the author indicates as most appropriate for 'converting the multiple classification scheme of referents [their relative importance] and levels [of interaction] in a set of related hypotheses' are those relative to a complex procedure of multivariate analysis, originally formulated by Guttman (1968), called 'facet analysis' (Canter, 1983, p. 671).

Referring to Canter's (1983) detailed illustration, we would like to emphasize the theoretical valency he attributes to this procedure. Considering that the procedure allows one to discover the 'structure' of the evaluation of a place (through the identification of its most elementary facets), Canter claims that this model can be generalized to many environmental settings. However, it must be noted that, although his proposal found great response in the area of applied research, the same cannot be said about the development of further theoretical suggestions.

Apart from more specific considerations, one of the most evident characteristics of the proposed approach consists in the assumption of an exclusively individualistic perspective in the study of environmental evaluation.

In effect, it seems to preclude *a priori* the possibility of ascertaining if and how needs and goals, through which individuals face and evaluate places in their environment, also reflect areas of sharing, as well as being the expression of isolated individuality. In particular, there is no consideration of the fact that the social exchange between individuals and groups in contexts, which are always governed by social rules, constitutes a premise for structuring these areas of sharing.

This is an issue which is to some extent present in the proposal advanced by Stokols (1981) for studying evaluation in terms of 'group–environment congruence'.

Also in this case, the analysis of processes of evaluation is approached through the 'motivational saliency' of places, once it is defined as a function of the goals of action individuals intend to pursue in the environment.

The concept of 'environmental congruence', used by the author in this regard, outlines the 'degree to which the environment favors relevant goals and activities', and in particular describes the outcome of the comparison individuals make between subjectively relevant goals and 'environmental opportunities' perceived as facilitating/impeding.

Stokols moves in this direction, placing himself within a transactional approach and departing from a more general interest in the study of the 'interface (or degree of interdependence)' between 'social units' and the respective socio-physical environment.

His primary purpose is to emphasize the importance of a research approach that assumes structured social units as the main unit of analysis (such as social or residential community groups/categories), rather than single individuals. Stokols considers that this has been neglected by e.p. and he advances his specific methodological suggestions aimed at studying the 'shared' aspects around which the processes of environmental evaluation can be articulated. This proposal indicates a parallel and integrated gathering of two series of data: those relative to the hierarchies in which the components of a certain social unit place the various environmental properties (perceived as relevant with respect to their objectives/goals); and those relative to the type (positive/negative) and degree of evaluation they express when the same characteristics are adopted for describing and qualifying the specific environmental settings they use. Through this procedure (for details, see Stokols, 1981), there is the guaranteed possibility of studying environmental evaluation using reference parameters which, besides mirroring the motivational saliency of the various aspects and environment components, also become the expression of positions shared within a group and/or a community. In fact, through the comparison between hierarchies of 'ideal' properties and evaluations of properties referred to the 'real' environment (reconstructed through the positions expressed by components of the social unit considered), the author proposes to clarify what he defines as the perceived 'group–environment' congruence. Focusing on aspects of sharing, Stokols's suggestions outline an alternative to the exclusively individualistic approach favoured by environmental-psychological research. However, the functionalist-pragmatic criteria, which this proposal seemed to respond to primarily, have allowed for the emergence of some other theoretical limitations' in particular, those deriving from a static view of the social dimension of human behaviour in accounting for the outcome of psychological processes (not only those regarding evaluation) which intervene to characterize the complex relationships that are established and/or changed between persons and their environment.

Knowing the environment

The centrality which e.p. has assigned to processes of perception in defining the relationships which link persons with the environment has been widely discussed. The theme of perception and the theoretical reflections which have developed around it remain the main point of reference for an adequate understanding of studies concerned with environmental knowledge.

This is the reason why the first section of this review is dedicated to 'environmental perception' and to the specific contribution outlined by e.p. with respect to the most general proposals advanced by other disciplinary sectors. Besides an outline of the main theories (discussed more thoroughly in Chapter 2 of this volume), the specific theme of the perception of space will be explored here.

As will be shown in the following sections dealing with 'cognitive maps' and 'cognition/representation', the study of the perception of space led e.p. to focus on the most stimulating points of departure and to formulate the premises for a deeper investigation (both empirical and theoretical) of the complex issue concerning 'environmental knowledge'.

Environmental perception The main question faced by environmental-psychological research to account for the psychological processes involved in environmental knowledge regards ways individuals 'perceive' the surrounding environment. To clarify the relations emerging between properties of the physical environment and ways individuals respond to them through perception is also one of the main purposes e.p. has always shared with other domains of environmental research: geography (Kates and Wohlwill, 1966) and planning (Lynch, 1960; de Jonge, 1962; Appleyard, 1969, 1970), and also anthropology (Romney and d'Andrade, 1964) and sociology (Strauss, 1961; Orleans, 1973).

Many authors have pointed out that the pluridisciplinary convergence of interests on the topic of environmental perception has been developed through research based on assumptions which are not so equally convergent. This has often produced conceptual imprecision and misunderstanding, deriving primarily from the use of the terms 'perception' and 'cognition' in a variety of extremely confusing contexts (Downs and Stea, 1973).

The main differences include the role and the functions assigned to perceptual processes in knowledge of the environment, the ways these processes are conceptualized with respect to behaviour, and the types of indications to be expected from the study of the output of the same processes.

Still today the term 'environmental perception' is often used interchangeably with 'environmental image', 'mental map' and 'cognitive map', reflecting not only the diversity of disciplinary connotations actually assumed by research on the topic, but also the articulation of approaches e.p. has followed, starting from the classical matrix of theories on perception (Downs and Stea, 1973).

In describing the specific characteristics assumed by this thematic area in environmental-psychological research, it must first be noted that, according to one of the most consolidated traditions of psychology, the perceptual component has been regarded as an emblematic expression of the relationships linking the 'external' world of the environment (and its objective properties) with the 'internal' world of the person. In this sense, empirical research has been mainly inspired by the classical theories regarding perceptual phenomena and has been particularly interested in the 'perceptual responses' persons give to the environment and to its physical characteristics, primarily with respect to the spatio-physical dimension.

According to this perspective, the topic of environmental perception has been primarily approached in terms of the 'information' provided by the formal organization of physical space as a function of the 'cognitive maps' persons structure about environmental settings on a large scale. Starting from a consideration of the perceptual response as the expression of the ways individuals mentally organize spatial information, a similar approach integrates the directions derived from the theories of perception with the models proposed by cognitive psychology.

In the following section it will be shown how environmental-psychological research, moving in this direction, has favoured questions on the functioning of processes of acquisition, organization and the use of spatial information, apart from the evaluative-affective component involved in these processes. Only more recently has this schema of analysis been enlarged to consider the relationships between knowledge and action. Particularly indicative of this tendency is the use of the term 'spatial cognition' – or, more generally, 'environmental cognition' – for classifying this area of investigation.

As we have already pointed out (see Chapter 2), in the study of environmental perception, an approach has been outlined in which the molar environment is considered as the object of perception. In this case, perception is also assigned the role of intermediary for defining the (psychological) relevance environments assume for the person. Therefore, this approach appears less tied to tradition and to models of perceptual studies and more clearly in line with the directions followed by social psychology in the study of 'social perception'. On the one hand, it expresses the ways the transactional school interprets the more general relationship between the individual and 'reality', and, on the other, it follows the directions proposed by Lewinian psychology through the concept of 'psychological field'.

Geographers have used this type of holistic approach in a series of studies classified in the literature by the term 'environmental perception'. However, it seems that the only objective animating this research is the discovery of the differences between 'objective/subjective' environment, apart from any hypotheses concerning the modalities and factors that account for 'transformations'. In this case, emphasis is centred exclusively on the evaluative dimension and on the personal meanings attributed by individuals to the environment. The idea of perception is so comprehensive that it does not allow space for any other type of psychological processes or for a hypothesis linking perception and action.

In contrast to the way it is applied in geography, the holistic approach to the study of environmental perception has constituted a relevant premise for further developments in psychological research on environmental knowledge.

In the final part of this chapter it will be seen how the molar perspective, which characterizes this approach in e.p., has contributed to a shift of interest from the solely formal aspects of organized physical space to the content components through which space is defined. The most evident methodological correlate of this change consists of a more integrated consideration of the cognitive, evaluative and behavioural components. These components are studied as interrelated variables in the structuring of environmental knowledge and its connotation in terms of meanings, which are actively made by individuals. This approach, on the one hand, assumes the socio-physical environment as object of knowledge, and, on the other, more adequately defines the processes involved in it as processes of 'cognitive representation'.

The synthetic presentation of the two main approaches referred to by environmental-psychological research certainly does not account for the rich debate which has always been associated with the topic of environmental perception and which involves several significant theoretical issues.

In order to trace the outlines of this debate, we must first go back to some critical considerations which have been formulated from a transactional point of view towards theories of perception. Together with the central role attributed to perception in processes of knowledge, these considerations emphasize the peculiarity perception assumes when its object is the environment.

According to Ittelson (1973a), 'living means perceiving' and no psychological study of relationships between persons and their environment can be thought of as apart from perception. But looking at the most important developments of the theories on perception, Ittelson interprets them as lost occasions for psychology to adequately consider the environment. His first criticism concerns what he considers the 'discovery' from which psychological research promoted its most significant developments; this regards the recognition of the 'complex' nature of perceptual processes in contrast to conceptions which interpret the relative outcomes as the 'conscious experience of sensory inputs'. As for Brunswik and the 'New Look' theoreticians of perception, as well as for Ittelson, one of the aspects neglected in studies on perceptual processes is the basic function of 'directive for action' which they carry out.

Projected onto the study of relationships between persons and the environment, these general premises serve Ittelson to emphasize the inadequacy of an analysis that brings the cognitive dimension of these relationships back into the most traditional and reductive schema of 'perception of the object'. From this perspective, several important aspects assumed by environmental perception would not be given due consideration. In this regard, the author gives a primary position to the 'multimodality' with which the environment provides information and to the involvement – which derives from it – of many sensory processes, besides the one linked to 'seeing'. 'The environments spoken of are large in relation to man [. . .] large enough to require movement in order to make contact with all aspects of the situation.' As such, they 'possess many properties that objects almost never have and generally cannot have. The quality of the surroundings, the first, the most obvious and which best defines the environment, obliges the observer to become a participant [. . .] the environment is not observed, it is explored' (ibid., p. 139).

Thus, on the one hand, Ittelson's proposal emphasizes the multi-dimensionality of the environment within which he distinguishes physical and social dimensions (Ittelson et al., 1974); on the other hand, it highlights the role played by the movement of exploration (and, thus, the many perspectives from which the perceiver knows the environment) in the process through which persons arrive at knowing/perceiving the environment. In this way he outlines a molar approach which seems to be very similar to the ecological one more explicitly developed in other directions by Gibson. However, unlike Gibson and also unlike the more classical tradition of studies on perception of the object, Ittelson characterizes his proposal by pointing out that the perceiver connects with the physical-environmental disposition by means of precise objectives and goals. He explicitly affirms that 'environmental perception always implies action, [but] not blind action or action without a goal' (Ittelson, 1973a, p. 141). Further, placing perceptual activity in the specificity of the complex situations individuals participate in, he points out that 'action and perception support each other reciprocally as a function of the goal' and that 'the way the environment is looked at is, in a very general sense, a function of what is done, including the strategies used in its exploration and conceptualization' (ibid., pp. 141, 144).

Besides these specifications, which in certain ways share the positions of the 'New Look' theorists, this author's suggestions are particularly innovative, primarily with regard to the properties he recognizes in the environment and to their nature. On the one hand, he calls attention to the fact that 'the environment has in itself the properties to provide symbolic meanings and motivational messages that can influence the direction taken by action: meanings and motivational messages are a necessary part of the content of environmental perception' (ibid., p. 141); on the other hand, he points out that environments can be considered, 'almost without exception, as part of a social activity; persons are always part of the situation, and environmental perception is mainly a social phenomenon' (ibid.).

Because of the wide range of problems they touch on, the suggestions offered by Ittelson only provide a general framework for research on environmental perception. And its effectiveness primarily derives from the attention the author pays to the relationships between perception and the functioning of cognitive processes. He starts by considering the 'stimulus', the classical referent of studies on perception, as a 'source of information'. In agreement with the perspective outlined by Tolman and Brunswik (1935) – but mainly by Brunswik (1957) – he specifies that 'the information refers to a wider context'. The stimulus information, as defined by scholars of perception, is the information that regards 'the environment in which the individual lives and acts and comes from' (Ittelson, 1973a, p. 135). Continuing along these lines, he points out that for a long time psychology operated with the 'wrong assumption that two distinct and separate systems – perceptual processes and cognitive processes – are linked by fixed and unidirectional bonds', and that the most recent research shows the importance of considering 'the entire perceptual-cognitive system as part of a larger system, whose basic function is the elaboration of information' (ibid., pp. 136–71). The final point also tends to be shared by the domain of study more specifically concerned with the perception of environmental space.

As some representative researchers in this area have pointed out, the term 'cognitive map' was proposed as an alternative to the term 'environmental perception' (Downs and Stea, 1973). This alternative calls attention to some conceptual differences between perception as it is considered by experimental psychology and perception which involves environmental space: a process, in the first case, carried out as a consequence of the presence of an object and regarding its immediate interception by one or more of the senses, and, in the second case, concerned with spatial contexts so broad as to not be perceptible or grasped instantaneously, or through a series of brief glances (Stea, 1969).

Primarily interested in the study of large-scale environments, this research sector recognizes that the type of space it is concerned with has the characteristic of being outside the immediate perceptual field of persons and, thus, requires the intervention of cognitive activity and/or the elaboration of spatial information. Moving from this premise, the adoption of the concept of cognitive map implies a modality of study which does not treat the perceptual and cognitive processes separately and distinctly.

The 'cognitive map' as a response to the spatial organization of the physical environment   The attention given by environmental-psychological research to the spatio-physical dimension has led to an approach to the study of environmental perception which is, in a certain sense, an alternative to the one proposed mainly by geographers. Through the specific reference to space, perception was reconsidered in the light of the cognitive activity persons carry out in elaborating 'spatial information'. In this way its exclusive and generic connotation as process, which transforms an 'objective' environment into a 'subjective' one, was contrasted. The term 'cognitive map' is actually used to designate the outcome of this activity, and 'cognitive mapping' refers to the activity itself.

The most consistent incentive received by e.p. in this direction has come from the works of the urban planner, Kevin Lynch, who was the first to develop a programme aimed at showing the ways persons form 'mental images' of the environment. With his now classic work, *The Image of the City* (1960) (referred to in Chapter 1 above), he meets the specific need of planners to understand the rules underlying 'visual comprehension' of the environment, starting from the premise that it is possible to establish optimal modalities for organization of the formal structure of a built space once the way its properties are perceived and cognitively organized by persons is known.

Lynch essentially moved in this direction in the study of various cities in the United States such as Boston, Jersey City and Los Angeles. Starting with a procedure based primarily on graphic responses (people's sketches of the city or some parts of it), he first proved the validity of a taxonomic system, developed intuitively and articulated around what he considers key elements for describing the shape of the physical environment of the city. Providing useful distinctions for recognition tasks of environmental space, these elements have been adopted by the author as the most probable categories of indicators used by persons for structuring a clear and 'strong image' of the city. They include 'paths', 'nodes', 'landmarks', 'districts' and 'edges'.

This taxonomic system has been not only validated by Lynch's research, but also through other experimental work (Magana et al., 1981; Aragones and Arredondo, 1985). For Lynch, the quality of the image of the city, structured by its inhabitants around these five types of spatial characteristics, is a rather direct correlate of the properties possessed by the physical configuration of the relative urban space. These same descriptive elements are, in fact, used by the author to define the degree of 'legibility' of different urban environments.

Regarding types and qualities of visual stimulations considered to facilitate or impede perception of the complex physical-geometric structure of urban space, legibility is mostly a question of 'good shape'; a quality of the entire spatio-physical disposition, which the positive or negative psychological response seems to depend on, and which individuals give to the city by means of image. Through the results of his research Lynch showed, for example, that Boston is a much more legible city than either Jersey City or Los Angeles.

The great reception of Lynch's suggestions by disciplines interested in environmental studies also involved psychologists; not only did they use the same procedures for studying the perception of city space, but they questioned the results of Lynch's initial studies by calling attention to the nature of the psychological processes involved in acquisition, organization and use of information about locations, distances and conformations of the physical setting in various types of environments, with particular reference to large-scale ones.

Moving in this direction, environmental-psychological research essentially set the goal of clarifying the ways people elaborate 'spatial information'. Besides hypotheses predicting inter-individual differences in the structuring of cognitive maps for representing this information, the main premises guiding research in this case regard, on the one hand, the limited quality of spatial information people are usually able to elaborate; on the other, the need they have to use reference systems (or maps) for resolving spatial problems, such as orientation and effective locomotion in the physical environment.

Empirical contributions were primarily focused on the 'map', considered as a distinct problem within the cognitive structure. This left the consideration of the more specific relations between cognition and spatial behaviours in second place. In fact, this issue has only recently become the object of reflections and systematic proposals of analysis. As the most recent reviews show (Evans, 1980; Golledge, 1987; Garling and Golledge, 1989), the issue most investigated concerns the formal properties of the maps themselves, rather than their relative contents, and the processes of acquisition and development of 'spatial knowledge' these maps are destined to represent at the cognitive level. This tendency confirms both the primary interest in studying the outcomes of cognitive mapping in more circumscribed terms of 'cognitive responses' people give to the spatio-physical properties of the environment and the assumption that these responses reveal transformations of the physical-environmental space and of its objective characteristics.

It must also be noted that the terms 'spatial cognition' and 'environmental cognition' have been used interchangeably in the literature to designate the specific field of investigation.

There has been long debate over the meaning of simple analogy or, instead, the more literal similarity attributed to the concept of cognitive map with respect to a cartographic representation of the physical environment (Kuipers, 1978). This is also in relation to the fact that the most diffused procedure for the empirical study of spatial cognition is the one developed by Lynch (1960), which consists in assigning individuals the task of reproducing the configuration and the spatial characteristics of specific environmental settings in drawings.

In spite of the function of metaphor, explicitly recognized in this concept (Downs, 1981), the purpose of clarifying the properties of cognitive maps has raised questions regarding the aspects these two types of representations have in common. Starting from the consideration that the cartographic representation 'transforms' the environment into an image which preserves some content and properties of the environment, but leaves out and distorts others, it was questioned whether the cognitive map also maintains the Euclidean geometric properties of the environmental space it represents, with particular reference to distance and direction.

As Baird et al. (1982) have reported, a number of studies on well-known or familiar environments conducted on adults, show that none of the properties found in the represented space are linearly correlated with those of real space. Even if directions are more accurately represented in some cases than distances (Garling et al., 1981), their prevalent non-Euclidean nature has also been demonstrated (Moar and Bowers, 1983).

As Evans (1980) and Garling and Golledge (1989) have pointed out, the question this type of investigation tries to respond to reflects the more specific cognitive problem of the 'format' the representation of spatial information can assume in memory, considered the visual imaginal characterization of this information. In this regard, some studies have proposed verifying which aspects of representations tend to be organized in a 'propositional' form (or abstract, in the sense that they have an arbitrary and/or symbolic relation with what they represent) or, vice versa, through an 'analogic' format (or isomorphic, in the sense that they maintain some of the characteristics of what they represent) (Kosslyn, 1980).

Recently this type of question has also received great attention as a consequence of the new possibilities of investigation opened up by computer simulation. Approached from this viewpoint, the topic of spatial cognition directly concerns the cognitive abilities involved in the most general processes of the functioning of thought, that is, the type of ability acquired over time, which follows complex developmental routes and is marked by continuous changes.

With the aim of finding out about the genesis and development of cognitive maps, another topic widely treated by research concerns cognitive mapping in subjects (such as children) who are in particularly significant moments of cognitive development. The various systematic reviews which have appeared in the literature (Hart and Moore, 1973; Moore, 1976; Evans, 1980; Axia, 1986; Heft and Wohlwill, 1987) show the richness of topics approached empirically with respect to this aim.

Although the main issue faced by research on this concern will be outlined, a more thorough analysis requires detailed reference to the original works.

What has always characterized researchers' reflections in this area is the intention of describing the developmental processes of cognitive mapping in the light of psychological theories of development. In this sense, Piaget's stage theory takes on particular importance with reference to the development of spatial notions (Piaget and Inhelder, 1947; Werner, 1948).

Besides the possibility of focusing on the developmental dynamics characterizing the progressive transition from 'egocentric' space to 'decentralized' (or 'allocentric-objective') space (Moore, 1976), this theory constitutes a useful reference point not only for specifying differences in modalities of knowledge regarding space, but also for assuming these differences as indicators of a sequence which is hierarchically ordered over time.

The most significant example in this regard is surely provided by Siegel and White's (1975) proposals. According to them, the development of cognitive mapping is articulated in five stages, and is outlined on a parallel with the more general development of cognitive abilities concerning both symbolic abstraction and the simultaneous organization of multiple information inside an objective system of reference.

The initial stage is identified with a sort of 'photographic' knowledge, carried out in the memory of single and isolated points of reference in environmental space. In the four subsequent stages, the development of spatial cognition progresses respectively towards: (a) an initial use of the single points of space as references for organizing routes; (b) the appearance of a first integrated organization of cognitions regarding distinct and limited parts of an environment; (c) the formation of an objective system of reference (expressed primarily through orientation ability); (d) the appearance of the ability to coordinate routes in the area of this system of reference. According to this perspective, what seems re-proposed primarily is the primacy assigned by Piaget to visual memory in the development of spatial knowledge (Piaget and Inhelder, 1968).

The development of cognitive mapping is also linked to the acquisition of those spatial notions which respond to the principle of reversibility and are particularly representative, in Piagetian psychology, of the stage reached in the more general process of cognitive development.

As Heft and Wohlwill (1987) report, many studies concerning cognitive maps in developmental age subjects have followed this approach. The questions most frequently concern the type and content of cognitions structured by children in different age groups on the spatio-physical disposition of various types of environments (Acredolo et al., 1975; Bremner and Bryant, 1977; Acredolo, 1978), as well as the ways they evaluate the distances between different points in space (Kosslyn et al., 1974; R. Cohen et al., 1978; Cohen and Weatherford, 1980).

As already mentioned, the interest environmental-psychological research has dedicated to the substantial aspects of cognitive mapping primarily relates to the scale dimensions of the physical-environmental space people have to deal with, or, better, the different degree of complexity these dimensions involve with respect to the processes of spatial cognition.

The literature reports examples of studies on very different types of environmental space going from those of entire cities to those defined by single buildings. As proof of the interest raised by Lynch's work, the primary and most representative object of study is the environmental space of the city. In fact, the methodology proposed by Lynch has been used in studies conducted in cities in various countries: Amsterdam, Rotterdam and L'Aja (de Jonge, 1962); Ciuda Guayana in Venezuela (Appleyard, 1969, 1970); Rome and Milan (Francescato and Mebane, 1973); New York (Milgram et al., 1972); and Paris (Milgram and Jodelet, 1976).

However, these studies have often highlighted conspicuous limitations to Lynch's proposals from a psychological point of view. These limitations are mostly theoretical and they cast doubts upon the effectiveness of the methodological procedure as a general framework for the study of cognitions people make about an environmental space as complex as a city.

On the theoretical side, the most evident problem derives from the use of the concept of image. As Downs and Stea (1973) have pointed out, the almost exclusive emphasis which has been placed on the activity of 'seeing' has led many researchers to consider the images themselves as 'the cognitive equivalent of vision', thus, creating confusion between perception and cognition.

Further, assuming the formal aspects of geometric space as equally exclusive criteria for the analysis of cognitive maps, research has abstracted the problem of spatial knowledge from the content dimension characterizing various environments. Finally, the role of various forms of person–environment interaction on the outcome of spatial cognitions has received no consideration.

Numerous studies have shown the existence of connections between the degree of familiarity persons have with the various parts of their own urban environment and the characteristics of relative spatial maps, as well as between spatial maps and the ethnic-cultural and/or social position variables people start from in structuring relationships with their own city.

With regard to the first, we need only mention the studies comparing spatial representations both as a function of the distance between resident's home and place of work in urban environments (Saarinen, 1969; Lynch, 1977) and as a function of length of residence in the city (Ladd, 1970; Moore, 1974). In these cases, the results have shown how accuracy and degree of descriptive details of the maps tends to increase in relation to the increase both in distances between home and place of work, and in length of residence in the city.

With regard to socio-cultural variables, one of the most frequently cited studies, conducted in Rome and Milan by Francescato and Mebane (1973), was based on the procedures suggested by Lynch. This study shows how several differences regarding size of the represented space, as well as quantity and types of content elements, are associated with differences in socio-economic level. In both cities subjects belonging to the lower classes tend to trace maps reproducing more reduced urban areas with fewer details. This tendency has also been confirmed by a study conducted in

Paris (Milgram and Jodelet, 1976). In this case, the socio-economic variables are directly correlated with a different knowledge of the various parts of the urban space. Besides representing the city differently from higher class subjects, those belonging to the lower classes demonstrate less knowledge about several areas of the city.

Looking at the most recent research developments on spatial cognition, the most significant emerging tendency is the decrease in the emphasis previously placed on the formal characteristics of physical space and a more attentive consideration of the contents composing that space. This tendency seems greater the more explicit reference becomes to a holistic conception of environmental perception, that is, the more attention is oriented towards assuming the spatial dimension as one of the many components constituting the complex environmental situations individuals are part of and interact with.

Although remaining focused on the function assigned to cognitive maps to facilitate movements and locomotions of persons in medium and large-scale environments, in this case research is oriented towards analysing cognitive mapping in the light of the relations linking knowledge of the environment and aims of actions carried out in it.

Particularly representative of this perspective is the systematic activity (both empirical and theoretical) conducted in recent years in Europe at the Umea Environmental Psychology Research Unit (Sweden). According to Garling and Golledge (1989), both working in this group, in order to understand how persons mentally form cognitive maps, the 'travel plans' they propose and carry out in their environment must be considered. On the one hand, this suggestion assumes an already-acquired degree of familiarity with environments and, thus, primarily regards those constituting the socio-physical context of the individual's daily life. On the other hand, the spatial dimension figures as a component within which units or environmental elements are placed; their specificity is marked by functional and symbolic-representative attributes as well as perceptual ones. In its role as synthetic but effective guide to action, the cognitive map is meant to represent at least three interrelated components: information regarding units or elements constituting environmental space; the spatial relations which can be established between them in terms of 'inclusion', 'direction-distance' and 'proximity' – but with respect to references which have a particular perceptual and/or symbolic saliency for persons; and 'travel plans', which include indications about the ways they can reach others, starting from a determined point in environmental space (Garling et al., 1984).

Although they agree with the general approach which considers the cognitive map as an outcome of the processes of elaboration of spatial information, these authors define environmental space as an entity that fills with precise contents in relation to the management plan individuals are pursuing. And this is the type of space they consider as the object of perception-knowledge. In this sense – and because it serves to guide the 'route' followed by people during the execution of a travel plan in the environment – the cognitive map contains the representation of information, not so much regarding the formal properties of physical-geometric space as the characteristics and locations of places (Canter, 1977, 1986) for formulating predictions about action.

Other studies have started from a different perspective and have shown how the differences cognitively traced by persons between places are associated with both habitual actions (Mannetti et al., 1987; Bonnes et al., 1990) and actions perceived as appropriate with respect to these places (Genereux et al., 1983).

Although basically associated with the tradition of the study of perceptual phenomena, these recent orientations of spatial cognition studies can be considered representative of the more general tendency to analyse the processes of environmental knowledge in connection with goals and plans of action people propose to accomplish in the respective environments; that is, to recognize these goals as general references which, analogously with what Neisser (1976) indicated with the concept of 'schema', direct both processes of perception and processes regarding the elaboration of environmental information, represented at the cognitive level (Garling and Golledge, 1989).

Beside the broadening of perspective in studies on spatial cognition, a similar theoretical orientation offers an effective framework for an integrated approach towards the more general issue of environmental knowledge, primarily when research adopts an interactive view of relationships between persons and environments and emphasizes the constructive function of cognitive processes.

As we will attempt to show in the next section, following this framework the focus of analysis is meant to shift from the outcome of perceptual and/ or cognitive processes to the modalities and content of 'representations'.

The cognition/representation of socio-physical environments Using a metaphor, Russell and Ward (1982) hold that in order to move and act in a specific environment it is necessary to possess a type of knowledge which, besides carrying out the function of atlas, also carries out the function of mental encyclopedia. This is to point out how the knowledge generally acquired by persons with respect to the environments in which they live not only consists in a static mental representation of 'where' a thing is located in physical space, but also includes specifications about 'what' this entity is. This is one way of calling attention to the fact that environmental knowledge constitutes the dynamic outcome of processes which involve locomotion in space and occur over time.

In the preceding section, it was partly illustrated how research focused on spatial cognition has recently turned its attention to this type of suggestion, facilitating a more integrated analysis of the formal aspects and content of the environmental space represented in a cognitive map. This occurs through a preliminary consideration of the strict correlation linking knowledge with action. The increasing emphasis on this issue calls attention primarily to the fact that individuals, in structuring their cognitive maps, assume 'significant units' of the environment (or places) as reference points. In this respect the spatial dimension becomes strictly interconnected with the content dimension. A more general hypothesis deriving from the active position recognized for persons is that concerning the interrelation between environmental knowledge and types/degrees of involvement persons have with the places in their environment.

Studying the spatial cognition that inhabitants of Cambridge (UK) have about their neighbourhood, Lee (1968, 1976) found positive correlations between the spaciousness of the area they indicate as spatially defining the neighbourhood and the degree to which respective behaviours are oriented towards an active participation in and/or integration with the surrounding physical and social environment. On the basis of these findings, Lee defined cognition of the neighbourhood as a 'socio-spatial schema'. His major aim was to point out how the spatial attributes of the cognitive map reflect knowledge relative to both the physical and social components of the environment, and primarily how these attributes are correlated with the range and frequency of activities people carry out in their socio-physical environmental context.

The findings provided by Lee have been used to interpret the results of an initial study of Milan's city centre (Bonnes and Secchiaroli, 1979). As a consequence of the inter-individual variability found in the representations of a sample of residents, the hypothesis was formulated that this variability might be associated with the different degree of integration/ marginality characterizing the subjects' relationships with the socio-physical environment of their city.

This hypothesis was tested in a study which more thoroughly analysed data regarding cognitions of the centre of Milan, and also investigated cognitions regarding the centre of Bologna (Bonnes and Secchiaroli, 1982a, 1982b). In both cases attention was first focused on the modalities used by residents to represent the centre with respect to its spatio-physical characteristics. The main indicators assumed were the spaciousness of the area identified as the centre and relative spatial location with respect to the topographical configuration of the two cities.

Empirical data were gathered from graphical responses, that is, the subjects were asked to circle the zone they considered as the centre on a scale-size map of the two cities. The study also included the use of a questionnaire to gather data on motives for going to the centre and frequency of access.

With regard to the spatial dimension, representation of the centre was primarily structured around the 'monumental landmarks', with particular reference to the architectural structure that was symbolically representative in a historical sense, such as the cathedral and its square in the case of Milan and the main square in the case of Bologna. This first result is different from what usually emerges in research based on Lynch's perspective and concerning cities which are very different from the Italian ones. In the Italian case, the spatial representation is, in fact, primarily structured on 'paths'.

Other specifications characterize the descriptive contents of the centre. These are primarily the clear tendency to include components regarding the functional structures and/or urban services within the respective spatial area.

Here the centrality that the dimension of 'meanings' (symbolic and functional) tends to assume in processes of knowledge concerning urban environmental space is particularly evident. In this regard, an equally clear concomitance of variations was found between extension and location of the area of the centre and the types of 'functional meanings' residents of the two cities attribute to it (Bonnes and Secchiaroli, 1979, 1982b). The size of the centre area tends to increase the more the subjects make specific use of its structures, primarily those meant for socializing functions (or for meeting/communication with other persons).

These studies have provided findings about the relationship between modality of environmental cognitions and positions characterizing the various persons in terms of integration/marginality with respect to the environment of the city centre (Bonnes and Secchiaroli, 1983). In this regard, attention was centred on the condition of marginality, after defining it at both a subjective and an objective level. In the first case it referred to a more undifferentiated attribution of functional meanings to the centre and to less use of the relative structure, and in the second case the variables assumed as indicators were concerned with socio-economic status, seniority and location of residence, age and sex. The more the subjects' condition was marginal, according to both of these parameters, the more accentuated the tendency to represent the centre as less extended spatially and less rich and differentiated in its imaginal components.

The study of less complex environments, besides being less extended spatially than that of the city, also provides useful material for a more thorough analysis. In fact, these cases usually provide the opportunity for making more precise verifications, primarily with respect to hypotheses centred on relations between knowledge and behaviours and actions effectively carried out by persons in the environment.

In this regard, we will briefly discuss the results of two studies which respectively studied the environment of a university campus in the United States (Holahan and Bonnes, 1978) and of an Italian industrial concern (Bonnes et al., 1980) using this type of hypothesis. In both cases the subjects were asked to trace a map of the environment in question on a sheet of white paper.

Confirming the tendencies that have emerged from studies on the city centre, in both cases the results primarily show consistent correlations between the spatial characteristics of the environments represented graphically and the symbolic and functional meanings attributed by subjects to them. This tendency is particularly accentuated with respect to those very circumscribed environmental areas where the maximum degree of agreement is found among subjects. In fact, these areas correspond to environmental spaces where significant components are located. Besides their perceptual saliency, these components seem to provide a particular symbolic value, primarily in relation to the activity persons tend to carry out in the two environments, that is, the tower of the administration building in the case of the university campus; the main entrance and the area in which the machines and most important equipment for production are located in the case of the factory.

Other indications emerge concerning the more specific objectives of the two studies: a verification of the role played by 'familiarity' and by the different nature of work tasks in knowledge and representation of space in the industrial environment; a comparison between spatial cognitions and modalities of use of the various spaces on the university campus.

With regard to the factory, the results show that more details and less 'spatial distortion' (meaning degree of proportionality in reproducing the size of different spaces) correlate with work tasks involving 'supervisional' activities, rather than with partial and 'prescribed' tasks; and this is more consistent than what occurs regarding greater seniority in the factory. In this case, environmental knowledge is more clearly connected with the opportunity for 'control' (in a physical and social sense) permitted by the overall situation than the greater chance for learning linked to growing familiarity with the factory environment.

In the case of the campus, the tendency to represent spatial shapes in a distorted way and to include/exclude various environmental spaces has been compared with (a) the students' opinions as to the areas considered to be most adequate for different types of use behaviours (simple crossing, a solitary break, a break for social relations) and with (b) the data from direct observation of behaviours accomplished through the technique of 'behavioural maps' (Ittelson et al., 1970).

The outcome of these comparisons again confirms the hypothesis of a correlation between spatial characteristics of cognitions and types of activity carried out by persons in these environments: the subjects who reproduce the areas with more detail are also those who use them more frequently.

This type of research seems to indicate that the study of environmental knowledge overflows the boundaries traced by the cognitive map construct around the formal aspects of the spatio-physical dimension.

On the other hand, it reflects the more general perspective in e.p. which emphasizes a molar approach to the environment (Craik, 1970) and to the processes that control its perception/cognition (Ittelson, 1973b). This approach becomes more necessary, the more complex the nature of the environmental settings people interact with; that is, the more environments figure as socio-physical contexts which specify the organization of people's daily lives, as is the case with urban environments.

In connection with the emphasis cognitive psychology has placed on the concept of information (as an alternative to the objectivity of the stimulus), the possibility has opened up in e.p. of analysing knowledge about these environments in terms of the complexity (primarily informational) they pose for respective users.

Starting from these premises, a model of analysis is proposed which identifies knowledge with the representation of the external world to the mind and describes this representation as the outcome of constructive activity carried out by cognitive processes. Therefore, an active role is recognized for individuals with respect to these processes, primarily in the sense that the approach they have with information coming from the environment is considered to be guided by pre-existing structures of knowledge (or 'schemata') (Neisser, 1976).

In any case, focusing on the ways information is elaborated and organized mentally, this model seems to preclude the possibility of an integrated analysis of cognitive and affective dimensions. Further, as Saegert and Winkel (1990) point out, since this model refers to the environment exclusively in terms of source of information, it tends to reduce the multiform nature of person–environment interaction to outcomes of the functioning of the person's internal processes.

Both of these aspects constitute major issues for environmental-psychological research, considering, on the one hand, the role played by the evaluative component of processes leading individuals to trace differences between generic environments and more specific places; and, on the other hand, the importance the social component can assume in outlining shared reference points concerning attributions of meaning to environments, especially through exchange and social interaction. In effect, e.p. has dedicated more and more attention to these issues in studying environmental cognition.

As shown in the following pages, the increasing emphasis on the construct of 'place' (Canter, 1977; Stokols, 1981) and of 'social image-ability' (Stokols, 1981) has emerged as the most significant sign in this direction. These constructs outline a theoretical framework that is consistent with the more general perspective followed by contemporary social psychology, particularly in the European context. In fact, contrasting the images of individuals as pure 'active thinking organisms' and/or 'information processors', the European approach to social cognition is based on the hypothesis of a strict relationship between cognitive (individual) and social processes.

According to several authors (Doise, 1976, 1982; Farr and Moscovici, 1984; Tajfel, 1984; Palmonari, 1989), the articulation of this general hypothesis lies in the following premises: (a) cognitive processes are considered as properties of individuals-in-context and not as autonomous peculiarities of mental functioning. The cognitive man/woman is conceived as someone who looks for information (and does not only receive it from the environment) in connection with his/her own goals; (b) 'implicit theories' or 'images of reality' which guide information processing are considered as representational and symbolic frames of reference whose structure and/or change are established during the many and various interactions individuals engage in and with the physical and social contexts they live in.

Following these premises, the research is not so much interested in the outputs of perception/cognition as in the processes and conditions generating the collectively shared 'representations' which allow individuals to master the complex world they are part of.

As will be shown in more detail (Chapter 5), this dynamic approach to the study of the symbolic dimension of human behaviour has its major focus in the complex interactions involving individual, inter-individual and collective processes. The most significant suggestions in this direction have certainly been proposed by Moscovici (1961–76, 1981, 1982, 1984a, 1984b) in his 'theory of social representations'.

5

Paradigms and Psycho-social Constructs in Present-Day Environmental Psychology

Plurality and convergence of paradigms

The authors who have considered the paradigmatic orientation of e.p. have primarily noted that the field is characterized by a 'plurality of paradigms' (Altman, 1973; Craik, 1977; Moore, 1986, 1987; Saegert and Winkel, 1990), although in some cases they are not very clearly distinguished (Craik, 1977; Moore, 1986). Certainly the heterogeneity presented by the field, not only at the beginning but still today, gives the impression of variety; however, Saegert and Winkel's (1990) most recent work has proposed a more synthetic and convincing framework for it.

We agree with the point of view expressed by various authors concerning the co-existence of several paradigms within the field, and we believe these paradigms can be primarily traced to the two previously mentioned traditions of psychological research in conceptualizing the physical environment in relation to psychological processes: on the one hand, the physical environment of psychology of perception, with a physicalist-molecular and individualistic paradigm; and, on the other, the physical environment of social psychology, characterized in both a molar and social sense, corresponding to the paradigm of the psycho-social approach.

The four major paradigms singled out by Saegert and Winkel (1990) can be traced back to these two main theoretical orientations. The first orientation seems to coincide with the first paradigm, defined by them as (a) the 'adaptation' or 'adaptive paradigm', and the second orientation seems primarily associated with the other three paradigms, defined as (b) 'environment as opportunity structures for goal-directed action', (c) 'socio-cultural forces' and (d) 'cross-paradigm historical synthesis'.

These authors tend to single out the various paradigms also in relation to the topics treated by environmental-psychological research, pointing out the prevalence of each paradigm according to the area of interest.

According to the authors, the 'adaptive paradigm' has inspired several areas of environmental-psychological research considered by them 'theoretically and methodologically more mature', such as those dealing with 'environmental stress', 'environmental perception and cognition' and 'environmental assessment' (see Chapter 4). The authors point out that these areas of research tend to 'derive their main theoretical constructs from an assumption that the goal of biological and psychological survival motivates behavior. The biological and psychological individual attempts to cope with threats, to meet basic biological needs and to restore and expand capacities for coping and flourishing' (Saegert and Winkel, 1990, p. 446). The same authors emphasize the limits of this paradigm, pointing out that studies both on environmental stressors and on environmental cognition conducted within this paradigm 'leave inexplicit the trans-actional nature of many of the processes and variables they employ (social relationships, interpretations). They also fail to place their data in the context of policy options, political influences and economic and cultural factors' (ibid., p. 452).

These authors continue by singling out the primary weakness of this paradigm in the tendency to 'treat the person as a biological and psychological individual and the environment as naturally given'. They observe that 'despite the constant identification of real and perceived control, as mechanisms for effective coping, the social, political and economic processes that distribute control among people have been largely ignored' (ibid.).

The second paradigm singled out by the authors, which they term as being 'of the environment as opportunity structure for goal-directed action', is, in our opinion not so well-defined from the psychological point of view as the previous and the subsequent ones, even if it is more clearly oriented towards the psycho-social perspective.

> Unlike the adaptive paradigm, work in this tradition presents environmental experiences primarily as a process of selecting the best options within a system of sociophysical constraints and opportunities. The rational planning aspect of human nature is emphasized rather than the biologically responsive aspects. (ibid.)

The area of research inspired by this paradigm seems to be primarily related to geography, with particular reference to the time-geography school of the University of Lund and its followers (Parkes and Thrift, 1980; Carlstein, 1982; Hagerstrand, 1983), or to sociology, in relation to time-budget studies (Andorka, 1987; Michelson, 1987). Overall, these studies pay little attention to the psychological (that is, individual) dimension of the processes studied, which seem to be generated by the physical-geographical 'opportunities' of the environment, as also indicated by the terminology chosen for defining this paradigm.

We believe that this second paradigm has a weak identity from the psychological point of view; the authors' primary concern of outlining a general framework to include all the literature on the person–environment relationship forced them to also include contributions coming from different disciplines and, thus, weakly characterized under the psycho-logical profile.

On the contrary, the third paradigm singled out by Seagert and Winkel and defined as 'socio-cultural forces' seems clearly characterized in a psycho-social sense. They indicate the following characteristics for this paradigm:

> The most important of these is the emphasis on the person as a social agent rather than an autonomous individual having needs for survival or desires to carry out personal projects. The person as a social agent seeks and creates meaning in the environment. Since social interaction is a central feature of this paradigm, a second important process issue involves the understanding of interrelationships between the environment on the one hand and group formation and maintenance on the other. The emphasis on individual survival in the adaptive paradigm has its social counterpart in research documenting efforts to deal with environmental threats, not as an individual concern, but as a problem for the social structure within which the individual is embedded. (ibid., p. 457)

Further, 'the paradigm explicitly recognizes that environmental meanings and actions are not solely individual constructions. The individual both defines and is defined by the groups in which he/she participates' (ibid., p. 465).

To complete the picture traced by the authors with regard to the various paradigms co-existing in e.p., the fourth paradigm defined by them as 'interparadigm historical synthesis', aims at representing the broader perspective of integration between the previous paradigms and, contrary to them, is mainly oriented towards social change. In this sense Saegert recalls her distinction (1987) between research having specific 'transformative intentions' and research aimed only at understanding the phenomena observed and, thus, having 'technological' or 'interpretive intentions'. According to the authors, these various paradigms, rather than being in opposition – in the way they are outlined by Craik (1977) and Moore (1986) – should be considered as connected and in particular linked by a relationship of progressive inclusion, one within the other: the first paradigm of adaptation should be considered the most internal one, that is, included within all of the others, which should be subsequently more and more external and, thus, progressively more comprehensive, shifting from the first (adaptative paradigm) to the last (cross-paradigm historical synthesis).

Nevertheless, the modalities for realizing the expected connections between paradigms at the level of empirical research are not clear from the authors' proposal; on the contrary, the impression remains of difficulty in operating in an integrated way between the various paradigms.

Again in this case a theoretical divergence seems to emerge between the tradition of psychology of perception, on the one hand, and the tradition of social psychology, on the other. This occurs not so much through the opposition of the various subject areas treated by research (as the authors seem to believe) as within the single areas of research. Also in this case the divergence is evident through the tendency towards opposition, rather than integration, between the two main paradigms, represented, on the one hand, by the 'adaptive' paradigm, characterized in both a physicalist and individualistic sense, primarily localized in the direction of psychology of perception, and, on the other hand, by the 'socio-cultural' paradigm, characterized in both a molar and social sense, primarily coinciding with the direction of social psychology.

It should also be noted that one of the main difficulties of the field seems to be that of operating, at the level of empirical research, on the basis of the molar and psycho-social direction almost unanimously affirmed at the theoretical level – as shown previously (see pp. 68–72).

It should also be noted that the tendency towards divergence, both between paradigms and between theoretical intentions and research practices, seems to characterize e.p.'s first period of work primarily; however, in more recent years various authors have worked in the direction of a greater integration between these different theoretical perspectives, primarily through the introduction of new, useful constructs, which we will now pause to consider.

In effect, the possibility that the emerging field of e.p. will succeed in realizing the molar and psycho-social approach, so unanimously affirmed by the intentions of its principal theoreticians, seems to be linked to the possibility of developing adequate conceptual instruments. The main problem for the field seems to be the capability of developing and applying suitable constructs for dealing with the so-called 'social dimension' (Tajfel, 1984) implicit in every relationship between the individual and the socio-physical environment, allowing for research less anchored to the 'adaptive paradigm' of the physical-perceptual tradition and more oriented towards the 'socio-cultural' paradigm, typical of the social-psychological tradition.

Main psycho-social constructs

Person–environment transactions

The transactional-contextual perspective   Over the years the need for e.p. to assume a theoretical perspective defined as 'transactional' (Ittelson, 1973b; Stokols and Altman, 1987), or 'ecological' and 'socio-systemic' (Altman, 1973; Ittelson et al., 1974; Stokols, 1987), or also 'transactional-contextual', as Stokols and Altman propose in the recent *Handbook* (1987), has been increasingly affirmed by various authors.

In reality, this agreement, although followed more in programmatic intentions than in research practice, translates the main theoretical concerns of e.p. previously indicated represented by the holistic intention, on the one hand, and the psycho-social perspective, on the other.

On the other side, the transactional theoretical perspective is the one explicitly indicated from the beginning by the first founding psychologists,

Ittelson and Proshansky, and still remains the one confirmed most systematically by the various authors concerned with the theoretical aspects of the field. This perspective has been re-proposed recently as the theoretical foundation of the monumental *Handbook*, primarily in the work of Stokols, Altman and Wapner (Stokols and Altman, 1987).

Both the choice of the term 'transaction' and the theoretical implications underlying it refer back to the transactional school of the Princeton group (see pp. 33–8), even if the emphasis shifts here from the prevalent interest in the perceptual phenomenon to the more general problem of the person–environment relationship.

The authors who most systematically point out the need for this theoretical perspective are from the group at the City University of New York primarily through Ittelson (1973b; Ittelson et al., 1974) – coming directly from the Princeton group – and more recently Altman, with his collaborators (Altman, 1976; Werner et al., 1985; Altman and Rogoff, 1987), and Stokols (1987).

In affirming the need for the transactional perspective as the theoretical foundation of the psychological approach to the person–environment relationship, the aim is to free this investigation from both perspectives, on the one hand too 'objectivist' and, thus, biased by 'environmental determinism', and, on the other, too 'subjectivist', that is, exclusively centred on the psychological phenomena in individualistic and intra-psychical terms, with scarce interest in extra-individual or 'contextual' factors in a collective or physical sense.

The two main psychological theoretical traditions the transactionalist perspective opposes are, on the one hand, the behaviourist tradition, with its 'environmental objectivism' based on the reality of the 'stimuli', and, on the other, all the subjectivist traditions variously centred on individualistic or personalogical perspectives often based on innatist viewpoints (for example, the principle of isomorphism of the Gestalt school or that of libido of the psychoanalytic school), in any case affirming the primacy of experienced reality, considered as a direct outcome of intra-psychic individual processes.

The transactional perspective basically aims at re-composing the subject–object dichotomy and more particularly the dichotomy between the person and the environment; it suggests a dynamic relationship between the two, no longer considered as independent units but as interdependent aspects of the same unit. The modalities followed by the various authors to express their adherence to this transactional perspective often vary according to different tendencies in emphasizing the peculiarity of this perspective and to different modalities in using the term 'transactional'.

For several authors this approach is essentially characterized by its aim of dynamically reconciling the opposition between personal factors and environmental factors. In this sense they are primarily interested in pointing out the following peculiarities of the approach. On the one hand, there is the dynamic reciprocity or 'mutual causation' of the person–environment relationship; not only does the environment influence the person or the person the environment, but there is always a simultaneous reciprocity of influences going from the environment to the person and vice versa. On the other hand, both the 'active' (not purely 'reactive') character, that is, intentional, planned, oriented by goals of human behaviour/action in the environment, and the central role held by cognitive-perceptual processes, understood in a 'constructive' sense in orienting this action in the environment. In order to indicate the peculiarity of this perspective, in certain cases the term 'interactional-transactional' approach (Moore and Golledge, 1976; Holahan, 1978) is used, with the intention that the two terms, 'interactionism' and 'transactionalism', are synonymous. 'Our use of the term transactional is intended to reflect the dynamic, two-way interaction between the person and the environment. Of course this view does not imply that in every transaction personal and situational factors are of equal importance' (Holahan, 1978, p. 171). Or:

> In this view, experience and behavior are assumed to be influenced by intraorganismic and extraorganismic factors operating in the context of ongoing transactions of the organism-in-environment. Transactions between the organism and the environment are viewed as mediated by knowledge or cognitive representations of the environment; but these representations are treated as constructed by an active organism through an interaction between inner organismic factors and external situational factors, in the context of particular organism-in-environment transactions [. . .].
>
> Far from being passive recipients of external forces moving them to conform to the demands of the external stimulus situation, and far from being driven simply by biological factors and inherited patterns of response, in this view persons are conceived of as active organisms adapting to the world in response to both internal and external demands. (Moore and Golledge, 1976, p. 14)

On the contrary, other authors point to the tendency of the transactional approach towards a holistic and systemic perspective and to the centrality of aspects of change – rather than of stability – in the definition of phenomena. In this case, besides affirming the interactive nature of the person–environment relationship, the systemic character of the approach is highlighted, which considers the elements of that relationship as inseparably connected with each other rather than as discrete units. In this way the impossibility of considering the two elements of the relationship separately is specified, as well as their reciprocal influence, in which one of the two elements is alternatively considered object or subject of influence by the other; and so is the need to give attention to the aspects of relation and exchange which characterize that relationship.

This holistic perspective no longer considers the elements of the relationship as units of analysis, that is, the person on the one side and the environment on the other; instead, the focus is on the relation between the two elements, in this case considered as a single 'unit' (Altman, 1973) or a 'totality' (Ittelson, 1973b): the unit of the 'person-environment' (Saegert and Winkel, 1990) or of the 'person-in-environment' (Wapner, 1987), or finally, as Altman (Stokols and Altman, (1987) says, of the 'person-environment socio-physical unity'. With the intention of synthesizing the main characteristics of the transactional approach, Saegert and Winkel (1990, p. 443) define the following five dimensions:

(a) 'the person-in-environment' provides the unit of analysis;
(b) both person and environment dynamically define and transform each other over time as 'aspects' of a unitary whole;
(c) stability and change co-exist continuously;
(d) the direction of change is emergent, not preestablished;
(e) the changes that occur at one level affect the other levels, creating new person—environment configurations.

In this perspective, the possibility of using the term 'transactional' as a synonym for 'interactive' is excluded, pointing out the diversity of the transactional perspective with respect to the interactive one.

For example this is Altman's (Altman and Rogoff, 1987) position; he has been the one most recently involved in outlining this transactional approach for environmental psychology and defining it as 'transactional world view'. In presenting this perspective in the introductory chapter of the recent *Handbook*, he tends to oppose it not only to the interactionist viewpoint but also to other major theoretical perspectives in psychology considered as having mainly limiting characteristics, namely those designated by him as 'trait', 'interactional' and 'organismic'.

For each of these perspectives he specifies the diversity of the units of analysis, the assumptions relative to the aspects of change and of stability and the underlying philosophical concepts, and he points out that 'the transactional world view emphasizes the study of holistic units of analysis, with phenomena defined in terms of inseparable psychological, contextual and temporal facets' (Altman and Rogoff, 1987, p. 34).

For example, with regard to the diversity of units of analysis assumed in the various perspectives, he distinguishes that in 'the trait world view' this primarily regards 'the person and his psychological characteristics'; in 'the interactional world view' this regards the 'psychological qualities of the person and the physical or social environment considered as separate, underlying entities, with interaction between parts'; in 'the organismic world view' the 'holistic entities [are] composed of separate person and environment components, elements or parts whose relations and inter-actions imply qualities of the whole, which are "more than the sum of its parts"'; and finally, in 'the transactional world view' the 'holistic entities [are] composed of aspects, not of parts or separate elements; aspects which define each other; the temporal qualities are aspects intrinsic of the whole' (ibid., p. 28).

Further, he points out that, unlike other orientations, the transactional approaches include temporal qualities and change as intrinsic aspects of psychological phenomena:

The transactional view shifts from analysis of the causes of change to the idea that change is inherent in the system and the study of its transformations is necessary to understand the phenomena. In the transactional perspective the changing configuration itself is the focus of analysis. [. . .] Change is viewed more as an ongoing, intrinsic aspect of an event than as the outcome of the influence of separate elements on each other. (ibid., p. 25)

In this case the author concludes with the hope that the transactional world view will find greater use in psychology in general and e.p. in particular.

Further, in the proposal to associate the term 'contextual' with the term 'transactional', thus using the 'transactional-contextual' designation, Stokols and Altman (1987) point out the specific attention that both the transactional perspective and e.p. have for the characteristics of the 'context' in which psychological phenomena occur. Stokols (1987, p. 42) observes: 'A fundamental feature of transactional research is its emphasis on the dynamic interplay between people and their everyday environmental setting, or "contexts".'

In order to specify the characteristics of the transactional approach, Moore and Golledge (1976, p. 14) observe: 'the position is taken that behavior can only be fully understood in the context of the total organism-in-environment situation and as a function of the particular ongoing transaction between the two'.

By using the term 'transactional-contextual' the authors seem to highlight various aspects:

(a)   first, the interest of the transactional orientation in contextual problems in general;
(b)   second, the specific attention that e.p. in particular, unlike 'other psychologies', dedicates to contextual aspects, that is, the setting in which the considered phenomena occur, as Stokols specifies;
(c)   third, they refer indirectly to what several authors have defined as the 'contextual revolution' (Little, 1987) occurring in psychology in general and in personality psychology in particular over the past thirty years.

In this way, Little (1987) synthesizes the salient features of this 'psychological revolution', essentially represented by the change towards a more situationist perspective and, thus, also in the psycho-social direction. This was marked by the publication of volumes such as Mischel's (1968) and supported by new theories of personality, that is, ego psychology (Hartmann, 1958), Kelly's (1955) theory on personal constructs and even more by the previous works of Lewin (1936) and Murray (1938); thus, Little (1987, p. 211) affirms:

The contextual revolution shifted the search for laws in psychological research from the self-contained individual to the natural milieu within which that individual was located. Moreover, in its extreme form, contextualism stripped personality psychology of the exclusive right to explanatory primacy making a strong case that the claim of the context was causally significant.

On the other hand, this situationist 'contextual' orientation of personality psychology tends to converge with the other orientation of the same type, defined in this case as 'ecological' (see pp. 20–2), coming from various areas of psychology such as perception-cognition (Tolman, 1932; Brunswik, 1947; Gibson, 1979; Neisser, 1976, 1987) and social and developmental psychology (Lewin, 1936; Barker, 1968; Bronfenbrenner, 1979; Wapner and Kaplan, 1983) as specifically treated in Chapter 2.

Furthermore, we can note how the convergence of both the situationist orientation of personality psychology and the ecological orientation of the psychology of perception-cognition and of social and developmental psychology has tended in recent years to animate the psychologists' debate around the problems of 'contextualism' and the 'contextual approach' to psychological phenomena (Sarbin, 1976; McGuire, 1983; Veroff, 1983; Georgoundi and Rosnow, 1985).

The salient aspects of this approach can be synthetically outlined: a holistic approach in a systemic sense; descriptive not only causative research orientation; the search for relations outside of the unidirectional model of causality; the study of phenomena in the context in which they naturally occur; the recognition of the context as constituting the dimension of the psychological phenomena under examination.

It is not surprising that psychologists with psycho-social training show particular interest in this framework, considering that a large part of the 'contextualist' demands tend to coincide with those which have always been present in social psychology: holism; explanations of psychological phenomena outside the exclusively intrapsychic view; and linking of these phenomena with contextual factors in a socio-cultural, historical and physical-geographical sense (Manicas and Secord, 1983; Gergen and Gergen, 1984; Moscovici, 1984b).

Person–environment transactions   The increasing use of the term 'person–environment transactions' in e.p. is the most explicit sign of the adherence of these authors to the above-mentioned transactional-contextual perspective.

More and more often the use of this term is preferred in referring to problems of the relationship between the person and the socio-physical environment. Actually, through the use of this construct of 'person–environment transaction' the authors aim to point out a series of specific modalities for understanding both the person and the environment and their reciprocal interdependence, in agreement with the 'transactional-contextual' perspective discussed previously.

Ittelson et al. (1974) systematically summarized these theoretical peculiarities, underlying the simple choice of the term 'person–environment transaction'.

In analysing them we will define these characteristics in terms of the person, on the one hand, and the environment, on the other, even if – as we have already shown – the characteristic of the transactional perspective remains that of considering these two elements as interdependent and, thus, not analysable separately.

With regard to *person*, the 'person–environment' transaction points out the following main characteristics.

1   The person is to be considered in his/her entirety, as a dynamic whole, that is, as

> *a dynamically organized system* whose behavior and experience at all times expresses the interactive consequences of these processes and functions [. . .]. The unit of analysis here is not an isolated stimulus–response sequence, but the intact individual behaving and experiencing in the context of a specific ongoing physical setting. To understand the nature of this complex event which is the primary objective of the environmental psychologist, it is necessary to extract and study particular psychological functions and processes (for example, the commuter's searching perceptions of the train as he enters) but never when removed or in isolation from their relationships to other psychological functions and processes. (ibid., p. 83)

2   The organizing and integrating factor of the above-mentioned dynamically organized system, constituted by the person, is the character of human activity which is primarily 'goal-directed'; that is, individual behaviour is motivated, intentional, meaningful; thus, it is oriented towards integrating aspects of activity pertaining to 'doing' with those of experience relative to 'thinking'.

3   The motivational processes underlying behaviour are to be understood not as the exclusive outcome of intrapsychic processes, but as the result of a continuous confrontation/exchange between internal motives or 'needs' of the individual and opportunities and objects/aims present in the environment:

> To understand human motivation of the goal-directed nature of human behavior, it is important to identify its essential components. The initiation of behavior will depend not just on the existence of a need but the extent of the arousal of that need. Such arousal may result from factors within the person or from events and stimuli in the environment [. . .]. The occurrence of actual behavior depends not only on *need arousal* but also on availability of the appropriate *goal-object*. (ibid., p. 84)

4   This behaviour motivated towards goal-objects is connected to other aspects of the context in which this correspondence motives/goal-objects takes place, such as the characteristics of 'value' of the objects available and the perceived probability of success in achieving objectives. Overall this involves recognizing the importance of the social context in orienting processes of motivated behaviour with regard to goal-objects:

> The need arousal is a necessary, but far from sufficient, condition for determining behavior [. . .] behavior is also influenced and determined by the broader social context in which our relations with other people, social

constraints, opportunity, the degree of skill and talent we possess, and the nature of the physical setting all play a role. (ibid., p. 85)

5   In the individual's relationship with his/her environment, a central role is assigned to cognitive processes, considered as typical transactive processes at the individual level for 'constructing' and orienting the individual's relationship with his/her environment:

> Man is a *cognitive* animal. He does far more than see, hear, feel, touch, smell, in the simple sense of 'recording' his environment. He interprets it, makes inferences about it, dreams of it, judges it, imagines it, and engages in still other human forms of knowing. It is all of these forms of knowing that permit the individual to accumulate a past, think on the present, and anticipate the future. (ibid.)

6   Further, cognition is considered as 'an emerging transactional process involving the interaction of the characteristics of the person with those of the event to be perceived'. The 'emerging' character of the resulting perceptions or experiences is emphasized; that is, the cognitive result is not determined by the characteristics of the known object or those of the knowing subject but by the 'emerging experience':

> . . . out of the interaction of person and place may come an entirely new, or emergent, kind of experience that is quite independent of the intrinsic nature of either party to the transaction. (ibid., p. 86)

7   The centrality attributed to cognitive processes in the relationship between the individual and the environment recognizes a selective role for cognition in perceived reality:

> The influence of the behavioral factors we have been discussing determines not only how we perceive the objects and events that concern us, but also what we perceive. As complex changing systems in their own right, the environments that confront goal-directed man must be and are selectively perceived. (ibid., p. 87)

8   An equally important role is recognized in affective-emotional processes for orienting human behaviour with regard to goal-objects:

> . . . the various emotions have the properties of need states. They can initiate and guide behavior. They are not merely epiphenomena that accompany other motivated states, but, as reactions to oneself, to others, or to physical settings and their objects, they direct behavior with respect to particular goals or ends. (ibid., p. 88)

9   Aspects of change, more than those of stability, characterize the person in his/her relationship with the environment:

> Psychologically speaking, the individual represents a dynamic system which is characterized by both constant change and relative stability. (ibid., p. 89)

Parallel to the above-mentioned aspects characterizing the person within the person–environment transaction, a series of equally implicit assumptions can be listed with regard to the environment, again referring to Ittelson et al. (1974).

1   The environment primarily consists in a setting, that is an organized

whole in space and time of physical aspects, social activities and symbolic aspects or meanings:

> We emphasize here that the 'demand' character of an environment is more than the sum of its ongoing social activities. Individuals, as members of broad social groups, are socialized not just to behave, but to behave appropriately in relation to relevant physical settings; and not simply to the immediate sensory stimuli of the setting, but to its symbolic qualities as well – the 'meanings' suggested by outward appearances. (ibid., pp. 90–1)

2   In every environmental setting physical aspects are closely linked to social and socio-cultural ones, giving spatial and temporal regularity to their occurrence in the settings:

> . . . the regularity and consistency of behavior in given physical settings over time and space occur because such settings are closely and tightly interwoven with the fabric of social organizational, and cultural systems that circumscribe the day-to-day life of any group of individuals. In effect, any given physical environment is not only a behavior environment but also a social, organizational, and cultural environment. (ibid., p. 91)

3   Environmental settings must be considered as open, not closed, systems without pre-established spatial and temporal borders, and as dynamically organized:

> If a physical setting is an open system characterized simultaneously by change and stability because of its interrelatedness with corresponding and more embracing social, normative, and organizational systems, then its organization is dynamic. A change in any component of the setting has varying degrees of effects on all other components in that setting, thereby changing the characteristic behavior pattern of the setting as a whole. (ibid.)

4   The character of 'wholeness' of the environment remains even when the need for analysis focuses attention on sectorial aspects of it; in any case, every partial aspect takes on complete meaning only from its relations with the other aspects:

> . . . it should be clear that regardless of such designations as 'physical environment', 'social environment', 'family', 'the individual' and so on, in reality there is only the *total environment*. While the extraction of any one of these environmental aspects is possible and useful for purposes of analysis and research, it cannot be stressed too strongly that first, they are merely different ways of analyzing the same situation, and second, that each one exists and derives meaning only by its relationships to the others. (ibid., p. 92)

5   The environment is conceived in terms of processes rather than characteristics; underlying the aparent stability, aspects of change over time prevail, with necessary attention to their temporal dimension:

> . . . we have objects, people, activities, interactions, relationships, spatial arrangements, as well as other components that interact with and relate to each other. The inclusive environment then is an active and continuing process whose participating components define and are defined by the nature of the inter-relationships among them at a given moment and over time. [. . .] Environment is unique at any given time and place. Its stability over time is remarkable in

that like the eddy of a whirlpool, it emerges out of a process of constant change. (ibid.)

6   Considering the importance of the time dimension, environments must be conceptualized as time-related phenomena, assigning importance to the natural history of their use and to how their history regards the same participants in the same environment:

> The [environments] have a natural history of use, and, like human beings, are not simply to be viewed at isolated points in time. Rather, they must be conceptualized as time-related phenomena, some of whose properties emerge from the sequence and interactions of a succession of events in the continuous use of these settings. Patterns of behavior in a given setting are rooted not only in the dynamics of the immediate environmental process, but also in the history of that process. Physical settings change as a function both of their continued use and of their place in a changing social system in which technological innovations, altered human relationships, and changing values are at one and the same time the causes and consequences of the changes in this system. (ibid.)

7   In each moment the environment will be perceived as unique by the perceiving individual: 'Considering all of the many possible factors of individual differences, the uniqueness of surroundings for each of them is a self-evident proposition' (ibid.).

8   Environments are typically neutral. Awareness of their characteristics occurs when a change is introduced or when an unfamiliar setting is encountered.

9   Even though environments are open systems, they present physical limits which can be primarily described as 'resistant', 'supportive' or 'facilitative' with regard to the participants' behaviours. 'Behavior in the total environmental context will always be affected by the physical opportunities that exist for expressing a desired behavior' (ibid., p. 96).

Overall, on the one hand it can be easily noted that many of these assumptions are similar to those often stressed by social psychology when defining its disciplinary orientation. On the other hand, the theoretical framework underlying these assumptions, with regard to the specific authors involved (Koffka, 1935; Murray, 1938; Murphy, 1947; Lewin, 1951; Barker, 1968), seems to assimilate this transactional orientation of e.p. within social psychology.

On the whole the construct of 'person–environment transaction' seems a typical construct able to orient environmental-psychological research in a psycho-social direction.

From behaviour setting to place

'Place-specific' behaviour and the phenomenological contributions to place
In recent years the term 'place' has been used increasingly in e.p., although often with a non-univocal theoretical perspective. In certain cases it is simply used as a synonym for the more consolidated construct of 'setting',

162   *Environmental psychology*

derived (as we have already noted) from Barker et al.'s ecological psychology (see pp. 45–53). In other cases it is used with precise theoretical intentions (Canter, 1977, 1986; Russell and Ward, 1982; Proshansky et al., 1983; Altman, 1986), with the aim of developing a 'place theory' (Canter, 1977, 1988).

These authors intend not only to bring the extra-psychological construct of place into e.p., but to assign it a central position as the main construct characterizing the entire disciplinary area.

Russell and Ward (1982) point out how the peculiarity of e.p. with respect to other areas of psychology is its primary assumption regarding the place-specific character of human behaviour: 'Behavior that occurs in one place would be out of place elsewhere. This place specificity of behavior is the fundamental fact of e.p.' (ibid., p. 652).

Canter (1986) points out that e.p. should be considered 'the study of situated human action': 'The central postulate is that people always situate their actions in a specifiable place and that the nature of the place, so specified, is an important ingredient in understanding human action and experience' (ibid., p. 8).

Actually, the progressive relevance of the 'place' construct in e.p. was initially supported by the attention given to this construct by other disciplinary areas outside of psychology; before psychology, both architectural design and geographical research began to work with this concept, mainly following the philosophical phenomenological school (Merleau-Ponty, 1945; Schütz, 1962–6; Husserl, 1970).

The architectural field was the first to be oriented in this direction since the task of architects is usually to plan specific places such as homes, schools, hospitals, churches, etc., rather than environments in general. Thus, we can say that architectural design was initially oriented towards environmental-psychological research with a prearranged 'interest in place'.

Not by chance, at the beginning of e.p., when Altman (1973) analysed the possible sources of difficulty for collaboration between 'practitioners' of the environment and 'social researchers and, thus, environmental psychologists', he singled out as the first difficulty the diversity of the unit of analysis taken as the point of reference, by these two sides; in the first case this was represented by 'places' and in the second by 'psycho-environmental processes', which tend to be 'trans-places' (for example, territoriality, privacy, environmental cognitions, etc.).

At the beginning, interest in the environment considered as place seemed to create opposition and difficulty in comprehension rather than collaboration and convergence between the sciences of design/architecture and environmental-psychological research. At the same time it should be noted that the sciences of design, in outlining the theoretical foundation of their interest in the unit of analysis of place, tended to search for support primarily in the contributions of the philosophical phenomenological school – both classical (Husserl, 1960, 1970) and existential (Merleau-Ponty, 1945, 1951; Heidegger, 1962, 1975, 1982; Schütz, 1962–6, 1967).

Obviously these perspectives could not be easily integrated within the tradition of psychological research.

Particular attention is given to those authors who write from the phenomenological perspective about the experience of the physical environment, of space and its places, such as Merleau-Ponty (1945), Bachelard (1969), Heidegger (1975) and Norberg-Schulz (1971, 1980).

The contribution of the philosopher Heidegger (1975) is emblematic in this sense. He investigates the phenomenon of 'dwelling', trying to define the process by which people make their place of existence a home. Heidegger arrives at the conclusion that dwelling involves a super-imposition of four principal elements: earth, sky, gods and man. Through earth and sky dwelling incorporates the natural world and environment, while gods and man incorporate individual, interpersonal, ecological and spiritual dimensions. Interpenetrating all these dimensions and providing the basis for their potentially positive relationship is what Heidegger calls 'sparing and preserving', that is, the kindly concern and care for things, places, persons, for what they are and for what they can become. According to Heidegger, dwelling identifies the essential element of what it means 'to be a human being living in the world'.

It should also be noted that the interest of architectural design in the approach of the phenomenological school tends to merge with the parallel route taken by geographical research, through the work of authors such as Tuan (1961, 1974, 1977), Relph (1970, 1976) and Buttimer and Seamon (Buttimer, 1976; Seamon, 1979, 1982; Buttimer and Seaman, 1980) regarding what is defined as 'the phenomenology of the geographical world'.

The concept of 'place' holds a central position for these authors also; in this construct they tend to bring together the many individual experiences about the 'world', characterized by features of necessity, immediacy and idiosyncracy typical of the phenomenological view. Seamon (1982, p. 130) affirms:

> Place refers not only to geographical location but also to the essential character of a site which makes it different from other locations. Place, in this sense, is the way in which dimensions of landscape come together in location to produce a distinct environment and particular sense of locality.

For example, the authors speak of 'natural places', that is, those which people belong to 'naturally', which represent for them 'the zero point of their reference system' (Bollnow, 1967, p. 180); in this sense, the home is immediately indicated as typical. Norberg-Schulz (1980) affirms the existence of what he defines as *'genius loci'*, that is, 'the spirit of the place'. According to this author, every place has its *genius loci*, whose roots are in the natural environment or in what he calls the 'natural place'. This natural place not only represents 'a mere flow of phenomena, but has a structure and incorporates meanings' (ibid., p. 23). In this sense he singles out five main dimensions, represented respectively by thing, order, character, light and time. Thing and order refer to the spatial quality of the landscape, and character and light refer to the overall atmosphere. Time involves both constancy and change in the landscape, especially with regard to the daily and seasonal rhythm of weather, climate, vegetation and animal life. From the various combinations of these five dimensions, four different types of natural places emerge, corresponding to the various landscapes and various *genii loci*: the *romantic* landscape, characterized by change, diversity and detail, best represented by Scandinavian forests (the author is Scandinavian); the *cosmic* landscape, characterized by continuity and extension, best exemplified by the desert; the *classical* landscape, in which there is a balance between variety and continuity, best represented by the Greek landscape; and finally, the *complex* landscape, represented by a mix of the three preceding ones and best representing most actual places, which in general are not pure in their natural expression.

Norberg-Schulz proposes an immanent and static view of places, which are outlined as a function of their intrinsic physical characteristics. Human activity and intervention in places are considered more successful the more they succeed in identifying the essential character of the place and in creating human environments in syntony with this. Science and technology are considered as forces destined to provoke a loss of contact with the *genius loci* and, according to the author, to encourage the erroneous conviction that people are free from 'a direct dependence on places' (Norberg-Schulz, 1980, p. 18). According to the author, current problems of the environment and of human alienation are in part due to this error in evaluation, and he affirms the need for a return to place, arising out of self-conscious understanding and design.

The concept of place also occupies a central position in geographical theories such as those of Tuan (1974, 1980) and Relph (1976). Relph (1976), in particular, attempts to outline what is called the 'phenomenology of place': places are defined in exclusively experiential terms, and the constituting aspects of this experience are characterized (in a dialectic sense) by many 'intrastructural tensions' (Seamon, 1982). Relph (1976, p. 114) defines places as 'fusions of human and natural order [. . .] and significant centres of our immediate experience of the world'. The central aspect of human place experience is singled out in the dialectic between 'existential insideness – the degree to which people feel part of a place, corresponding to a situation of unself-conscious immersion in the place – and 'existential outsideness', which involves feelings of strangeness and separation from the place. Through different degrees of insideness/outsideness different places assume different identities for different people. For Relph, existential insideness is the foundation of the place concept, because place 'experienced without deliberate and self-conscious reflection yet is full with significances' (ibid, p. 55).

Tuan (1974, 1979) approaches the theme of place in order to investigate the problem of the affective ties people establish with the surrounding physical environment. In this case, the concept of 'topophilia' is proposed to indicate 'all the affective ties of the human being with the material environment' (Tuan, 1974, p. 3), with particular reference to positive feelings. In contrast, 'topophobia' is proposed to indicate affective ties with distressful places capable of inducing anxiety and depression (Tuan, 1979). The author also examines the phenomenon he defines as 'sense of place' in contrast to that of 'rootedness' in places (Tuan, 1980). The latter is characterized as a simple and unself-conscious familiarity and occupation of a place; the former is presented as the product of an intentional capacity to reflect on that place and, thus, to appropriate it at the affective level in a self-conscious way. 'Rootedness implies being at home in a place in an unself-conscious way [. . .] it is a long habitation at one locality [. . .]. The sense of place, on the other hand, implies a certain distance between self and place, that allows the self to appreciate the place' (Tuan, 1980, p. 4).

In this regard, consistent with the central assumption of the phenomenological school, emphasis is placed on the capacity of human 'intentionality' to enlarge the cognitive horizon, in both a spatial and a temporal sense; in this way, the extended temporal perspective – defined as 'the sense of extended time' – is acquired, which is not exclusively focused on the present, typical of the condition of rootedness.

> Subjectively rootedness is a state of being made possible by an in-curiosity toward the world at large and an insensitivity toward the flow of time. (ibid.)

> It excludes not only anxiousness and curiosity about what lies beyond the next hill, but also of what lies beyond present time. (ibid., p. 5)

> Rootedness is an unreflective state of being in which the human personality merges with its milieu. (ibid., p. 6)

In this regard, Tuan cites the distinction between 'knowing,' as the result of simple familiarity with the object and 'knowing about' as the result of conscious cognitive effort, thus 'explicit knowledge'; the former generates a sense of stability and rootedness, the latter a 'sense of place'.

Therefore, emphasis is given to the character of human intentionality through which people assume the 'sense of place'. Thus, for Tuan, places are not direct results of physical characteristics of the environment but products of intentional human acts turned towards the 'creation of places': 'There are the deliberate acts of creating and maintaining place for which speech, gesture and the making of things are the common means. [. . .] Gestures, either alone or in association with speech and the making of things, create place' (ibid.). Here again he uses examples to show how in certain cultures and in certain cases the creation and maintenance of the sense of place are entrusted to the rituality of words and gestures more than to the presence of manufactured goods: 'The Australian aborigines maintain their awareness of place not so much with material fabrication, as with words and gestures – with stories that tell and the rituals that perform.' He continues, exemplifying:

The power of words is further illustrated in the settlement of a new land. Explorers conjure places out of the wilderness by simply naming certain peaks and rivers. [. . .] Words and gestures are ephemeral compared with objects. Yet not only do objects themselves vary greatly in durability, but their role in sustaining a sense of place may not depend on their permanence. (ibid.)

Again he takes examples from anthropology, citing cases of sacred rituals based on perishable objects and, thus, necessitating continuous reconstruction. In these cases the capacity of the rite to emphasize the existence of the community and of its place is entrusted to the shared action of reconstruction of the object more than to the sacred object itself: 'What unifies the far-flung members of the Mbona cult and gives the cult center its special aura is not the shrine, but the act of building it – not so much the final material product, as the cooperative effort and gesture' (ibid.).

In this regard it is interesting to note that Tuan foresees a dynamism of places entrusted to shared, not individual, human activity such as language and common activities, capable of not only creating but also continuously recreating places. As an example he cites the fact that inhabitants speak of the various places in the city; this not only has a determining role in giving a stable image to places, but may also create and destroy the same places:

The city is a built environment, full of places. Still, the reality of these places in individual minds lacks stability. City people are constantly 'making' and 'unmaking' places by talking about them. A network of gossip can elevate one shop to prominence and consign another to oblivion . . . in a sense, a place is its reputation. (ibid.)

However, Tuan also underlines the capacity of built objects to 'create places':

A built object organizes space, transforming it into place. This object may be a piece of sculpture. A jar put on a hill, the poet Wallace Stevens says, can tame the surrounding space, which rises up to the jar and no longer seems wild. The object may be an ordinary house or a monument such as the Eiffel Tower in Paris, a warehouse or a striking office building such as the Transamerica skyscraper in San Francisco. (ibid.)

He also considers the case in which very different objects are introduced into the environment which are dissonant with people's pre-existing 'sense of place', and, therefore, destined to 'trample on the residents' traditional sense of place' (ibid.); the construction of the Eiffel Tower and the Transamerica skyscraper are cited as examples of this. People's initial hostility towards these objects can lead over time to a change in their sense of place, and they end up identifying these objects as distinctive elements characterizing the entire surrounding environment.

Overall, the phenomenological approach to the concept of place and to the analysis of the person–environment relationship presents contrasting valencies for the emerging field of e.p. On the one hand, holistic intentions, programmatic interest in 'meanings', situationism, and the centrality attributed to the spatial and corporeal dimension of human experience are important points of departure for a molar approach to the person–socio-physical environment relationship, which is one of the main aspirations of the developing field of e.p.

On the other hand, the epistemological and methodological starting points of the phenomenological approach, especially in its radical form, appear from many points of view completely in opposition with those of the tradition of psychological research, that is, an exclusively descriptive and qualitative method, extraneous to any form of systematic and quantifying observation, total idiosyncrasy of every interpretive situation both for the researcher and for the subject investigated.

In an article illustrating the phenomenological contribution to e.p., Seamon (1982) points out the epistemological differences between the phenomenological approach and the approach of conventional scientific methodology; he outlines a series of contrasts between what he defines as 'positivist' and 'phenomenological' e.p. However, besides the radical contrast between the two approaches, the author points out the existence of an intermediate level, which he defines 'less radical', where the two perspectives can attempt to collaborate; in this direction he hopes that concepts and theoretical formulations generated in the phenomenological area can be translated into objects of study for more conventional research.

The work carried out by various authors around the construct of place, which we will discuss in the next section, is oriented in this direction, even though the references they make to the phenomenological school are in general vague and in some cases absent.

Revision of behaviour setting in the direction of place The growing attention that e.p. has given to the construct of place over the last ten years can be traced to two main factors. On the one hand, this tendency can be positioned within the above-mentioned perspective advanced by Seamon (1982) regarding the possibility of collaboration between the phenomeno-logical approach and psychological research. This is due to the undoubted stimulating role that phenomenological studies have on the theme of the person–socio-physical environment relationship. Confirmation of this is found in the works of various authors such as Carl Grauman (1974, 1988), who repeatedly emphasizes the importance of this collaboration; another example is the environmental-psychological research which is still being carried out in a completely phenomenological way by various authors, especially in Europe (Dovey, 1985; Korosec-Serfaty, 1988; Barbey, 1990).

On the other hand, the limits of the constructs initially used by e.p. are being increasingly noted, in particular 'behaviour setting', which can be considered as one of the main theoretical constructs in this area.

The contributions of many authors (Wicker, 1987; Kruse, 1988; Fuhrer, 1990; Rapoport, 1990), even if not explicitly involved with the construct of 'place' but working critically for a revision of the construct of 'behaviour setting', can be considered as equally oriented towards developing the so-called 'place perspective' or 'place theory' more specifically indicated by authors such as Canter (1977) and Russell and Ward (1982).

This revision of the 'behaviour setting' construct, as initially outlined by Barker et al.'s ecological psychology (see pp. 45–53), has been mainly carried out by some students of Barker's school, such as Wicker (1987) and Schoggen (1989), and by the German school defined as 'eco-psychology' or 'psychological ecology', (Lewin's term) with the aim of taking up the Lewinian tradition more directly (see pp. 38–45) Kruse, 1978; Kaminsky, 1983; Fuhrer, 1990).

The criticisms of Barker et al.'s perspective regarding 'behaviour setting' are generally concentrated around the following two points.

1 The psychological perspective (understood as the phenomenological-subjective perspective) is substantially absent. Therefore, on the one hand, there is excessive emphasis on supra-individual characteristics of the settings and, thus, on the complete interchangeability between persons inside the same setting; and, on the other, there is a lack of attention to cognitive processes occurring in the setting participants, not only in view of maintenance, but also in view of possible changes within the setting.

With regard to this, it is proposed that the construct of setting first recovers its psychological dimensions, in particular those relative to the cognitive processes of *interpretation*, that is, of attribution of *meaning* to the settings. Here, the vast literature existing on 'social cognitions' is called upon; in various ways it shows the existence and use of organized cognitive systems at the individual level which affect interaction with persons and social situations. The constructs of 'schema' or 'prototypical situations' (Cantor, 1981; Cantor et al., 1982), 'scripts' (Schank and Abelson, 1977; Abelson, 1981) and 'frames' (Goffman, 1974; Forgas, 1985) are examples of this. So, too, is Wicker's proposal to include in the study of setting what he calls the 'cognitions of the setting program' (1987, p. 624). Moreover, Fuhrer's interest in considering the 'denotative and connotative meanings' (1990, p. 527) of objects making up specific settings, as well as those relative to the settings, moves in the same direction.

2 Barker et al.'s theory of behaviour setting is characterized by an eminently intra-setting view point. On the one hand, this appears primarily as a homeostatic theory of maintenance of individual settings, which are considered both independent of their respective context and as 'natural data', not as products of the socio-cultural peculiarities of the context; on the other hand, there is no possibility of dealing with the dimension of setting change, which can be approached only by means of an inter-setting perspective.

In contrast to this, a dynamic and contextualized viewpoint – that is, not exclusively intra-setting – is proposed for behaviour settings: 'One regards settings as social constructions that are continually being built and rebuilt through the deliberate actions of individuals [. . .] then explanations are needed for the organizing and operating of processes' (Wicker, 1987, p. 623). In this direction, Fuhrer proposes supporting this dynamic view of settings by Moscovici's (1984a) theory of 'social representations', pointing out the explicative potential of this construct for the comprehension of settings, in particular with regard to the existence of 'social conventions, norms, and values [which] are part of culture [. . .]: these as social representations are collective representations, or socio-culturally shared symbolic imagery of ideas and beliefs that represent action-related components of regulation on the aggregated level' (Fuhrer, 1990, p. 526).

In this same direction, Wicker (1987) proposes the more direct linking of the theory of behaviour setting with that of the social psychology of the organization (Weick, 1979), particularly with regard to its capacity to consider aspects not only of stability, but also of flexibility, change and possible internal differentiation of the organizational settings considered.

All these speculations tend to converge with the proposals of several other authors to support the above-mentioned theoretical positions in terms of the 'place' construct rather than the behaviour setting construct (Canter, 1977, 1986, 1988; Stokols and Shumaker, 1981; Russell and Ward, 1982).

By means of this construct, the aim is to affirm the centrality of the so-called 'psychological aspects' – and, thus, aspects of both cognitive and affective *meaning* – as regulators of the individual's relationship with the socio-physical environment; at the same time, the latter is not considered in a molecular sense, but as organized into 'socio-physical units' represented by settings or places. Thus, place is defined as a 'unit of environmental experience' (Canter, 1986) or as a 'psychological or perceived unit of the geographical environment' (Russell and Ward, 1982). In this way, through place, the socio-physical unit of the setting finds direct reference in the 'perceived reality' of subjects, rather than in the reality singled out by the researcher.

As will be clarified later, by means of the 'place perspective' in e.p. a series of crucial modalities are outlined for understanding the person–socio-physical environment relationship; for many reasons these modalities seem to summarize the major earlier theories in e.p., such as the behaviour setting theory of ecological psychology and that of the transactional-contextual and phenomenological approaches.

Supported by the construct of place, e.p. aims at recovering the entire theoretical tradition of behaviour setting, at the same time affirming what was initially ignored by that tradition, that is, the centrality of the area of meanings for understanding human behaviour in the environment. In the same way, both the active and the intentional roles – that is, cognitively oriented, guided by goals – of human behaviour in the environment are affirmed as well as the continuous integration between cognitive and affective aspects and between individual and shared aspects for human behaviour/action in the environment.

Therefore, on the one hand, this proposal seems primarily aimed at shifting the behaviour setting perspective of ecological psychology into environmental-psychological research, because of its attention to:

(a)   the 'organized' properties in a systemic sense of the units of analysis taken as reference points;
(b)   the objective aspects of manifest behaviours and of the surrounding physical reality;
(c)   the social perspective, based on the supra-individual properties of the contexts in which the individual action takes place.

On the other hand, the phenomenological and holistic interests of the phenomenological and transactional approaches are recovered through the integration of these two perspectives, primarily by means of:

(a)   the use of empirical-experimental methodology;
(b)   the attention centred on perceptual-cognitive processes, both aspects being characteristic of the transactional approach.

Place according to David Canter   Already at the end of the 1970s there were initial efforts aimed at incorporating the construct of place within traditional environmental-psychological research: the first attempt was made at the University of Surrey (Guildford) in the work of David Canter. In 1977 the author published *The Psychology of Place*, in which he began to advance a systematic proposal, which he continued to develop in the following years: 1983, 1986, 1988. In the 1980s other authors also made relevant contributions in this area, in particular a Canadian group in British Columbia led by Russell and Ward (Russell and Ward, 1982; Genereux et al., 1983; Ward et al., 1988) and authoritative researchers in the United States, such as Stokols (Stokols and Shumaker, 1981) Proshansky (Proshansky et al., 1983) and Altman (1986).

This area of studies is moving towards developing what can be defined as 'place theory' in e.p., but although several steps have been taken in this direction, a great deal of work still remains to be done.

The first steps can be found in Canter's initial works. Still of interest today is his proposal of outlining an approach to the construct of place as systematically as possible, starting from its redefinition in terms which can be dealt with within the traditional perspective of psychological research.

> This book is about the psychological processes which enable us to understand places, to use them and to create them. It is not about any of those topics so favoured by experimental psychologists; space perception, object perception, colours or shapes. Rather it is concerned with those situations in which people live and work, converse with others, are alone, rest, learn, are active or still. This does not mean it is concerned with activities alone, or only with the buildings which house them. It is about those units of experience within which activities and physical form are amalgamated: places.

Canter (1977, p. 1) presents his book by expressing the desire that his work move in an antithetical direction to that of the molecular tradition of experimental and perception psychology, proposing instead a molar approach oriented towards units of significant experience. Therefore, the construct of place is proposed in psychological investigation primarily with the intention of affirming the need to orient environmental-psychological research towards molar units of the environment, that is, towards 'wholes endowed with significance' and not towards simple elements or 'variables'.

It is interesting to note that in formulating this proposal Canter prefers to link himself with a tradition more endogenous to psychology, such as the cognitive orientation of Bartlett's school, rather than trying to go back to the tradition of the phenomenological school. He tends to single out an ideal route which goes from Bartlett's (1932) 'serial reproductions' of studies on memory to the 'socio-spatial schemata' singled out by Terence Lee (Bartlett's student and Canter's teacher) on the study of the neighbourhood (1968), to Kevin Lynch's (1960) 'spatial maps and images of the city'. It should be noted that Canter tends to develop his proposal for a 'psychology of place' by paying attention to processes of cognitive representation of the surrounding environment, giving particular attention to all those phenomena that e.p. tends in general to define as 'cognitions', maps or cognitive representations, or knowledge of the environment (see Chapter 4). In his introduction, Canter affirms that 'If we are to understand people's responses to places and their actions within them, it is necessary to understand what (and how) they think; and thus this book will concentrate more upon conceptual systems than behavioural systems.' Thus, he affirms his desire to 'look within the individual for the *causes* of his actions, at his interpretation of the context within which he finds himself' (Canter, 1977, p. 1).

His work, which in this case he defines as aimed towards 'studying the cognitive systems pertinent to the environment', is oriented in the following two directions: (a) 'development of a theory which enables us to describe and understand the structure of these systems' and (b) 'examination of the procedures available for bringing these internal processes into public view' (ibid., p. 3).

In this way Canter provides a series of interesting insights such as that of the internal organization (in a hierarchical sense) of the cognitive systems relative to places, and that of 'specificity', or of 'diffusion', and of the different degree of 'differentiation' presented by the same systems in relation to the characteristics of the relative internal organization. He also shows the close connection between cognitive systems, affective reactions and actions carried out concerning the physical characteristics of the environment. Then he treats the problem of the differentiations of places in relation to individual differences and, in this regard, he proposes the construct of 'environmental role', with a meaning similar to – even if more limited than – the construct of 'social role' used by social psychology. The environmental role 'refers only to that aspect of a person's role which is related to his dealing with his physical environment' (ibid., p. 128). The example of the doctor, the patient and the hospital cleaner helps to clarify the diversity of environmental roles that each of them carries out in the hospital place.

Environmental psychology

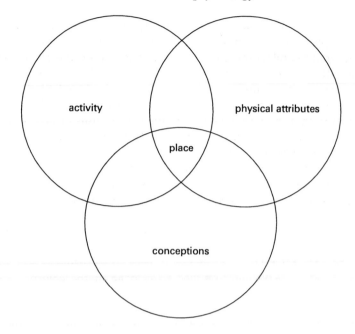

Figure 5.1   *Place according to Canter (1977 , p. 158)*

At the end of his work, he proposes a definition of place on the basis of the preceding: to the question 'which are the main constituents which amalgamate to form places?', he responds by singling out three main constituents, which are presented in Figure 5.1.

'A place is the result of relationships between actions, conceptions and physical attributes.' From this it follows that place cannot be fully identified if you do not know:

(a)   what behaviour is associated with it or it is anticipated will be housed in a given locus;
(b)   what the physical parameters of that setting are;
(c)   the descriptions or conceptions which people hold of that behaviour in that physical environment (ibid., p. 159).

Canter returns later to these theoretical positions attempting further investigation of the construct of place both from the individual side, specifically pointing out the *purposive* aspects of individual 'place' activity (1983) – that is, active gaol-directed and cognitively organized action – and specifying the nature and reciprocal connections of the constituting components (1986).

He specifies that these three components are to be considered 'three sets of properties which they have which is the key to their distinctness. Taken together they describe much of what is psychologically significant about a place.' He also points out that they are not to be considered simply as 'variables' to be dealt with independently and intercorrelated but as 'aspects of place to be explored' (1986, p. 8). He also affirms that 'for study and analysis purposes it is necessary to divide up the components of places into their constituent parts but the essence of the argument here is that they are always components of an integrated system' (ibid., p. 9).

It is interesting to note how, following the holistic proposal, he expresses the conviction that the best examples of the descriptions of places are to be found in the work of novelists, rather than scientists, and he cites Proust and several passages from Milne (1928).

Actually, Canter's proposal encounters some difficulty, primarily in the attempt to outline a systematic approach in an area in which the tradition of the phenomenological approach has widely operated, leaving 'indelible marks' such as the undoubted holism of its 'results'.

On the whole, summarizing Canter's proposals, the main components constituting the construct of place can be expressed as follows (as already illustrated in Figure 5.1):

(a) the activities which are understood to occur at a location and the reasons for them. Here we would add the consideration of the individuals – actors of these activities – as parts of the same component of activities;

(b) the evaluative conceptualizations, or, better, the representations which are held of the occurrence of those activities; and

(c) the physical properties of the place, as they are evaluated – or better represented – in relation to the activities.

In any case, beyond the discussion of how complete the components indicated by Canter are in constituting place (Giuliani et al., 1988), the proposal seems an interesting point of departure for looking at the psycho-social developments of environmental-psychological research, aiming in particular at systematically reorienting the reflections of the phenomeno-logical approach around the construct of place – attempting to establish a link between them and the tradition of ecological psychology on behaviour setting.

Canter (1986, p. 8) affirms:

> . . . places can be readily distinguished from behaviour settings and situations. Unlike behaviour settings a) they are not created by the investigator on the basis of observing behaviour and b) they have distinct evaluative and physical components. Unlike situations, they have a distinct enduring existence as well as being inevitably intertwined with the physical properties of their location.

On the other hand, Canter points out the usefulness of supporting environmental-psychological research with the construct of place with particular attention to social psychology; he proposes it as the specific 'bridge-construct' capable of linking e.p. and social psychology. In particular, he points out not only the possibility but also the necessity of linking the 'perspective of place' and the most recent interests of social psychology oriented towards situationism (Argyle et al., 1981; Magnusson, 1981), with attention to 'situations' and 'social episodes' (Forgas, 1979). According to the author, from this bridging not only should further possibilities for investigation of the place perspective occur but also new possibilities for social psychology to enrich or locate its situationist perspective through the perspective of place; that is, 'putting situations in their place', as Canter says in the title to his article:

> Both behaviour settings and situations occur within places. One place may house many of Barker's behavioural settings or of Argyle's situations, at the same or different points in time. It must be emphasized, though, that places are part of experience. They cannot be specified independently of the people who are experiencing them. The central postulate is that people always situate their actions in a specifiable place and that the nature of the place, so specified, is an important ingredient in the understanding of human actions and experience. (1986, p. 8)

Actually, there are many perspectives for integrating the construct of place, as outlined by Canter, in social psychology, even if they are still mostly to be developed. For example, besides the specific link with the situationist view of social psychology, proposed by Canter, other specific links could be established with the other main research areas of social psychology, especially European ones, dealing with the topic of social representations (Moscovici, 1984a); these theoretical assumptions seem equally relevant for the 'place perspective', as we will try to show in the next section.

Overall it should also be considered that the contributions of many authors working with the construct of place have often shown the usefulness of Canter's proposal (Genereux et al., 1983; Ward et al., 1988; Bonnes et al., 1990) and have provided contributions which can integrate and enrich this proposal (Stokols and Shumaker, 1981; Proshansky et al., 1983).

Social representations of place

Social imageability, place-dependence and social representations of place
Daniel Stokols's (1981; Stokols and Shumaker, 1981) contribution to the development of the construct of place appears to move in the same direction as Canter's. Stokols also tends to consider the construct of place as a successive step and, thus, as an enrichment of the primitive construct of behaviour setting, in this case primarily pointing out the symbolic implications of this new construct with respect to the preceding one: places are seen as the 'physical and symbolic context of human action' (Stokols and Shumaker, 1981, p. 443). 'Places are viewed not only as composite of behavior-shaping forces, but also as the material and symbolic product of human action' (ibid., p. 442).

At the same time the author notes the insufficient specification that both the theory of behaviour setting of Barker's ecological psychology and the other 'ecological' approaches, such as that of Bronfenbrenner, give to the physical-architectural characteristics of the setting considered: 'Previous analyses of settings have emphasized the social and behavioral aspects of settings, [. . .] while neglecting to consider the relationships between these dimensions and the architectural-geographical milieu' (ibid.). Thus, Stokols also tends to define place as a relational entity between physical properties, aspects of meaning and relative activity. However, Stokols's analysis tends to touch on some aspects relative to the construct, proposing further investigation of the dimension of 'shared meanings'. In this way Stokols proposes new conceptualizations of the construct of place which seem to be able to orient environmental-psychological research with increasing clarity in the direction of social psychology; this is true with particular reference to the more recent area developing from it, especially in Europe, as an intersection between the Lewinian tradition and symbolic interactionism, and tending to gravitate around the theory of social representations (Doise, 1982; Moscovici, 1984b; Tajfel, 1984).

Stokols points out how his perspective aims mainly at recomposing the fundamental dualism between the 'objectivist' and 'subjectivist' perspective which environmental-psychological research has traditionally confronted. Even more specifically, this perspective overcomes the tendency towards an individualistic view which environmental-psychological research has generally assumed in studying the phenomena of representation of the environment, dealing with them in terms of 'cognitive or mental maps', 'cognitive representations', 'cognitions' and 'environmental knowledge' (see Chapter 4). As the author observes:

> . . . whereas most research on environmental cognition has emphasized the individual's perception of the environment (cf. Moore & Gollege, 1976), the present analysis encompasses the phenomena of social perception – that is, the processes by which setting members collectively perceive and ascribe meaning to their sociophysical milieu. By focusing on the common or widely recognized meanings that become associated with the molar environment, our analysis offers a 'middle ground' between subjectivist perspectives, which construe environmental perception as essentially a personal, idiosyncratic phenomenon, and objectivist views of the environment, which avoid reference to perceptual processes altogether. (Stokols and Shumaker, 1981, p. 445)

He proposes basing this investigation of the shared meanings of places on the construct of 'social imageability' specifying how with this term he is attempting to understand 'the perceived social field of the physical environment'. It should be noted how this term is proposed as an analogy to (and in partial revision of) Kevin Lynch's (1960) initial proposal concerning the urban environment; that author, primarily interested in the design of the physical form of the city, was one of the first to pose the problem of the 'imageability' or memorability of its physical form. 'Just as environments can be described in terms of the imageability (or memorability) of their physical elements, they also can be characterized in terms of their *social imageability* – that is, their capacity to evoke vivid and collectively held social meanings among the occupants and users of a place' (ibid., p. 446).

In this regard Stokols specifies the possibility that this imageability of places can also be supported by a 'perceptual salience' connected to the 'number and intensity of highly noticeable features within an environment'; these elements include those also indicated by the tradition of experimental and cognitive aesthetics (Berlyne, 1960; Wohlwill, 1976; Kaplan and Kaplan, 1982): 'stimulus contrast, novelty and complexity' (Stokols, 1981, p. 398).

Together with perceptual salience, a salience of 'significance' or of 'sociocultural meanings' can also be identified which 'encompasses collectively shared images' : 'The widely recognized images or meanings conveyed by places constitute the non-material properties of the physical milieu, the sociocultural "residue" or residual meaning that becomes attached to places' (ibid.).

Stokols also singles out several possible strategies for examining the images of places in terms of their 'social imageability' or 'perceived social field', to arrive at determining the respective degrees of 'complexity', 'clarity', 'heterogeneity', 'distortions' and 'contradictions'.

He also examines the characteristics of settings which he believes most contribute towards orienting the social imageability of places, singling out three main dimensions (ibid., p. 398):

(a) *functions* represented 'by individual or group specific activities that occur within places on a regular basis (including) the norms associated with these activities, as well as descriptive information regarding the identities and social roles of setting members' (ibid.);
(b) *goals* personal and collective goals and purposes;
(c) *evaluations* of occupants, physical features and/or social functions typically associated with a place.

Within this perspective the author defines 'the perceived social field of the place as the totality of functional, motivational and evaluative meanings conveyed by the physical environment to current or prospective occupants of the place' (ibid.). As can be noted, this proposal tends to point out the same aspects already indicated by Canter's analysis in defining the concept of place, although a central role is recognized here for the functional aspects of place.

The author's proposal (Stokols 1981; Stokols and Shumaker, 1981) continues with a closer examination of the phenomenon defined as 'the social imageability of places', pointing out two main problematic aspects:

(a) the problems of link/attachment or, as he says, of 'dependence' of people on places they occupy;
(b) the possibility of defining taxonomy of places in relation to both the type of social aggregation of the occupants (individual, aggregate,

group) and to the phases of the transformative processes of the place (processes of maintenance, modification and termination).

The points he makes about the first aspect are particularly interesting; he proposes a direct link between the social imageability of places and what he defines as 'place-dependence' of the occupants: 'As a place becomes increasingly "layered" with social meanings, the interdependence among social and physical components of the setting is assumed to increase. Thus, the sociocultural meanings associated with a setting are viewed as the "glue" that binds groups to particular places' (Stokols, 1981, p. 396). In this way Stokols introduces the construct of 'place-dependence' to define 'the subjective quality of the relationship between occupants and places [. . .] when occupants perceive themselves as having a strong association with a place, we describe them as *place-dependent*. Thus place-dependence describes an occupant's perceived strength of association between him or her self and specific places' (Stokols and Shumaker, 1981, p. 457). Actually this construct of place-dependence seems in many ways to deal with those phenomena of the person–environment relationship which other authors investigate with reference to the 'place attachment' construct (Fried, 1982; Shumaker and Taylor, 1983; Giuliani, 1991); on the other hand, it also seems partially linked to the 'place identity' construct advanced by Proshansky (1978; Proshansky et al., 1983), which we will return to later (see pp. 186–92).

Overall these constructs aim at foregrounding the need to explore the affective and motivational processes of the relationships of individuals with the socio-physical environment: on the one hand, they suggest that these processes occur with modalities tending to be stable and lasting over time (for example, the establishment of attachment 'bonds' or of 'place-dependence'); on the other hand, they could also be interpreted in relation to the broader phenomena of personal identity on which psychology has a long tradition of studies with various theoretical perspectives.

At the same time, through these constructs the emphasis is on the possibility of exploring these processes only when the environment is defined in terms of 'units of wholes', that is, of 'place/s', considering them as socio-physical units of environmental experience, and not in terms of simple, physical, discrete and molecular properties.

Several specific features can be recognized in these constructs; their different use underlies several different theoretical interests and research objectives. We will return to 'place identity' in detail later (pp. 186–92). Here we wish to make a distinction between the two apparently very similar constructs of 'attachment' and 'place-dependence'.

It seems that 'place-attachment' has a stronger individualistic connotation than 'place-dependence'; this can also be seen in the choice of the term 'attachment' – of ethological, that is, biological origin – and in the type of studies of developmental psychology this construct is linked with (Bowlby, 1969, 1973; Ainsworth et al., 1978, Brotherton, 1985). Through the 'place-attachment' construct the main aim is to study the affective and personal components of the establishment of the 'attachment bond' with places, although the most recent developments in this area of research tend to be more detailed on this topic (Shumaker and Taylor, 1983; Lee, 1990; Giuliani, 1991).

The place-dependence construct, as proposed by Stokols and Shumaker (1981), aims instead at emphasizing the 'shared' components of the bond between people and places and the 'shared' origin of that bond; thus, they consider the person as always part of social groups/categories, and places as socio-culturally significant objects. This construct can be more directly linked with that of place identity, and in the same way with the entire psycho-social tradition of research on the topic of 'identity/self' and 'social identity' (Doise, 1976; Palmonari et al., 1979; Tajfel, 1981; Bonnes, 1988); This will be discussed in more detail on pp. 186–92.

Overall Stokols's proposals seem interesting due to their possibility for psycho-social development in environmental-psychological research. However, the author does not fully develop the various implications of his proposals and gives priority to the primarily functional perspective. In fact, his attention is mainly on the functional aspects of places and on the activities occuring there, tending to derive exclusively from them the social imageability of places and the place-dependence of the occupants.

Actually, Stokols's proposals on the 'social imageability of places', like place-dependence, are interesting mainly because they foreground an aspect not fully explored by e.p. in general or by 'place theory' in particular. We are referring to the possibility of linking the construct of 'social imageability of places' – and, thus, 'place theory' – with the theory developed in social psychology on social representations for the study of the relationship between shared and individual aspects of social experience:

> Social representations are cognitive systems with their own logic, their own language [and] having implications relevant both for values and for concepts [. . .] they do not simply represent 'opinions on', 'images of', 'attitudes toward', but real theories or branches of knowledge for discovering and organizing reality; [they are] a system of values, notions and practices with two main functions: first to establish an order which allows individuals to orient themselves and to master their material world and, second, to facilitate communication between the members of a community providing them with a code for naming and classifying the various aspects of their world and their individual and group history. (Moscovici, 1961–76, p. xiii)

This theory will not be discussed in detail here since there is already a wide body of literature developed around it (Farr and Moscovici, 1984; Jodelet, 1989; Palmonari, 1989). However, we would like to emphasize that this theory, since it primarily focuses on the processes of cognitive construction and symbolic representation of social reality, may be crucial also for the study of the person–socio-physical environment relationship, particularly when the latter is defined in terms of places (as discussed above), with particular attention to the component of cognitive representation of place.

The theory of social representations aims at understanding both the dynamic modalities with which shared and personal aspects of social experience take shape and the interconnections between cognitive and affective aspects of these processes; in this way it seems particularly appropriate for reframing the theory of place and its various constructs, especially those related to the processes of representation of places, such as social imageability, place-dependence and place identity.

Within this perspective, it seems that the first construct can be directly translated into that of 'social representation of place' the second, together with place identity, can be linked to 'social identity', which also tends to be considered as part of the theory of social representations (Tajfel, 1981; Turner, 1981; Bonnes, 1988; Palmonari, 1989).

Orienting the environmental psychology of place with this perspective, it becomes possible to take into consideration the area of 'place communication and denomination', in order to study what in this case would be named 'place discourse' (Potter and Wetherell, 1987), similar to the recently identified 'environmental discourse' (Kruse and Grauman, 1990).

In this perspective, the phenomenon cited by Tuan (1979) according to which places are also 'created, re-created and undone' by speaking of them and, thus, by means of language and discourse (see pp. 161–7) would also be investigated in terms of research. Following this perspective, the view e.p. has often been concerned with of 'environmental meaning and communication' (Krampen, 1979; Kaplan and Kaplan, 1982; Rapoport, 1982) should be reoriented; in these studies attention is mostly focused on the physical-visual-perceptual characteristics of the environment, treating the corresponding psychological processes of environmental representation as dependent on them through the processes of 'elaboration of environmental information'.

On the contrary, following the perspective of 'social representation of place', the paradigm tends to shift from the visual-perceptual one of 'adaptation' to the psycho-social or 'socio-cultural' one (see pp. 149–52); this means implicitly favouring 'thinking' – considered as theory-dependent and, thus, deriving from categorization processes, also in a social sense (Tajfel, 1981) – with respect to 'seeing', according to the distinction proposed by Neisser, discussed previously (see pp. 32–3). This means accepting a paradigm which, instead of assuming these two processes as parallel, affirms their interdependence and, in particular, the priority of 'thinking' with respect to 'seeing', or the possible dependence of the latter on the former, as the first studies of the 'New Look' perceptual school began to show (Postman et al., 1948).

Perhaps it is worth recalling that all of Henry Tajfel's (1969, 1981) work in the psycho-social direction started from this kind of study, that is, from cognitive to social categorization, to the intergroup conflict, to the most ambitious project of promoting the development of a European social psychology less oriented in individualistic terms with respect to the then prevailing social psychology of the United States (Israel and Tajfel, 1972). Moscovici's theory of social representations gave crucial support to this project (Tajfel, 1984).

It is not surprising that there are no explicit suggestions in this research direction by the environmental psychologists (Stokols, Proshansky) who formulated the previously discussed constructs, considering the general reluctance of the academic world in the United States to join the European research on social representations. On the contrary, European authors often make specific proposals oriented in this direction (Jodelet, 1987; Kruse and Gauman, 1987; Bonnes, 1980; Bonnes and Secchiaroli, 1982a, 1986; Bonnes and Giuliani, 1987).

Actually, environmental-psychological investigation in terms of social representations of 'place' has still to be developed, although several studies more or less explicitly oriented in this direction show interest in the area, as will be illustrated below.

Social representations of place in the urban environment: some research results Most of our research in e.p. is oriented towards the theoretical perspective of 'social representations of place'.

Specifically, with this theoretical view we have considered the person–urban environment relationship in various studies, in part referred to in Chapter 4.

The point of departure for many of these studies has been the 'place naming' used by inhabitants in urban environments in large- and medium-size Italian cities (Milan, Rome, Bologna, Lecce), in order to:

(a) single out the most significant units of place at the level of inhabitants' urban experience (Bonnes and Secchiaroli, 1979, 1982a, 1982b);

(b) determine the correspondence between 'naïve naming' and 'official naming', with regard to the differentiation of urban environment into sub-units of place (neighbourhood, district, etc.) (Bonnes et al., 1987a).

With regard to the first objective, three main sub-units of place were identified through the naming of 'the centre', 'my neighbourhood' and 'the periphery', the characteristics of the social representations of place corresponding to each of these urban sub-places were studied with regard to physical attributes, evaluations and corresponding activities, with particular reference to the city of Rome (Bonnes, 1986; Bonnes et al., 1987b; Bonnes et al., 1990). A heterogeneous sample (for age, gender, socio-economic level, length of residence) of inhabitants (465) was considered; all subjects were living in the same city neighbourhood (Aurelio quarter), in an intermediate position with respect to the centre and the periphery.

The overall representations shown by the inhabitants were analysed, also taking into consideration the categories suggested by Stokols (1981) for the analysis of social imageability of places in relation to aspects of both content (cognitive and affective) and form (complexity and clarity of cognitive contents). The results show systematic differences in the three place representations with particular reference to their nucleus, that is, the aspects which show greatest agreement (Bonnes and Secchiaroli, 1986; Bonnes et al., 1987a). The main results regarding the aspects of content of the nucleus of the three representations are summarized in Table 5.1.

The cognitive content of the three representations differs with regard to the characteristics of spatial delimitation of the area and of the elements composing the 'imaginal visualization' of each sub-place. A different incidence is noted between aspects of physical-'perceptual relevance' and aspects of 'social-meaning relevance' for the visual images of the three sub-places: the former dominate the nucleus of the representation of the centre and of the neighbourhood, although the pre-eminence of the type of elements differs – in the case of the centre, the elements are primarily concerned with the architectural structure of the place (buildings and monuments); in the case of the neighbourhood, they are primarily concerned with the functional structure (elements of the commercial and communication structure). The nucleus of the representation of the periphery is, on the contrary, much more vague at the physical-perceptual level, where aspects with 'social-meaning relevance' prevail, concerned with the elements of the 'atmosphere-context'.

Overall the representations of the centre and the neighbourhood seem much more linked to a defined and also differentiated physicality compared with the periphery, where the representation seems much more vague at the physical-spatial level. The representation of the centre seems to have an intermediate position between the 'realism' of the neighbourhood and the vagueness of the periphery.

On the one hand, the image of the centre is strongly linked to the physical-perceptual components related to its architectural-monumental structures; on the other, it is similar to the representation of the periphery due to the strong relevance that the vague traits of atmosphere-context assume, although with different cognitive-affective contents, that is, variety, beauty, history/antiquity, happiness and interest for the centre; sadness, poverty and monotony for the periphery.

A strong differentiation also emerges for the affective content of the three representations; above all a clear and contrasting polarization is found between the centre (primarily valued in a positive way) and the periphery (almost exclusively valued in a negative way).

The existence of a prevailing internal ambivalence is found in the representation of the neighbourhood of residence; a contradiction emerges between general evaluations (oriented positively) and the specific content of the imaginal representation (oriented negatively).

Thus, the formation of the representation of the neighbourhood of residence seems to present greater problems with regard to the possibility

Table 5.1 *Main characteristics of representations of three urban places*

Place	Spatial definition	Focal components of image	Affective/evaluative orientation	Dominant symbolic dimension in user–place relationship
Centre	Circumscribed within the confines of the most relevant historical area of the city (Aurelian walls); shifting towards neighbourhood	Elements of perceptual relevance (descriptive of architectural structure)	Area of positive polarization (on overall evaluation and on single relevant components)	'Aspecific-observative use': contemplative use diffused over different components of environment, but hardly linked with goal-oriented action
Periphery	Diffused/indeterminate; specified more by lines of demarcation than by delimitation of areas	Elements of meaning relevance (descriptive of atmosphere of the place)	Area of negative polarization (both levels)	'Non-use extraneousness' evoked by the place
Neighbourhood	Notably restricted compared with conventional borders; axial configuration, lengthened towards the centre	Elements of perceptual relevance (descriptive of functional structures)	Area of ambivalences/contradictions (overall positive evaluation; negative on components)	'Specific-instrumental use' which takes shape in terms of goal-oriented actions/uses

Source: Bonnes and Secchiaroli, 1986, p. 38

of integration of its affective and cognitive aspects, probably because the processes of 'place identity' are more involved with this urban sub-place than with the other two sub-places considered.

With regard to the formal aspects of the three representations, 'complexity' and 'clarity' were analysed: 'complexity' refers to the variety of environmental features comprising the cognitive content of the representations and 'clarity' pertains to the degree of sharing existing for the main cognitive contents of these representations. No differences in the complexity of the three place representations emerge, but the representation of the centre has greater overall clarity than the other two.

Furthermore, these place representations are strongly differentiated with regard to the perspectives of use and activity according to which a different symbolic-functional dimension emerges for each sub-place (Bonnes et al., 1990). This dimension can be defined (see Table 5.1) as mainly of 'aspecific-observative' use in the case of the centre, since it includes many activities not linked to the functional structure of the place, consisting more of 'looking around' or simply 'being in the place'; of 'specific-instrumental' use in the case of the neighbourhood, since it involves activities more related to the functional structure of the place (stores, public parks, sports facilities); and of 'non-use-extraneousness' in the case of the periphery, where the absence of functional activities emerges.

Analysis of the most shared aspects of these three place representations reveals some insights about the relationship the individual has with his/her urban environment. The differences shown for the nuclei of the three representations seem particularly appropriate for placing them within the theory of social representations in outlining various modalities according to which the place-city representation is constructed by the inhabitants.

The different representations identified seem to indicate reciprocal interdependencies, aimed at singling out the existence of a 'naïve theory of the city', that is, as predicted by the theory of social representations:

> . . . a system of notions, values and practices for the discovery and organization of reality (in this case, urban reality), in order to establish an order which allows individuals to orient themselves and master their material world (in this case the city), and facilitates communication between members of the community providing a code for naming and classifying. (Moscovici, 1961–76, p. xiii)

The various differences found in the nuclei of the urban sub-places' representations seem to indicate the possibility of considering these place representations as symbolic systems for differentiating and organizing the wide and complex urban environment with the aim of ordering it, that is, mastering it from the cognitive and affective point of view. On the basis of these preliminary results, the study has continued in various directions in order to investigate both the hypothesized aspects of interdependence between sub-places (Bonnes et al., 1990; and see pp. 192–7) and the connections between the most shared aspects and most personal aspects of the place representations (Mannetti et al., 1987; Bonnes et al., 1991a, 1991b). Specific investigations have taken up the representation of 'one's neighbourhood of residence', which seemed particularly problematic (Ardone et al., 1987; Bonnes et al., 1991a, 1991b), and the centre representation, which seems equally crucial in orienting inhabitants' urban representations.

The sub-place centre has emerged with particular relevance in other studies carried out in the city of Rome on the relationship between naïve knowledge and naming of the various parts of the city and official toponomy in use (subdivision of the city into thirty-four neighbourhoods and twenty districts) (Bagnasco, 1987).

Overall the results showed that social representation of the Roman urban area is weakly linked to the official toponomy of neighbourhoods and districts, contrary to what has been found for other large European cities, particularly Paris (Milgram and Jodelet, 1976).

The inhabitants' knowledge is often erroneous and confused with regard to naming and spatial localization of their neighbourhood. Instead, what we have defined as an 'improper toponymic naming' emerges with regard to the neighbourhoods, which tends to be used more than the official one. In any case, the representation of the city toponymy seems much more precise for the inhabitants at the level of naming – whether proper or improper – than that of spatial memory: the inhabitants' capacity to correctly locate the names of neighbourhoods and areas remembered verbally is very low.

If these results are compared with those regarding the history of various parts of the city and the relative toponymic subdivision (Bagnasco, 1987), it is found that the scarce clarity of representation, or social imageability of the various toponymic areas of the city, corresponds with low stability and historical continuity of the official toponymy.

It can also be noted that the places/parts of the city having greater clarity at the level of inhabitants' representation (EUR and Monte Sacro, centre) are also those that have greater continuity in the story of the city. Thus, a correspondence can be seen between the place representations of the city and the history of the city, that is, shared modalities in time of place actions. On the other hand, the tendency of urban representations to be differentiated in relation to some inhabitant peculiarities has been shown, such as gender and length of residence in the city; the representations are more confused for short-term and female inhabitants than for long-term and male inhabitants (Bonnes et al., 1987a).

Beside these studies pointing out the relevance of place-centre representations in orienting inhabitants' relationships with their urban environment, other aspects of place representations have been investigated in various studies – which we have already mentioned (see Chapter 4) – in several Italian cities (Milan, Bologna, Lecce).

In some cases the spatial characteristics of place representation were studied, referring to the location of the area (extension and focal point) and the types of elements characterizing the centre. In this way it was seen that the nucleus, in spatial terms, of this representation (also termed by us 'stereotyped centre') constitutes a very circumscribed zone, clearly focused on the main, central square, in the cities where the plan and urban history are strongly 'centralized' (that is, in Milan, Piazza Duomo, and in Bologna, Piazza Maggiore). In the case of cities where there is more than one symbolically relevant square, the nucleus of the representation presents less agreement and tends to unify these principal squares (in Rome, Piazza Venezia, Piazza Colonna and Piazza del Popolo and in Lecce, Piazza San Oronzo and Piazza Mazzini).

In any case this nucleus, which appears to refer to the areas with more symbolic meanings from both historical and architectural points of view, is much more circumscribed than the area officially considered the 'centre'. It has also been shown that besides this most shared area the overall representation tends to include a broad area in some cases extending beyond the conventional one.

However, systematic variations exist within this overall area on the sharing of the spatial representation, which appears connected to specific characteristics of the inhabitants. In particular, regardless of the city considered, the spatial representation of the centre tends to vary in the inhabitants in relation to the position of their residence, by sector and distance, with respect to the centre. Both the extension and the location of the area tend to be shifted in the direction of the inhabitants' residences; that is, the spatial representation tends to be shaped in a direction capable of reducing the distance between the point of residence and the area considered as the centre.

On the other hand, other characteristics of the inhabitants such as types of activities carried out and types of functional and affective meanings attributed to the centre have also been shown to influence the modalities of spatial representation, as have differences in socio-economic level and in length of residence. As already discussed (see Chapter 4), the more the centre is used actively, and not marginally, the more its spatial represen-tation is extended and complex (at the level of variety of imaginal elements present) and the less it coincides with the stereotyped centre, that is, with the maximum shared area at the representational level (Bonnes and Secchiaroli, 1982a, 1982b, 1983).

Overall the dynamic nature of the place-centre representations emerges from these studies, showing both the close connection between shared and individual aspects of this representation and its tendency to integrate cognitive, affective and behavioural aspects concerning this place experience.

On the other hand, similar results have been found in other studies involving other places (not only urban), such as a university campus in the United States in the representations of its students (Holahan and Bonnes, 1978) and a factory in the representations of the various categories of workers (Bonnes et al., 1980), discussed previously (see Chapter 4).

Place identity

The increasing interest of e.p. in cognitive, affective and motivational factors has revealed the complex nature of the relationships between individuals and their socio-physical environment. The growing emphasis on these factors has clearly supported a definition of person–environment relations in terms of 'interdependence' rather than of linear determinations. Since it is concerned with the relation between cognition and action, the theoretical construct of place proposed by Canter is particularly representative in this direction but it is not the only one worthy of attention.

Among others, Proshansky's (1978; Proshansky et al., 1979, 1983; Proshansky and Kaminoff, 1982) construct of 'place identity' offers a very promising perspective for research. In this case a particular centrality is assigned to the 'sense of belonging' in the definition of the relationship between individuals and the socio-physical environment, starting from the consideration of the latter as a multiplicity of 'places that define and structure day-to-day life'. Introducing the construct of place identity, the authors primarily focus attention on the role that can be played by the physical environment and its properties in processes of formation of the more comprehensive 'personal identity'. In this way they intend to fill what has been considered a relevant gap in the psychological theory on the development of identity (Fried, 1982).

According to Proshansky et al. (1983), the processes through which a person defines him/herself in a society are 'not restricted to making distinctions between oneself and significant others, but extend with no less importance to objects and things, and the very spaces and places in which they are found' (ibid., p. 57). Since places carry out a relevant role 'in the satisfaction of biological, psychological, social and cultural needs of the person' in the many situations faced in his/her lifetime, they assume the function of meaningful reference points in the processes of identity definition.

The limits these authors attribute to the classical theoretical principles guiding psychological research on self identity (see Mead, 1934; Erikson, 1950; Rosemberg, 1979) consist in the emphasis they have given to 'individual, interpersonal and group processes' as exclusive factors in the development of identity. Their critical position asserts that 'the subjective sense of the self is defined and expressed not simply by one's relationships to other people, but also by one's relationships to the various physical settings that define and structure day-to-day life' (Proshansky et al., 1983, p. 58). In support of this assertion, they point out the impact that phenomena such as deterioration of the neighbourhood, frequent change of residence and technological transformations of the surrounding landscape can have on self identity.

From these basic assumptions, Proshansky et al. move towards the perspective of integrating the study of developmental processes leading to the definition of self identity with the analysis of the more specific processes underlying the differentiation of places and their properties. Although the construct of place identity presents limits and incongruencies, which must still be clarified, it seems to offer interesting possibilities in this respect, particularly because it allows for a more specific and systematic approach to a problem also being confronted by geographers such as Relph (1976), Buttimer and Seamon (1980) and Tuan (1980).

In fact, what prevails in the latter cases is a phenomenological approach to the study of place identity. Following a similar approach, the conceptual definition of place identity recalls the idea of 'personal attachment' – or 'rootedness' – to places which are specified as precise geographical realities and which emphasize the 'sense of belonging' lived by the individual as the correlate of this attachment. This also involves an experience which the individual can be fully aware of only when the specific, necessary conditions are lacking. Only then may the experience become an object of reflection and, possibly, of more analytical definition.

According to Proshansky et al. (1983, p. 61), place identity is conceived instead as 'developed by thinking and speaking about places, through a process of distancing which allows for reflection and appreciation of places' and anchored to the particular possibility individuals have of perceiving and/or knowing that specific component of the self defined through interaction with the physical environment. In proposing a conceptual systematization for the notion of self, Neisser (1988) has more recently defined this component as the 'ecological self'.

Thus, contrasting the phenomenological approach in favour of a cognitive perspective, attention is oriented towards 'the wide range of person–physical setting experiences and relationships, based on a variety of physical contexts that from the moment of birth until death define people's day-to-day existence' (Proshansky et al., 1983, p. 62).

But, in carrying out relationships with the places in his/her own life context, the individual is not limited 'to experience and to record' the physical environment and its objective characteristics. Since individuals perform actions concerning the satisfaction of needs, what enters into the field are primarily values, attitudes and beliefs about the physical world in more general terms, that is, what can be expected of it and what assumes positive or negative valency. According to Proshansky et al., this is the way the physical environment and its characteristics become effective reference points for 'defining and integrating place identity' in the individual.

The ideas and feelings that individuals structure during the course of their many life experiences constitute a sort of matrix that can be anchored both to specific environmental settings and to more general typologies of settings. This is also the reason why place identity can be considered as 'sub-structure of the self identity of the person consisting of broadly conceived cognitions about the physical world in which the individual lives' (ibid., p. 59). The 'environmental past' is placed at the centre of these cognitions and defined as the totality of references to 'places, to spaces and to the relative properties' which have best contributed to the satisfaction of the person's needs. The centrality of this past implies that place identity is equivalent not to the development of a sense of belonging to particular places, but to a system of references regarding the environmental experience individuals structure over time; nor must it be considered as a premise for a 'stable' place identity, defined once and for all. In fact, the approach proposed by Proshansky et al. is based on a 'person who considers himself involved in transactions with a world in continuous change' (ibid., p. 59). In this sense, the past also contains the history of significant changes in the environment; parallel to these, changes emerge in the contents of individuals' place identity.

Place identity as cognitive system and its functions As 'personal construction' that accomplishes the more general integrative functions of the self, place identity is specifically defined as a 'cognitive sub-structure of self-identity [which consists] of an endless variety of cognitions related to the past, present, and anticipated physical settings that define and circumscribe the day-to-day existence of the person' (Proshansky et al. 1983, p. 62). These cognitions develop by means of a 'selective involvement of the person with his environment' and possess the typical characteristics of every other cognitive structure, first of all that of being organized in an interconnected way.

The structure of place identity is described as a grouping of cognitions regarding 'a complex of physical setting related clusters of cognitions in which component cognitions of a given cluster are related to each other, and also, to a greater or lesser degree, to the component cognitions of other clusters' (ibid.).

As the outcome of individual cognitive functioning, this double order of correlations mirrors not only how the individual 'habitually experiences' different places, but the relations he/she establishes through the daily actions carried out in these places.

Like every other cognitive system, place identity is meant to accomplish the 'cognitive backdrop' function which enables people to 'recognize' what they 'see, think and feel in their situation-to-situation transactions with the physical world' (ibid., p. 66). It primarily allows for discrimination between what is familiar and what is not familiar in different environments. Serving as cognitive reference points for comparisons between old and new, between what is known and what is perceived, place identity functions as a framework for the positioning of the various places and respective properties within broader and known categories. In this way individuals are assisted in maintaining a sense of continuity of their own self over time, even when changing environments.

Attempting to further clarify these primary functions of place identity, Proshansky et al. point out that the processes which generate it resolve not only problems of 'recognition' of facts but also those of 'understanding its intended purposes and activities in relation to its design and other substantive properties'. In this sense place identity becomes 'the source of meaning for a given setting by virtue of relevant cognitive clusters that indicate what should happen in it, what the setting is supposed to be like, and how the individual and others are supposed to behave in it' (ibid., p. 67).

Referring to 'meaningful environments', the authors not only indicate the knowledge people acquire about how to behave themselves and what to expect (in a strictly functional sense) from specific settings, but they also consider the 'symbolic and affective associations between the individual and the various parts of the physical environment'. Both are in any case considered as 'culturally transmitted and integrated into the place identity of the individual through his or her own experiences in the physical world' (ibid., p. 68). In this sense, they are subject to being shared with others either in terms of wide diffusion or as an expression of the specificity of some particular social groups.

The social dimension of place identity   To live in an environment does not mean structuring experiences only with respect to its physical reality. In fact, 'meanings and social beliefs' are always attributed to the physical environment both by those living in it and by those external to it. This is the reason why Proshansky et al. emphasize that there is no 'physical environment that is not also a social environment and vice versa', and point out the two connected indicators that confirm the role played by the social dimension in specifying the physical components of place identity. The first one consists in some basic 'uniformities' which result from belonging to a certain culture; the other concerns some 'differentiations' manifesting themselves within the same culture and linked to the specificity of different social groups.

It is in relation to these types of considerations that 'cognitive *clusters*', by means of which these authors describe the structure of place identity, become something more than a system of memories, feelings and personal interpretations about single physical settings. In the organization of these clusters, an important role is assigned to the 'social definitions of settings that consist of the norms, behaviors, rules and regulations that are inherent in the use of these places and spaces'. But it is also pointed out that 'however "physical" or objectively real, these settings are inextricably tied to the social and cultural existence of a group, as expressed by its valued activities, interpersonal relationships and individual and group role functions' (ibid., p. 64).

Stated in other terms, this means that the place identity of different groups in a certain society and culture is not to be taken only as differentiated with respect to the 'uses and experiences of space and place', but also with respect to the 'corresponding variations in the social values, meanings and ideas which underlie the use of those spaces' (ibid., p. 64).

The basic point of the described differentiation is identified in the 'major social roles and social attributes that distinguish different groups of individuals in our society (e.g., sex, occupation, social class, etc.)'. These roles and attributes are, in fact, considered 'the conceptual nexus for understanding the development of self identity via the socialization process that goes on throughout the life cycle'. The cognitions on which place identity is structured are in turn seen as the 'expression and reflection of physical settings and their properties that support and are directly relevant to the social roles and attributes that define who the person is, how he or she is to behave, and what he or she is worth' (ibid., p. 80).

On the basis of these considerations, the authors also emphasize how the construct of place identity can be used for describing the double possibility that cognitions of a given setting assume positive and/or negative valency. According to them, the first of these alternatives is linked to the degree of learned 'personal adaptability' to the physical and social characteristics of the environment. A good degree of adaptability would imply positive cognitions when individuals, faced with adverse socio-physical conditions, are oriented towards a perspective of 'transformation' to these conditions.

Within these conceptual references, the social dimension affects place identity primarily as a normative background; this is the same kind of background in which the more general processes of development-socialization bring individuals to define their own self identity. More recently, along these same lines, Proshansky and Fabian (1987) further investigated the analysis by paying particular attention to the development of place identity in childhood.

Starting from the more general interest in material objects and in the meanings they can assume in the life of individuals, other authors have pointed to the central role these objects can play in the definition of identity. Csikszentmihalyi and Rochberg-Halton (1981) have called attention to the fact that human history is broken down into periods by assuming as reference points 'things', or artefacts, such as iron and bronze. Investigating a sample of families in the United States, these authors have empirically reconstructed hierarchies of importance attributed to daily life objects. They found that even though they are differentiated by generation (children, parents, grandparents), these hierarchies have in common the centrality assigned in all three cases to the place-home. The subjects studied tended in particular to attribute a significance of safety to it and, in this way, focused on a relevant component for the definition of personal identity.

The growing interest that environmental-psychological research has dedicated to the place-home, with the aim of clarifying the complex relationships established between individuals and their own socio-physical environment, has led various authors to assume several of the main references offered by the concept of place identity (Giuliani et al., 1988; Giuliani, 1989; Feldman, 1990). In this direction, an attempt has been made to focus on the 'stable' or 'open to change' nature of the 'attachment' individuals establish with their own home. In particular,

Feldman (1990) has investigated this question with regard to the high residential mobility during the life cycle of the American population. The results from these studies have led the author to point out that it is not with a specific and familiar domestic environment that individuals establish psychological (cognitive-affective) links as much as with 'typologies of environmental settings' which ensure the presence of certain characteristics in any geographical area. What seems to play a crucial role is not the issue of individual familiarization with a physical setting but primarily the issue of the 'perspectives and collective practices' it is possible to achieve in that setting.

In research concerning the urban environment, particular attention has recently been dedicated to the interconnections between meanings the place-home can assume and the more general attributions of meaning that different social categories (by age, sex, socio-professional conditions and types of environmental activities carried out) structure with regard to one's total life environment in the city (Bonnes et al., 1990, 1991a).

The overall relevance that Proshansky et al.'s perspective assumes in environmental-psychological research must be outlined first of all in theoretical-methodological terms. The perspective clearly moves from a question in many ways analogous to the one other authors have defined in terms of 'attachment' and/or 'dependence' of individuals on places. But it is equally clear how the construct of place identity implies a specific consideration and analysis of the psychological processes that mediate the complex relationship, which is established and evolves over time, between individuals and their own socio-physical environment. Since Proshansky et al. have chosen to explain these processes in the light of the psychological theory of identity, their proposal is consistent with one of the most emblematic thematic areas in current (primarily European) psycho-social research. In this sense it may be considered a promising point of encounter between social psychology and e.p.

Starting from the basic classical references for the construct of self (Mead, 1934) and identity (Gordon, 1968; Gergen, 1971), social psychology has more recently articulated a substantial debate in this regard. In particular, a series of theoretical specifications have emerged which emphasize the crucial position occupied by identity between individual processes and social dynamics (Tajfel, 1981; Turner, 1981). In the light of these premises the proposal advanced by Proshansky et al. seems to offer space for the development of several of the possibilities the concept of place identity has for now only outlined. As has emerged from some reviews (Carugati, 1979) and as Palmonari (1989) has recently pointed out, orienting oneself in the vast and often contradictory literature on the notion of identity has not been an easy task even for social psychology. One of the basic problems is the fact that this notion seems to refer to many conceptual categories which are at times also very different from each other. A clarification Palmonari considers particularly useful for this purpose derives from the preliminary distinction between the two main modalities for proceeding to the conceptualization of identity: the first refers to the experience that the individual lives in terms of 'continuity of the self, over time and space, and of one's possibility of intervening autonomously (even if in a limited way) in the environment and the events in any given moment'. The second, instead, entrusts to the 'public image' (and, thus, to external criteria regarding personal history and experience) the definition of the 'precise place occupied by the individual in society' (Palmonari, 1989, p. 146); in this case 'types of identity' are defined as products of specific social structures (see Berger and Luckmann, 1966).

Although both of these conceptions present identity as a phenomenon emerging from the relationship/confrontation individuals establish with and practise in their own environment, the position and the role attributed to the individual in that relationship is very different in the two cases. When the sense of identity is emphasized, margins of 'freedom' remain open for the individual's active participation in interaction with the socio-physical environment and, thus, for the consideration of the 'constructive' nature of the transactions on which identity is structured and maintained in its various components. In contrast, when the perspective of typification is adopted, the deterministic function of the social environment becomes the major focus and identity can only be analysed as an expression of the adaptive processes to the environment which the individual will tend to undergo.

According to Codol (1980), identity, considered as experience of continuity of the self, designates a synthesis of all the cognitions regarding the relationship between the self and the objects of the physical and social world. In this sense, identity can be considered as the result of a socio-cognitive process that includes 'the whole knowledge, and its temporal evolutions, about oneself in the different relations with the world' (Palmonari, 1989, p. 145). As a consequence identity becomes one of the 'social factors [. . .] coming from the person-actor' which also 'control the action (or behavior toward aims)' (ibid., p. 147). Doise (1988) is also particularly representative of this perspective, even though he has investigated the topic of identity and of the self as correlated with relations between groups or social categories. In fact, one of the first conclusions this author draws from his broad and systematic research concerns the socio-cognitive nature of the processes controlling the formation and maintenance of identity. With particular reference to the construct an individual has of him/herself, he points out the important function of this construct as 'organizing principle of symbolic relations between social agents', and advances the proposal of considering and studying identity as a 'social representation' (Doise, 1988, p. 107).

From intra-place to multi-place

What we have discussed until now on the one hand points to the crucial role that the construct of place has assumed in recent years in e.p., and on the other illustrates several directions environmental-psychological research is taking in order to construct a theory of place able to give greater homogeneity and theoretical consistency to the field. It has also been shown that the more environmental-psychological research is supported by the construct of place, the more it tends to assume the psycho-social perspective.

Another perspective emerging from the most recent literature seems important for constructing the above-mentioned theory of place: this perspective can be variously defined as 'inter-place' or 'multi-place' or 'place system'; and until now it has only been explored initially (Rapoport, 1986, 1990; Bonnes et al., 1990, 1991b). This perspective aims at contributing to the theory of place by proposing a shift from the intra-place view, that is, centred on one place, to a broader, multi-place perspective. Single places are not treated separately but each place is situated within a broader 'place system', that is, within a complex of other places that seem more directly linked with it. In this way, the single place is situated within broader 'multi-place systems', in order to single out the most shared and most personal modalities the various sub-places tend to be linked with, through the relationships individuals establish with them. Thus, it also becomes possible to define different features of the multi-place systems in relation to the characteristics of both the places treated and the persons involved.

The point of departure for this perspective is the consideration of the 'organized' nature of the place-experience for the individual; that is, places tend to be connected at the level of both individual and collective experience. Russell and Ward (1982, p. 654) observe: 'The environment [. . .] is a complex of immediate and distant places, psychologically arranged into a hierarchy such that each place is part of a larger place and can be subdivided into smaller places.' In this way some main relations between places can be distinguished, such as those of inclusion/exclusion and nearness/farness; both these relations can be found at a spatial or categorial level: one place can be spatially included/excluded or near/far from another. For example, the neighbourhood is included in the city, and the periphery is excluded from the centre of the city; or the city centre can be near or far from a particular neighbourhood. On the contrary, in a categorial and non-spatial sense a place can be included/excluded or near/far from another; for example, two squares of two different cities can be close in a categorial sense even though they are far in a spatial sense.

Relations of inclusion allow for the distinction of sub-places, in the case of places included within broader places – spatially or categorially. The latter represent supra-places; for example, the city is a supra-place compared to the neighbourhood and the centre, which, in this case, represent sub-places.

On the basis of these premises it seems possible to affirm, in line with Bronfenbrenner's (1979) proposals for psychological development, that the experience of place tends to be organized for the person according to different levels; these include progressively broader systems of relations of place to be understood as included one within the other and in reciprocal relationship, but distinguishable from each other.

It would seem that the first-level relations regard what can be defined as the place 'microsystem', constituted by the relationship the person has with a single place (or single places), or better with the single sub-place, since the micro-level always tends to be inside a broader unit of place.

The successive level is what can be defined as the place 'mesosystem' or multi-place system; this system derives from the connections between the various microsystems of sub-places to form a broader place.

The place 'exosystem' level is reached when the relationships between the single place-system and broader place systems or supra-places are considered, to arrive at the 'macrosystem', regarding the 'macro-level', which includes all the preceding levels of place (see Chapter 2, pp. 53–8) This general framework includes the tendency of the person to organize his/her own place experience in a multi-place sense, that is, linking or, better, integrating the various levels of the different place systems implicated through his/her own experience/action in the socio-physical environment.

This framework is primarily a hypothetical suggestion for the development of future lines of research, given that the multi-place perspective is still mostly to be developed; however, various attempts are emerging in the literature (Canter, 1977; Rapoport, 1986, 1990; Bonnes et al., 1990, 1991b). Our recent studies have been particularly oriented in this direction. We have been attempting to investigate people's relationships with urban places, assuming as point of departure the above-mentioned 'inter-place' perspective, or aiming at outlining the ways in which the city as a whole tends to figure as a multi-place system for its inhabitants (Bonnes et al., 1990, 1991b).

We have primarily been analysing the micro-level of urban sub-places, represented in particular by 'home', 'neighbourhood', 'centre' and 'periphery' places, in order to arrive at the consideration of the place mesosystem represented by the city as a whole.

The studies conducted until now have examined the urban environment of a large city (Rome) and a medium-size city (Lecce). The fact that these two cities also belong to different geographical-regional areas (a central region in the first case and a southern one in the second) might also allow extension of the analysis to the 'esosystem' level, which can be identified here in relation to the different geographical-regional positions of the cities. The relationship of the inhabitants to the various urban sub-places has been studied by considering the type of activities or, according to Rapoport (1990), the 'system of activities' carried out by them in the urban sub-places considered (home, neighbourhood, centre, periphery).

In every city a heterogeneous sample (for age, sex and socio-economic level) of inhabitants was examined; all were residents in the same neighbourhood, situated in an intermediate position between the centre and the periphery of the city. The analysis was carried out in successive phases to investigate first the level of the place microsystem, according to a primarily 'intra-place' perspective relative to each place considered. Then the place mesosystem was examined to show the modalities with which the various sub-places are connected in the system of activities carried out by the inhabitants. Finally, we outlined the characteristics of the multi-place system represented by the city for the various inhabitants, in relation to the characteristics of both the sub-places involved and the inhabitants considered. In order to emphasize that the study was not so much focused on individual intra-place activities as much as on the system of these activities organized in an inter-place sense, the term 'place pragmatics' was proposed analogously to the way this term has been used in psycholinguistics (Bates, 1976; Levinson, 1983), because of the implicit assumption, in both cases, with regard to the character (goal-oriented also in a relational sense) of human activity (whether linguistic or place-specific).

This research has revealed various relevant aspects for the inter-place perspective and in particular for the consideration of the place-city in the multi-place sense. For example, it has been shown that the various sub-places tend to be connected through specific intra-place and inter-place dimensions of activity, capable of articulating the most shared modalities of activity relative to each of these sub-places.

In particular, this research has revealed the crucial role that places of residence (the home and the neighbourhood) have in the organization of the entire system of activities or 'urban pragmatics' of the inhabitants. Each of the main dimensions of intra-place activity of the centre and of the periphery appears to be regulated as a function of the specific dimensions of activities carried out in the places of residence. That is, the inhabitants seem to carry out specific activities in the centre or in the periphery according to the type of activity carried out at home and in the neighbourhood, just as they seem to carry out particular activities in the neighbourhood in relation to the more specific ones carried out at home. In both of the cities, the tendency to have many, varied activities in the centre (both of 'specific use', that is, connected to the use of the functional structures of the place, and of 'aspecific/evasive use', that is, not connected to these functional structures) is accompanied by an 'open', not 'closed', practice with regard to places of residence. This refers to Altman et al.'s (Altman and Gauvain, 1981) proposal about the existence of a main 'dialectical dimension' of 'openness/closedness' with which people orient themselves in the socio-physical environment, allowing the access of others to the self in the first case and impeding it in the second case (see Chapter 4). Here 'residential closedness' coincides with exclusive withdrawal and confinement to the home, while openness coincides with a limited use of the home – only in a socializing way (for receiving friends) – and a multi-use of the neighbourhood, with particular reference to its open spaces (green areas) and facilities for sports activities.

The 'aspecific/evasive' activities carried out in the centre (that is, not connected to its functional structures, such as, for example, walking, seeing beautiful things, being in the midst of people) are, especially in the large city, connected to the tendency to live in a 'closed' way, that is, confined to the home, in places of residence. In this case, for this type of inhabitant, who tends to be confined to the home, the perspective of use of the centre seems aimed at re-establishing the urban sociability rendered precarious by excessive residential closedness.

It has also been shown that, in both cities considered, inhabitants tend to organize their 'urban pragmatics' as a function of two main urban sub-places, which are different in relation to inhabitants' age, sex and socio-economic level: the home and the neighbourhood (especially for women who are not particularly young), the home and the centre (especially for the higher socio-economic levels), and the neighbourhood and the centre (especially for the young). Those inhabitants who have urban pragmatics regarding more than two places are in the minority. However, there are also groups that tend to live almost exclusively in only one of these various sub-places (mono-place urban pragmatics), or only in the home (the elderly of low socio-economic level), or only in the centre (the very young). Overall these groups show a 'marginal' relationship with the city.

Generally the city as a multi-place system presents different characteristics of spatial extension, differentiation and complexity shaped according to the different urban pragmatics of its inhabitants.

These urban pragmatics seem mainly differentiated in relation to the inhabitants' orientation either towards integration or towards urban 'marginality/confinement'. The various activities carried out seem to differ with regard to the 'type of action orientation', 'level of specificity', 'intra-urban mobility' and 'social exchange' performed through these activities. Together with urban integration, with respect to marginality, the orientation towards 'doing' rather than towards 'not doing' (type of action orientation) prevails, that is, 'use-specific' activities compared to 'use-aspecific' ones (degree of specificity), high intra-urban mobility compared to immobility (degree of intra-urban mobility) and interactive social exchange compared to its absence (degree of 'social exchange').

Furthermore, in both cities, a 'trajectory of urban pragmatics' in relation to age can be clearly seen. This seems to begin in post-adolescence with a phase of withdrawal, characterized by escape from places of residence (home and neighbourhood), with parallel interest concentrated in the centre, pursued for non-specific reasons; it is a simple physical occupation rather than an active and specific use of its functional structures.

With increasing age (until thirty-five), a condition of greater urban integration emerges, with a more specific and varied use of the centre; at the same time a partial return towards places of residence occurs, that is, the neighbourhood only for sports activities, home only for receiving friends. If the socio-economic level is sufficiently high, there is an increase in the tendency to use the centre for specific reasons and with qualified intentions (for example, cultural use), together with the capacity to appreciate time passed at home.

However, with increasing age, this new found interest in places of residence includes the risk of a new urban confinement – especially for women – which, in large cities, tends to lead to the complete domestic mono-place confinement of the elderly.

Overall, as can be deduced from this, the multi-place perspective seems capable of offering many interesting starting points for the development of the theory of place. Only the results of future research, oriented in this sense, will be able to tell just how profitable this direction is for the further development of environmental psychology or, as we prefer to say, with other authors (Canter et al., 1988), of an environmental social psychology.

References

Abelson, R.P. (1981), 'Psychological Status of the Script Concept', in *American Psychologist*, 36, pp. 715–29.

Acking, C.A. and Kuller, R. (1973), 'Presentation and Judgement of Planned Environment and the Hypothesis of Arousal', in A.F. Preiser (ed.), *Environmental Design Research*, vol. 1, *Selected Papers*, Proceedings of the 4th International Environmental Design Research Association Conference, Dowden, Hutchinson & Ross, Stroudsburg, PA, pp. 72–83.

Acredolo, L.P. (1978), 'Development of Spatial Orientation in Infancy', in *Development Psychology*, 14, pp. 224–34.

Acredolo, L.P., Pick, H.I. and Olsen, M.G. (1975), 'Environmental Differentiation and Familiarity as Determinants of Children's Memory for Spatial Location', in *Developmental Psychology*, 11, pp. 495–501.

Ahrentzen, S. and Evans, G.W. (1984), 'Distraction, Privacy and Classroom Design', in *Environment and Behavior*, 16, pp. 437–54.

Aiello, J.R. (1980), 'When Compensation Fails: Mediating Effects of Sex and Locus of Control at Extended Interaction Distances', in *Basic and Applied Social Psychology*, 1, pp. 65–82.

Ainsworth, M.D.S., Blehar, M.C., Waters, F. and Wall, S. (1978), *Patterns of Attachment: A Psychological Study of Strange Situation*, Lawrence Erlbaum, Hillsdale, NJ.

Allport, F.H. (1955), *Theories of Perceptions and the Concept of Structure*, Wiley, New York.

Allport, G. and Pettigrew, T. (1957), 'Cultural Influence on the Perception of Movement: the Trapezoidal Illusion among the Zulu', in *Journal of Abnormal and Social Psychology*, 55, pp. 104–13.

Altman, I. (1973), 'Some Perspectives on the Study of Man-Environment Phenomena', in W. Preiser (ed.), *Environment and Design Research Association Fourth International Conference*, vol. 1, *Selected Papers*, Dowden, Hutchinson & Ross, Stroudsburg, PA, pp. 99–113.

Altman, I. (1975), *The Environment and Social Behavior: Privacy, Personal Space, Territoriality and Crowding*, Brooks/Cole, Monterey, CA.

Altman, I. (1976), 'Environmental Psychology and Social Psychology', in *Personality and Social Psychology Bulletin*, 2, pp. 96–113.

Altman, I. (1986), 'Theoretical Issues in Environmental Psychology', paper presented to the 21st IAAP Congress, Jerusalem.

Altman, I. (1988), 'Process, Transactional/Contextual and Outcome Research: an Alternative to the Traditional Distinction between Basic and Applied Research', in *Social Behaviour*, 3, pp. 259–80.

Altman, I. and Chemers, M.M. (1980), *Culture and Environment*, Brooks/Cole, Monterey, CA.

Altman, I. and Gauvain, M. (1981), 'A Cross-Cultural and Dialectic Analysis of Homes', in L. Liben, A. Patterson and N. Newcomb (eds), *Spatial Representation and Behavior across the Life-Span: Theory and Application*, Academic Press, New York.

Altman, I. and Rogoff, B. (1987), 'World Views in Psychology: Trait, Interactional, Organismic and Transactional Perspectives', in D. Stokols and I. Altman (eds), *Handbook of Environmental Psychology*, vol. 1, Wiley, New York, pp. 7–40.

Ames, A. (1955), *An Interpretative Manual: The Nature of Our Perceptions, Comprehensions and Behavior*, Princeton University Press, Princeton.

Ames, A. (1960), *The Morning Notes of Adalbert Ames* (posthumous vol. ed. by H. Cantril), Rutgers University Press, New Brunswik, NJ.

Andorka, R. (1987), 'Time Budgets and Their Uses', in *Annual Review of Sociology*, 13, pp. 149–64.

Antil, J.H. and Bennet, P.D. (1979), 'Construction and Validation of a Scale to Measure Socially Responsible Consumption Behavior', in K.E. Henion and T.C. Kinnear (eds), *The Conserver Society*, American Marketing Association, Chicago.

Appley, N.H. and Turnbull, R. (1967), *Psychological Stress: Issues in Research*, Appleton-Century-Crofts, New York.

Appleyard, D. (1969), 'Why Buildings Are Known', in *Environment and Behavior*, 1, p. 131.

Appleyard, D. (1970), 'Styles and Methods of Structuring a City', in *Environment and Behavior*, 2, pp. 100–18.

Appleyard, D. (1973), 'Professional Priorities for Environmental Psychology', in R. Kuller (ed.), *Architectural Psychology: Proceedings of the Lund Conference 1973*, Dowden, Hutchinson & Ross, Stroudsburg, PA.

Appleyard, D., Lynch, K and Meyer, J.R. (1964), *The View from the Road*, MIT Press, Cambridge, MA.

Aragones, J.I. and Arredondo, J.M. (1985), 'Structure of Urban Cognitive Maps', in *Journal of Environmental Psychology*, 5, pp. 197–212.

Arca Petrucci, M. and Gaddini, S. (1985), 'Introduzione', in G. Gold, *Introduzione alla geografia del comportamento*, Franco Angeli, Milan.

Archea, J. (ed.) (1967–9), *Architectural Psychology Newsletter*, University of Utah, Salt Lake City.

Archea, J. (1977), 'The Place of Architectural Factors in Behavioral Theories of Privacy', in *Journal of Social Issues*, 33 (3), pp. 116–37.

Archea, J. and Esser, A.H. (1969), *Man–Environment Systems*, Association for the Study of Man–Environment Relations, Orangesburg, NY.

Ardone, R.G., de Rosa, A.M., Bonnes, M. and Secchiaroli, M. (1987), 'Dimensioni valutative del proprio quartiere de residenza, per uno studio de "congruenza ambientale"', in E. Bianchi, F. Perussia and M.F. Rossi (eds), *Immagine soggettiva e ambiente: Problemi, applicazioni e strategie de ricerca*, Unicopli, Milan, pp. 207–17.

Ardrey, R. (1966), *The Territorial Imperative*, Atheneum, New York.

Argyle, M. and Dean, J. (1965), 'Eye-Contact, Distance and Affiliation', in *Sociometry*, 28, pp. 289–304.

Argyle, M., Furnham, A. and Graham, J.A. (1981), *Social Situations*, Cambridge University Press, Cambridge.

Asch, S.E. (1952), *Social Psychology*, Prentice Hall, Englewood Cliffs, NJ.

Axia, G. (1986), *La mente ecologica: La conoscenza della mente nel bambino*, Giunti Barbera, Florence.

Bachelard, G. (1969), *The Poetics of Space*, Bacon Press, Boston (original edn. 1958).

Bagnara, S. and Misiti, R. (1978), *Psicologia ambientale*, Il Mulino, Bologna.

Bagnasco, C. (1987), 'La toponomastica romana: caratteristiche e sviluppo storico', in M. Bonnes (ed.), *Ecologia urbana applicata alla città di Roma*. Programma UNESCO MAB no. 11, Progress Report no. 3, Istituto Psicologia CNR, Rome, pp. 33–72.

Bagnasco, C. and Bonnes, M. (1991), 'Citizen's Participation in the Improvement of the Urban Environment in Italy', in T. Deelstra and O. Yanitzky (eds), *Cities of Europe: the Public's Role in Shaping the Urban Environment*. Mezhdumarodnye Otnoshenia, Moscow, pp. 135–49.

Bailey, R., Branch, C.H. and Taylor, C.H. (eds) (1961), *Architectural Psychology and Psychiatry*, University of Utah, Salt Lake City.

Bailly, A.S. (1981), 'La géographie de la perception dans le monde francophone: une prospective historique', in *Geographica Helvetica*, 36, pp. 14–21.

Baird, J.C., Wagner, M. and Noma, F. (1982), 'Impossible Cognitive Spaces', in *Geographical Analysis*, 14, pp. 204–16.

Baker, A., Davis, R. and Silvadon, P. (1960), *Psychiatric Services and Architecture*, World Health Organization, Geneva.

Barbey, G. (1976), 'The Appropriation of Home Space', in P. Korosec-Serfaty (ed.), *Appropriation of Space*, Proceedings of Third International Architectural Psychology Conference, Louis Pasteur University, Strasburg, pp. 215–328.

Barbey, G. (1990), *L'évasion domestique*, Presse Polytecnique et Universitaires Romandes, Lausanne.

Barker, M.I. (1976), 'Planning for Environmental Indices: Observer Appraisal of Air Quality', in K.H. Craik and E.H. Zube (eds), *Perceiving Environmental Quality: Research and Applications*, Plenum, New York, pp. 215–328.

Barker, R.G. (1960), 'Ecology of Motivation', in M.R. Jones (ed.), *Nebraska Symposium on Motivation*, vol. 8, University of Nebraska Press, Lincoln, pp. 1–49.

Barker, R.G. (1965), 'Explorations in Ecological Psychology', in *American Psychologist*, 20, pp. 1–14.

Barker, R.G. (1968), *Ecological Psychology: Concepts and Methods for Studying the Environment of Human Behavior*, Stanford University Press, Stanford.

Barker, R.G. (1987), 'Prospecting Environmental Psychology: Oskaloosa Revisited', in D. Stokols and I. Altman (eds), *Handbook of Environmental Psychology*, vol. 2, Wiley, New York, pp. 1413–32.

Barker, R.G. (1990), 'Recollections of the Midwest Psychological Field Station', in *Environment and Behavior*, 22 (4), pp. 503–13.

Barker, R.G. and Gump, P.V. (1964), *Big School, Small School: High School Size and Students Behavior*, Stanford University Press, Stanford, CA.

Barker, R.G. and Schoggen, P. (1973), *Qualities of Community Life: Methods of Measuring Environment and Behavior Applied to an American and English Town*, Jossey Bass, San Francisco.

Barker, R.G. and Wright, H.F. (1951), *One Boy's Day*, Harper & Row, New York.

Barker, R.G. and Wright, H.F. (1955), *Midwest and Its Children: the Psychological Ecology of an American Town*, Harper & Row, New York.

Baroni, M.R. and Mainardi Peron, E. (1987), 'Descriptions of an Urban Route in a Natural Setting: Effects of Familiarity', poster at the 2nd European Conference for Research on Learning and Instruction, Tübingen.

Baroni, M.R. and Mainardi Peron, E. (1991), 'Conveying Environmental Knowledge through Language: Methodological Issues', paper presented to the International Workshop on 'Home Environment: Physical Space and Psycho-Social Processes', Cortona, Italy.

Bartlett, F.C. (1932), *Remembering*, Cambridge University Press, Cambridge.

Bates, E. (1976), *Language and Context: the Acquisition of Pragmatics*, Academic Press, New York.

Baum, A. and Koman, S. (1976), 'Differential Response to Anticipated Crowding: Psychological Effects of Social and Spatial Density', in *Journal of Personality and Social Psychology*, 34, pp. 526–36.

Baum, A. and Paulus, P. (1987), 'Crowding', in D. Stokols and I. Altman (eds), *Handbook of Environmental Psychology*, vol. 1 Wiley, New York, pp. 553–69.

Baum, A. and Valins, S. (1977) *Architecture and Social Behavior: Psychological Studies of Social Density*, Lawrence Erlbaum, Hillsdale, NJ.

Baum, A., Singer, J.F. and Baum, C. (1982), 'Stress and the Environment', in G.W. Evans (ed.), *Environmental Stress*, Cambridge University Press, New York.

Bechtel, R.B. (1977), *Enclosing Behavior*, Dowden, Hutchinson & Ross, Stroudsburg, PA.

Bechtel, R.B. (1988), 'Back to the Future . . . Again. A Perspective on Ecological Psychology', *Looking Back to the Future, Proceedings of IAPS 10th Conference*, Delft University Press, Delft, pp. 87–91.

Becker, F.D. (1981), *Work Space: Creating Environments in Organizations*, Praeger, New York.

Bell, P.A., Fisher, J.D. and Loomis, R.J. (1978) *Environmental Psychology*, W.B. Saunders, Philadelphia.

Bennet, C. (1977), *Spaces for People: Human Factors in Design*, Prentice Hall, Englewood Cliffs, NJ.

Berger, P.I. and Luckmann, T. (1966), *The Social Construction of Reality*, Doubleday, New York.

Berlyne, D.F. (1960), *Conflict, Arousal, Curiosity*, McGraw-Hill, New York.

Bernard, Y. and Bonnes, M. (1985), 'Strutturazione, organizzazione, animazione dello spazio domestico', in A. Piromallo and R. Savarese (ed.), *Oggetti, arredamento e comunicazione*, Liguori, Naples.

Bernard, Y., Lebeau, O., Giuliani, M.V. and Bonnes, M. (1987), 'Pratiques de l'habitat et mondes sociaux: Recherche comparative', in *Psychologie Française*, 32 (1/2), pp. 65–75.

Bianchi, E. (1980), 'Da Lowenthal a Downs a Fremon: Aspetti della geografia della percezione', in *Rivista Geografica Italiana*, 1–2, pp. 97–107.

Blundell, V. (1983), 'Comments', in *Current Anthropology*, 24, p. 58.

Bollnow, O. (1967), 'Life-Space', in N. Lawrence and D. O'Connor (eds), *Readings in Existential Phenomenology*, Prentice Hall, Englewood Cliffs, NJ.

Bonnes, M. (1977), 'Profilo dell'emergente psicologia ambientale', paper presented to the XVIIth SIPS Congress, Viareggio.

Bonnes, M. (1978), 'L'emergenza della psicologia ambientale: Verso un nuovo ambientalismo?', in *Rivista di Psicologia*, 1–2, pp. 97–107.

Bonnes, M. (1979a), 'Profilo critico dell'emergente psicologia ambientale', in *Ricerche di Psicologia*, 10, pp. 161–89.

Bonnes, M. (1979b), 'Il problema del rapporto tra psicologia ambientale e progettazione attraverso l'esame di alcuni risultati di recerca in tema di insoddisfazione circa l'ambiente residenziale', in G.A. Della Rocca and B.F. Padula (eds), *Atti del seminario su Insoddisfazione ambientale negli insediamenti umani*, Fondazione Aldo Della Rocca – Programma MAB-UNESCO, Rome, pp. 62–81.

Bonnes, M. (1980), 'La rappresentazione cognitiva dello spazio ambientale come possibile "concetto cerniera" tra lo psichico ed il sociale', in P. Amerio and G.P. Quaglino (eds), *Mente e società nella ricerca psicologica*, Book Store, Turin, pp. 235–51.

Bonnes, M. (1984), 'Mobilizing Scientists, Planners and Local Community in a Large-Scale Urban Situation: the Rome Case Study', in F. di Castri, F.W. Baker and M. Hadley (eds), *Ecology in Practice*, Tycooly, Dublin, vol. 2, pp. 52–67.

Bonnes, M. (1986), 'An Ecological Approach to Urban Environment Perception', in D. Frick (ed.), *The Quality of Urban Life*, Walter de Gruyter, Berlin, pp. 189–202.

Bonnes, M. (ed.) (1987), *Urban Ecology Applied to the City of Rome*, MAB-UNESCO Project 11, Progress Report no. 3, Istituto Psicologia CNR, Rome.

Bonnes, M. (1988), 'Mascolinità e femminilità', in G.V. Caprara (ed.), *Personalità e rappresentazioni sociale*, La Nuova Italia Scientifica, Rome, pp. 190–209.

Bonnes, M. (1990), 'Percezione dell'ambiente urbano in approccio multidisciplinare integrato: Il Programma MAB-UNESCO sulla città di Roma', report to the national interdisciplinary conference on 'Ambiente, territorio, nuovi bisogni sociali', Department of Political and Social Studies, University of Pavia, Pavia.

Bonnes, M. (ed.) (1991), *Urban Ecology Applied to the City of Rome*, MAB-UNESCO Project 11, Progress Report n. 4, MAB Italia, Rome.

Bonnes, M. (ed.) (1993), *Perception and Evaluation of Urban Environment Quality: A Pluridisciplinary Approach in the European Context*, Proceedings of MAB-UNESCO Symposium, MAB Italia, Rome.

Bonnes, M. and Bagnasco, C. (1988), 'The Active Participation of Scientists and the Public in Urban Planning: The Rome Case Study', in UNESCO–MAB Programme, *Cities and Ecology*, vol. 2, Centre of International Projects of the USSR State Committee for Sciences and Technology, pp. 121–7.

Bonnes, M. and Giuliani, M.V. (1987), 'Preface', in M.V. Giuliani, M. Bonnes and C. Werner (eds), *Homes Interior: a European Perspective*, Special Issue of *Environment and Behavior*, 19 (2), pp. 150–3.

Bonnes, M. and Secchiaroli, G. (1979), 'Il centro di Milano: Spazio e significato nella rappresentazione cognitiva di una grande città, in *Applicazioni Psicologiche*, 2, pp. 25–45.

Bonnes, M. and Secchiaroli, G. (1981a), 'A Transactional and Psychological Approach to Environmental Cognition', paper presented to International Symposium on 'Toward a Social Psychology of the Environment', Maison des Sciences de l'Homme, Paris.

Bonnes, M. and Secchiaroli, G. (1981b), 'The Study of Environmental Perception in View of an Integrated Approach to the Urban Ecosystem', in UNESCO–MAB Italia, *Urban Ecology Applied to the City of Rome*, Progress Report no. 2. MAB Italia, Rome, pp. 205–20.

Bonnes, M. and Secchiaroli, G. (1982a), 'Il rapporto individuo-ambiente urbano: la cognizione del centro cittadino in una prospettiva "transazionale costruttivista"', in *Giornale Italiano di Psicologia*, 9 (3), pp. 433–47.

Bonnes, M. and Secchiaroli, G. (1982b), 'Aspetti socio-spaziali nella rappresentazione cognitiva del centro cittadino', in *Ricerche di Psicologia*, 22–3, pp. 155–69.

Bonnes, M. and Secchiaroli, G. (1983), 'Space and Meaning of the City-Centre Cognition: an Interactional Transactional Approach', in *Human Relations*, 36 (1), pp. 23–36.

Bonnes, M. and Secchiaroli, G. (1986), 'Rappresentazioni cognitive della città e processi di costruzione delle realtà ambientali', in *Rassegna di Psicologia*, 3 (3), pp. 25–38.

Bonnes, M., Misiti, R. and Secchiaroli, G. (1980), 'Spatial Cognitive Representation of Working Environment and Working Experience in the Factory', in *Italian Journal of Psychology*, 7 (1), pp. 1–11.

Bonnes, M., Paola, F. and Poggiali, B.M. (1987a), 'I quartieri di Roma nelle conoscenze e preferenze degli abitanti', in M. Bonnes, (ed.), *Ecologia urbana applicata alla città di Roma*, Progetto UNESCO MAB no. 11, Progress Report no. 3, Istituto di Psicologia CNR, Rome, pp 73–108.

Bonnes, M., Secchiaroli, G. and Rullo, G. (1987b), 'Il quartiere di residenza, il centro, la periferia della città di Roma: Dalle "cognizioni" degli abitanti alla "immaginabilità sociale" dei luoghi urbani', in M. Bonnes (ed.), *Ecologia urbana applicata alla città de Roma*, Progetto UNESCO MAB no. 11, Progress Report no. 3, Istituto Psicologia CNR, Rome, pp. 275–94.

Bonnes, M., De Rosa, A.M., Ardone, R.G. and Bagnasco, C. (1988a), 'Perception of the Quality of the Residential Environment and Temporal Dimension of the Residential Experience', paper presented to the IXth IAPS Conference, Delft.

Bonnes, M., De Rosa, A.M., Ardone, R.G. and Bagnasco, C. (1988b), 'Urban Vegetation and Perception of the Quality of the Urban Environment', paper presented to 31st IAVS International Symposium on Spontaneous Vegetation in Settlements, Frascati.

Bonnes, M., Mannetti, I., Secchiaroli, G. and Tanucci, G. (1990), 'The City as a Multi-Place System: An Analysis of People–Urban Environment Transactions', in *Journal of Environmental Psychology*, 10, pp. 37–65.

Bonnes, M., Bonaiuto, M., Ercolani, A.P. and De Rosa, A.M. (1991a), 'Soddisfazione residenziale in ambiente urbano: un approccio contestuale dinamico', in *Rassegna di Psicologia* 3, VIII, 49–79.

Bonnes, M., Secchiaroli, G. and Mazzotta, A.R. (1991b), 'The Home as an Urban Place: Inter-Place Perspective on Person–Home Relationship', paper presented to the International Workshop on 'Home Environment: Physical Space and Psychosocial Processes', Cortona, Italy.

Bowlby, J. (1969), *Attachment and Loss*, vol. 1, *Attachment*, Basic Books, New York.

Bowlby, J. (1973), *Attachment and Loss*, vol. 2, *Separation: Anxiety and Anger*, Basic Books, New York.

Bowlby, J. (1980), *Attachment and Loss*, vol. 3, *Loss: Sadness and Depression*, Basic Books, New York.

Bremner, J.G. and Bryant, P.F. (1977), 'Place versus Response as the Basis of Spatial Errors Made by Young Infants', in *Journal of Experimental Child Psychology*, 23, pp. 162–71.

Bretherton, I. (1985), 'Attachment Theory: Retrospect and Prospect', in I. Bretherton and F. Waters (eds), *Growing Points in Attachment Theory and Research*, Monographs of Society for Research in Child Development, 50 (1–2 Serial no. 209), pp. 3–35.

Broadbent, D.F. (1957), 'Effects of Noise of High and Low Frequency on Behavior', in *Ergonomics*, 1, pp. 21–9.

Broadbent, D.F. (1958), 'Effects of Noise on an Intellectual Task', in *Journal of the Acoustical Society of America*, 30, pp. 824–7.

Broadbent, D.F. (1971), *Decision and Stress*, Academic Press, New York.

Broadbent, D.F. (1978), 'The Current State of Noise Research: Reply to Poulton', in *Psychological Bulletin*, 85, pp. 1052–67.

Broadbent, G. and Ward, A. (eds) (1969), *Design Methods in Architecture*, Lund Humphries, London.

Bronfenbrenner, H. (1977a), 'The Ecology of Human Development in Retrospect and Prospect', in H. McGurk (ed.), *Ecological Factors in Human Development*, North-Holland, Amsterdam, pp. 275–86.

Bronfenbrenner, H. (1977b), 'Toward an Experimental Ecology of Human Development', in *American Psychologist*, July, pp. 513–31.

Bronfenbrenner, H. (1979), *The Ecology of Human Development*, Harvard University Press, Cambridge, MA.

Brown, B.B. (1987), 'Territoriality', in D. Stokols and I. Altman (eds), *Handbook of Environmental Psychology*, vol. 1, Wiley, New York, pp. 505–31.

Brown, B.B. and Altman, I. (1983), 'Territoriality, Street Form and Residential Burglary: an Environmental Analysis', in *Journal of Environmental Psychology*, 3, pp. 203–20.

Bruner, J. (1957), 'Going beyond the Information Given', in J. Bruner et al. (eds), *Contemporary Approaches to Cognition*, Harvard University Press, Cambridge, MA.

Bruner, I., Goodnaw, J.J. and Austin, G.A. (1956), *A Study of Thinking*, Wiley, New York.

Brunswik, E. (1943), 'Organismic Achievement and Environmental Probability', in *Psychological Review*, 50, pp. 255–72.

Brunswik, E. (1947), *Systematic and Representative Design of Psychological Experiments*, University of California Press, Berkeley.

Brunswik, E. (1957), 'Scope and Aspects of Cognitive Problems', in J. Bruner et al. (eds), *Contemporary Approaches to Cognition*, Harvard University Press, Cambridge, MA, pp. 5–31.

Buttimer, A. (1976), 'Grasping the Dynamism of Lifeworld', in *Annals of the Association of the American Geographers*, 66, pp. 277–92.

Buttimer, A. and Seamon, D. (eds) (1980), *The Human Experience of Space and Place*, Croom Helm, London.

Cannon, W.B. (1932), *The Wisdom of the Body*, Norton, New York.

Canter, D. (1970), *Architectural Psychology*, Royal Institute of British Architects, London.

Canter, D. (1972), *Psychology for Architects*, Applied Sciences, London.

Canter, D. (1977), *The Psychology of Place*, Architectural Press, London.

Canter, D. (1983), 'The Purposive Evaluation of Places: a Facet Approach', in *Environment and Behavior*, 15, pp. 659–98.

Canter, D. (1986), 'Putting Situations in Their Place: Foundations for a Bridge between Social and Environmental Psychology', in A. Furnham (ed.), *Social Behaviour in Context*, Allyn and Bacon, London, pp. 208–39.

Canter, D. (1988), 'Action and Place: an Existential Dialectic', in D. Canter, M. Krampen and D. Stea (eds), *Environmental Perspectives, Ethnoscapes: Current Challenges in Environmental Social Sciences*, Avebury, Aldershot, pp. 1–18.

Canter, D. and Craik, K. (1981), 'Environmental Psychology', in *Journal of Environmental Psychology*, 1, pp. 1–11.

Canter, D. and Donald, I. (1987), 'Environmental Psychology in the United Kingdom', in D. Stokols and I. Altman (eds), *Handbook of Environmental Psychology*, vol. 1, Wiley, New York, pp. 128–31.

Canter, D. and Lee, T. (eds) (1974), *Psychology and the Built Environment*, Architectural Press, London.

Canter, D. and Stringer, P. (eds) (1975), *Environmental Interactions*, Surrey University Press, London.

Canter, D., Correira Jesuino, J., Soczha, L. and Stephenson, G.M. (eds) (1988), *Environmental Social Psychology*, Kluwer Academic Publisher, Dordrecht.

Cantor, N. (1981), 'Situations, Prototypes and Person–Situation Prototypes', in O. Magnusson (ed.), *Towards a Psychology of Situations: an Interactional Perspective*, Lawrence Erlbaum, Hillsdale, NJ, pp. 229–44.

Cantor, N., Mischel, W. and Schwartz, J. (1982), 'A Prototype Analysis of Psychological Situations', in *Cognitive Psychology*, 14, pp. 45–77.

Cantril, H. (1950), *The 'Why' of Man's Experience*, Macmillan, New York.

Caplan, R. (1982), 'Person–Environment Fit: Past, Present and Future', in C. Cooper (ed.), *Stress Research: Where Do We Go from Here?*, Wiley, Chichester, pp. 35–78.

Caramelli, N. (1983), 'Introduzione', in N. Caramelli (ed.), *La psicologia cognitivista*, Il Mulino, Bologna, pp. 7–25.

Carlstein, T. (1982), *Time, Resources, Society and Ecology: On the Capacity for Human Interaction in Space and Time, Preindustrial Societies*, Allen & Unwin, London.

Carp, F.M. and Carp, A. (1982), 'Perceived Environmental Quality of Neighborhoods: Development of Assessment Scales and Their Relation to Age and Gender', in *Journal of Environmental Psychology*, 2, pp. 295–312.

Carugati, F. (1979), *Il sé e l'identità: Alla ricerca di una nuova teoria*, Stabilimento Grafico F.lli Lega, Faenza.

Castri, F. di, Baker, F.W. and Hadley, M. (eds) (1984), *Ecology in Practice*, vols 1–2, Tycooly, Dublin.

Castri, F. di, Hadley, M. and Dalmanian, J. (1981), 'MAB: The Man and the Biosphere Program as an Evolving System', in *Ambio*, 10 (2–3), pp. 52–7.

Cormak, G.W. and Cornillion, P.C. (1976), 'Multidimensional Analyses of Judgements about Traffic Noise', in *Journal of the Acoustical Society of America*, 59, pp. 1412–20.

Chapman, D. and Thomas, G. (1944), *Lighting in the Dwellings. The Lighting of Buildings: Post War Building Studies*, 12, Appendix VI, London.

Codol, J.P. (1980), 'La quête de la similitude et de la differentation sociale: une approche cognitive du sentiment d'identité', in P. Tap (ed.), *Identité individuelle et personalisation*, Privat, Toulouse.

Cofer, C.N. and Appley, N.H. (1964), *Motivation: Theory and Research*, Wiley, New York.

Cohen, R., Baldwin, L.M. and Sherman, R.C. (1978), 'Cognitive Maps of a Naturalistic Setting', in *Child Development*, 49, pp. 1216–18.

Cohen, R. and Weatherford, D.L. (1980), 'Effects of Route Travelled on Distance Estimates of Children and Adults', in *Journal of Experimental Child Psychology*, 29, pp. 403–12.

Cohen, S. (1978), 'Environmental Load and the Allocation of Attention', in A. Baum, J.E. Singer and S. Valins (eds), *Advances in Environmental Psychology*, vol. 1, Lawrence Erlbaum, Hillsdale, NJ.

Cohen, S. (1980), 'After-Effects of Stress on Human Performance and Social Behavior: A Review of Research and Theory', in *Psychological Bulletin*, 88, pp. 82–108.

Cohen, S. and Weinstein, N. (1981), 'Non-Auditory Effects of Noise on Behavior and Health', in *Journal of Social Issues*, 37, pp. 36–70.

Cohen, S., Glass, D.C. and Singer, J.F. (1973), 'Apartment Noise, Auditory Discrimination and Reading Abilities in Children', in *Journal of Experimental Social Psychology*, 9, pp. 407–22.

Cohen, S., Glass, D.C. and Phillips, S. (1979), 'Environment and Health', in H.E. Freeman, S. Levine and L.G. Reeder (eds), *Handbook of Medical Sociology*, Prentice Hall, Englewood Cliffs, NJ, pp. 134–49.

Cook, M. (1970), 'Experiments on Orientation and Proxemics', in *Human Relations*, 23, pp. 61–76.

Cooper, C. (1972), 'The House as a Symbol of Self', in J. Lang, C. Burnett, W. Moleski and D. Vachon (eds), *Designing for Human Behavior: Architecture and the Behavioral Sciences*, Dowden, Hutchinson & Ross, Stroudsburg, PA., pp. 130–46.

Cooper Markus, C. and Sarkissian, W. (1986), *Housing as if People Mattered*, University of California Press, Berkeley.

Corcoran, D.W.J. (1962), 'Noise and Loss of Sleep', in *Quarterly Journal of Experimental Psychology*, 14, pp. 178–82.

Cornwell, M.L. (1982), 'Sex Differences in Environmental Concern', in *Environmental Sociology*, 31, pp. 9–11.

Craik, K.H. (1966), *The Prospects for an Environmental Psychology*, IPAR Research Bulletin, University of California, Berkeley.

Craik, K.H. (1968), 'The Comprehension of the Everyday Physical Environment', in *Journal of the American Institute of Planners*, 34 (1), pp. 646–58.

Craik, K.H. (1970), 'Environmental Psychology', in K.H. Craik, R. Kleinmuntz, R. Rosnow, R. Rosenthal, J.A. Cheyne and R.H. Walters (eds), *New Directions in Psychology,*vol. 4, Holt, Rinehart & Winston, New York, pp. 1–120.

Craik, K.H. (1971), 'The Assessment of Places', in P. McReynolds (ed.), *Advances in Psychological Assessment*, vol. 2, Science and Behavior Books, Palo Alto. CA, pp. 40–62.

Craik, K.H. (1973), 'Environmental Psychology', in *Annual Review of Psychology*, 24, pp. 403–22.

Craik, K.H. (1977), 'Multiple Scientific Paradigms in Environmental Psychology', in *International Journal of Psychology*, 12, pp. 147–57.

Craik, K.H. (1981), 'Environmental Assessment and Situational Analysis', in D. Magnusson (ed.), *Toward a Psychology of Situations*, Lawrence Erlbaum, Hillsdale, NJ, pp. 37–48.

Craik, K.H. (1983), 'A Role Theoretical Analysis of Scenic Quality Judgement', in R.D. Rowe and L.G. Chestnut (eds), *Managing Air Quality and Scenic Resources at National Parks and Wilderness Areas*, Westview Press, Boulder, CO, pp. 67–105.

Craik, K.H. and Feimer, N. (1987), 'Environmental Assessment', in D. Stokols and I. Altman (eds), *Handbook of Environmental Psychology*, vol. 2, Wiley, New York, pp. 891–918.

Craik, K.H. and Zube, F. (eds) (1976), *Perceiving Environmental Quality: Research and Application*, Plenum, New York.

Craik, K.H., Dake, K.M. and Buss, D.M. (1982), 'Individual Differences in the Perception of Technological Hazard', paper presented to the Meeting of the American Psychological Association, Washington, DC.

Csikszentmihalyi, M. and Rochberg-Halton, E. (1981), *The Meaning of Things*, Cambridge University Press, New York.

Daniel, T.C. and Ittelson, W.H. (1981), 'Conditions for Environmental Perception Research: Comment on the Psychological Representations of Moral Physical Environments by Ward and Russell', in *Journal of Experimental Psychology: General*, 110, pp. 153–7.

Davies, W.F. and Swaffer, P.W. (1971), 'Effect of Room Size on Critical Interpersonal Distance', in *Perceptual and Motor Skills*, 33, p. 926.

de Grada, F. and Mannetti, L. (1988), *L'attribuzione causale*, II Mulino, Bologna.

de Jonge, D. (1962), 'Images of Urban Areas: Their Structure and Psychological Foundations', in *Journal of American Institute of Planners*, 28, pp. 266–76.

Dewey, J. and Bentley, A. (1949), *Knowing and Known*, Beacon Press, Boston, MA.

Doise, W. (1976), *L'articulation psycho-sociologique et les relations entre groupes*, De Boeck, Brussels.

Doise, W. (1978), *Groups and Individuals: Explanations in Social Psychology*, Cambridge University Press, Cambridge.

Doise, W. (1982), *L'esplication en psychologie sociale*, Presses Universitaries de France, Paris.

Doise, W. (1988), 'Individual and Social Identities in Inter-Group Relations', in *European Journal of Social Psychology*, 18, pp. 99–111.

Dovey, K. (1985), 'Home and Homeless', in I. Altman and C.M. Werner (eds), *Home Environments*, vol. 8, *Human Behavior and Environment: Advances in Theory and Research*, Plenum, New York, pp. 33–64.

Downs, R.M. (1970), 'The Cognitive Structure of an Urban Shopping Centre', in *Environment and Behavior*, 2, pp. 13–39.

Downs, R.M. (1981), 'Maps and Mapping as Metaphors for Spatial Representation', in L.S. Liben, A.H. Patterson and N. Newcomb (eds), *Spatial Representation and Behavior across the Life Span*, Academic Press, New York, pp. 95–122.

Downs, R.M. and Meyer, J.T. (1978), 'Geography and the Mind: an Exploration of Perceptual Geography', in *American Behavioral Scientist*, 22, pp. 59–78.

Downs, R.M. and Stea, D. (eds) (1973), *Image and Environment: Cognitive Mapping and Spatial Behavior*, Aldine, Chicago.

Drottz-Sjoberg, B.M. and Sjoberg, L. (1990), 'Risk Perception and Worries after the Chernobyl Accident', in *Journal of Environmental Psychology*, 10, pp. 135–49.

Dunlap, E.E. and Van Liere, K.D. (1978), 'The New Environmental Paradigm: a Proposed Measuring Instrument and Preliminary Results', in *Journal of Environmental Education*, 9, pp. 10–19.

Dunnette, M.D. (1977), *Handbook of Industrial and Organizational Psychology*, Rand-McNally, Chicago.

Earle, T.C. and Cvekovich, G. (1990), 'What Was the Meaning of Chernobyl?', in *Journal of Environmental Psychology*, 10, pp. 169–76.

Eibel-Eibesfeldt, I. (1970), *Ethology, the Biology of Behavior*, Holt, Rinehart & Winston, New York.

Eiser, J.R., Hannover, R., Mann, L., Morin, M., Van der Pligt, J. and Webley, P. (1990), 'Nuclear Attitudes after Chernobyl: a Cross-National Study', in *Journal of Environmental Psychology*, 10, pp. 101–10.

Erdelyi, M.H. (1974), 'A New Look at the New Look: Perceptual Defense and Vigilance', in *Psychological Review*, 81, pp. 1–25.

Erikson, E.H. (1950), *Childhood and Society*, Norton, New York.

Evans, G.W. (1980), 'Environmental Cognition', in *Psychological Bulletin*, 88, pp. 259–87.

Evans, G.W. (ed.) (1982), *Environmental Stress*, Cambridge University Press, New York.

Evans, G.W. and Cohen, S. (1987), 'Environmental Stress', in D. Stokols and I. Altman (eds), *Handbook of Environmental Psychology*, vol. 1, Wiley, New York, pp. 571–610.

Evans, G.W. and Howard, R.B. (1973), 'Personal Space', in *Psychological Bulletin*, 80, pp. 334–44.

Farr, R. and Moscovici, S. (eds) (1984), *Social Representations*, Cambridge University Press, Cambridge.

Feldman, R.M. (1990), 'Settlement-Identity: Psychological Bonds with Home Place in a Mobile Society', in *Environment and Behavior*, 22, p. 183.

Festinger, L., Shachter, S. and Back, K. (1950), *Social Pressure in Informal Groups*. Stanford University Press, Stanford, CA.

Forgas, J.P. (1979), *Social Episodes: the Study of Interaction Routines*, Academic Press, London.

Forgas, J.P. (1985), *Language and Social Situations*, Springer-Verlag, New York.

Francescato, D. (1975), *Schemi e immagini di una città*, Bulzoni, Rome.

Francescato, D. and Mebane, W. (1973), 'How Citizens View Two Great Cities: Milan and Rome', in R.M. Downs and D. Stea (eds), *Image and Environment: Cognitive Mapping and Spatial Behavior*, Aldine, Chicago, pp. 131–47.

Fried, M. (1982), 'Residential Attachment: Sources of Residential and Community Satisfaction', in *Journal of Social Issues*, 38, pp. 107–19.

Friedman, S. (1974), 'Relationships among Cognitive Complexity, Interpersonal Dimension and Spatial References and Propensities', in S. Friedman and J.B. Juhasz (eds), *Environments: Notes and Selections on Objects, Spaces and Behavior*, Wadsworth, Belmont, CA, pp. 27–40.

Fuhrer, U. (1990), 'Bridging the Ecological-Psychological Gap: Behavioral Settings as Interfaces', in *Environment and Behavior*, 22 (4), pp. 518–37.

Garfinkel, N. (1967), *Studies in Ethnomethodology*, Prentice Hall, Englewood Cliffs, NJ.

Garling, T. and Golledge, R.G. (1989), 'Environmental Perception and Cognition', in H. Zube and G.T. Moore (eds), *Advances in Environmental Behavior and Design*, vol. 2, Plenum, New York, pp. 203–36.

Garling, T., Book, A., Lindeberg, E. and Milsson, T. (1981), 'Memory for the Spatial Layout of Everyday Physical Environment: Factors Affecting the Rate of Acquisition', in *Journal of Environmental Psychology*, 1, pp. 23–35.

Garling, T., Book, A. and Lindberg, E. (1984), 'Cognitive Mapping of Large-Scale Environments, Action Plans, Orientation and Their Inter-relationships', in *Environment and Behavior*, 16, pp. 3–34.

Gauvain, M., Altman, I. and Fahim, H. (1983), 'Homes and Social Change: a Cross-Cultural Analysis', in N.R. Feimer and F.S. Geller (eds), *Environmental Psychology: Directions and Perspectives*, Praeger, New York, pp. 180–218.

Gavin, J.F. and Howe, J.G. (1975), 'Psychological Climate: Some Theoretical and Empirical Considerations', in *Behavioral Sciences*, 20, pp. 228–40.

Genereux, R.L., Ward, L.M. and Russell, J.A. (1983), 'The Behavioral Components in the Meaning of Places', in *Journal of Environmental Psychology*, 3, pp. 43–55.

Georgoundi, M. and Rosnow, R.L. (1985), 'Notes toward a Contextualist Understanding of Social Psychology', in *Personality and Social Psychology Bulletin*, 11, pp. 5–22.

Gergen, K.J. (1971), *The Concept of Self*, Holt, Rinehart & Winston, New York.

Gergen, K.J. and Gergen, M.M. (1984), *Historical Social Psychology*, Lawrence Erlbaum, Hillsdale, NJ.

Giacomini, V. (1980), *Qualifying Aspects of the Project MAB 11 Applied to the City of Rome*, Report no. 5, MAB Italia, Rome.

Giacomini, V. (1981), 'Rome Considered as an Ecological System', in *Nature and Resources*, 17 (1), pp. 13–9.

Giacomini, V. (1983), *La rivoluzione tolemaica*, Editrice La Scuola, Brescia.

Giacomini, V. and Romani, V. (1982), *Uomini e parchi*, Franco Angeli, Milan.

Gibson, E.J. and Walk, R.D. (1960), 'The "Visual Cliff"', in *Scientific American*, 202, pp. 64–71.

Gibson, J.J. (1950), *The Perception of the Visual World*, Houghton-Mifflin, Boston.

Gibson, J.J. (1960), 'The Concept of Stimulus in Psychology', in *American Psychologist*, 16, pp. 694–703.

Gibson, J.J. (1966), *The Senses Considered as Perceptual Systems*, Houghton-Mifflin, Boston.

Gibson, J.J. (1972), 'The Affordances of the Environment', in E.Reed and R. Jones (eds), *Reasons for Realism: Selected Essays of James J. Gibson*, Lawrence Erlbaum, Hillsdale NJ, pp. 408–10

Gibson, J.J. (1978), 'A Note on what Exists at the Ecological Level of Reality', in E. Reed and R. Jones (eds), *Reasons for Realism: Selected Essays of James J. Gibson*, Lawrence Erlbaum, Hillsdale NJ, pp. 416–18.

Gibson, J.J. (1979), *The Ecological Approach to Visual Perception*, Houghton-Mifflin, Boston.

Gifford, R. (1980), 'Environmental Dispositions and the Evaluation of Architectural Interiors', in *Journal of Research in Personality*, 14, pp. 386–99.

Gifford, R. (1982), 'Projected Interpersonal Distance and Orientation Choices: Personality, Sex, and Social Situations', in *Social Psychology Quarterly*, 45, pp. 145–52.

Gifford, R. (1987), *Environmental Psychology, Principles and Practice*, Allyn and Bacon, Newton, MA.

Gifford, R. and Price, J. (1979), 'Personal Space in Nursery School Children', in *Canadian Journal of Behavioral Science*, 11, pp. 318–26.

Ginsburg, H.J., Pollman, V.A., Wauson, M.S. and Hope, M.L. (1977), 'Variations of Aggressive Interactions among Male Elementary School Children as a Function of Changes in Spatial Density', in *Environmental Psychology and Non-Verbal Behavior*, 2, pp. 67–75.

Giuliani, M.V. (1987), 'Naming the Rooms: Implications of a Change in the Home Model', in *Environment and Behavior*, 19 (2), pp. 180–203.

Giuliani, M.V. (1989), 'La casa come sistema territoriale', in *Edilizia Popolare*, 206/207, p. 58.

Giuliani, M.V. (1991), 'Toward an Analysis of Mental Representations of Attachment to the Home', in *Journal of Architectural and Planning Research*, 8 (2), pp. 133–46.

Giuliani, M.V., Bonnes, M., Amoni, F. and Bernard, Y. (1988), 'Home and Theory of Place', in D. Canter, M. Krampen and D. Stea (eds), *Ethnoscapes: vol. 1, Environmental Perspectives*, Avebury, Aldershot, pp. 39–53.

Glass, D.C. and Singer, J.F. (1972a), 'Behavioral After-Effects of Unpredictable and Uncontrollable Adversive Events', in *American Scientist*, 80, pp. 457–65.

Glass, D.C. and Singer, J.F. (1972b), *Urban Stress*, Academic Press, New York.

Glass, D.C., Singer, J.F. and Friedman, I.N. (1969), 'Psychic Cost of Adaptation to an Environmental Stressor', in *Journal of Personality and Social Psychology*, 12, pp. 200–10.

Glass, D.C., Reim, B. and Singer, J.E. (1971), 'Behavioral Consequences of Adaptation to Controllable and Uncontrollable Noise', in *Journal of Experimental Social Psychology*, 7, pp. 244–57.

Glass, D.C., Nayder, M.L. and Singer, J.E. (1973), 'Periodic and Aperiodic Noise: The Safety-Signal-Hypothesis and Noise After-Effects', in *Physiological Psychology*, 1, pp. 361–3.

Glass, D.C., Singer, J. and Pennebaker, J.W. (1977), 'Behavioral and Physiological Effects of Uncontrollable Environmental Events', in D. Stokols (ed.), *Perspectives on Environment and Behavior: Theory, Research and Applications*, Plenum, New York, pp. 131–51.

Goffman, E. (1959), *The Presentation of Self in Everyday Life*, Doubleday, New York.

Goffman, E. (1963), *Behavior in Public*, Free Press, New York.

Goffman, E. (1971), *Relations in Public*, Basic Books, New York.

Goffman, E. (1974), *Frame Analysis*, Harper & Row, New York.

Gold, J.R. (1980), *An Introduction to Behavioural Geography*, Oxford University Press, Oxford.

Gold, J.R. (1982), 'Territoriality and Human Spatial Behavior', in *Progress in Human Geography*, 6, pp. 44–67.

Golledge, R.G. (1987), 'Environmental Cognition', in D. Stokols and I. Altman, (eds), *Handbook of Environmental Psychology*, vol. 1, Wiley, New York, pp. 131–74.

Gordon, C. (1968), 'Self-Conceptions: Configuration of Content', in C. Gordon and K.J. Gergen (eds), *The Self in Social Interaction*, Wiley, New York, pp. 87–109.

Grauman, C. (1974), 'Psychology and the World of Things', in *Journal of Phenomenological Psychology*, 4, pp. 389–404.

Grauman, C. (ed.) (1978), *Ökologische Perspektiven in der Psychologie*, Huber, Berne.

Grauman, C. (1988), 'Towards a Phenomenology of Being at Home', in *Proceedings of the IAPS 10th Conference*, Delft University Press, Delft, pp. 56–65.

Guttman, I. (1968), 'A General Non-Metric Technique for Finding the Smallest Coordinated Space for a Configuration of Points', in *Psychometrika*, 33, pp. 469–506.

Hagerstrand, T. (1983), 'In Search for the Sources of Concepts', in A. Buttimer (ed.), *The Practice of Geography*, Longman, London, pp. 238–56.

Hall, E.T. (1959), *The Silent Language*, Doubleday, Garden City, NY.

Hall, E.T. (1963), 'A System for the Notation of Proxemic Behavior', in *American Anthropologist*, 65, pp. 1003–26.

Hall, E.T. (1966), *The Hidden Dimension*, Doubleday, New York.

Hansard, (1943), *House of Commons Rebuilding*, Parliamentary Debates House of Commons 393, no. 114, HMSO, London, pp. 404–74.

Hard, A. (1975), 'NCS. A Descriptive Colour Order and Scaling System with Applications for Environment Design', in *Man–Environment Systems*, 5 (3), pp. 161–7.

Hart, R.A. and Moore, G.P. (1973), 'The Development of Spatial Cognition: a review', in R.M. Downs and D. Stea (eds), *Image and Environment: Cognitive Mapping and Spatial Behavior*, Aldine, Chicago, pp. 246–88.

Hartley, L.R. and Adams, R.G. (1974), 'Effect of Noise on the Stroop Test', in *Journal of Experimental Psychology*, 102, pp. 62–6.

Hartmann, H. (1958), *Ego Psychology and the Problem of Adaptation*, International University Press, New York.

Heberlein, T.A. and Black, J.S. (1976), 'Attitudinal Specificity and the Perception of Behavior in the Field Setting', in *Journal of Personality and Social Psychology*, 33, pp. 474–9.

Heberlein, T.A. and Black, J.S. (1981), 'Cognitive Consistency and Environmental Action', in *Environment and Behavior*, 13, pp. 717–34.

Heft, H. (1981), 'An Examination of Constructivistic and Gibsonian Approaches to

Environmental Psychology', in *Population and Environment: Behavioral and Social Issues*, 4, pp. 227–45.

Heft, H. (1988), 'The Development of Gibson's Ecological Approach to Perception', in *Journal of Environmental Psychology*, 8, pp. 325–34.

Heft, H. and Wohlwill, F. (1987), 'Environmental Cognition in Children', in D. Stokols and I. Altman (eds), *Handbook of Environmental Psychology*, vol. 1, Wiley, New York, pp. 175–203.

Heidegger, M. (1962), *Being and Time*, Harper & Row, New York (original edn 1927).

Heidegger, M. (1975), 'Building, Dwelling, Thinking', in *Poetry, Language, and Thought*, Harper & Row, New York pp. 145–61 (original edn 1952).

Heidegger, M. (1982), *The Basic Problems of Phenomenology*, Indiana University Press, Bloomington (original edn 1927/1975).

Heider, F. (1958), *The Psychology of Interpersonal Relations*, Wiley, New York.

Heimstra, N.W. and McFarling, L.H. (1974), *Environmental Psychology*, Brooks/Cole, Monterey, CA.

Heller, K. and Monahan, J. (1977), *Psychology and Community Change*, Dorsey, Homewood, IL.

Helmholtz, H. (1866), *Handbuch der physiologischen Optik*, vol. 3, Leipzig.

Hershberger, R.G. and Cass, R.C. (1974), 'Predicting User Responses to Buildings. Man–Environment Interaction: Evaluations and Applications, vol. 4', *Proceedings of the 5th International Environmental Design Research Association Conference*, Environmental Design Research Association, Washington, DC., pp. 117–34.

Hinde, R. (1974), *Biological Bases of Human Social Behavior*, McGraw-Hill, New York.

Holahan, C.J. (1972), 'Setting Patterns and Patient Behavior in Experimental Dayroom', in *Journal of Abnormal Psychology*, 80, pp. 115–24.

Holahan, C.J. (1977), 'Rural Differences in Judged Appropriateness of Altruistic Responses: Personal versus Situational Effects', in *Sociometry*, 40, pp. 378–82.

Holahan, C.J. (1978), *Environment and Behavior: A Dynamic Perspective*, Plenum, New York.

Holahan, C.J. (1982), *Environmental Psychology*, Random House, New York.

Holahan, C.J. (1986), 'Environmental Psychology', in *Annual Review of Psychology*, 37, pp. 403–22.

Holahan, C.J. and Bonnes, M. (1978), 'Cognitive and Behavioral Correlates of Spatial Environment: an Interactional Analysis' in *Environment and Behavior*, 10 (3), pp. 317–33.

Holahan, C.J. and Saegert, S. (1973), 'Behavioral and Attitudinal Effects of Large-Scale Variation in the Physical Environment of a Psychiatric Ward', in *Journal of Abnormal Psychology*, 82, pp. 454–62.

Holahan, C.J. and Wandersman, A. (1987), 'The Community Psychology Perspective in Environmental Psychology', in D. Stokols and I. Altman (eds), *Handbook of Environmental Psychology*, vol. 1, Wiley, New York, pp. 827–62.

Honikman, R. (ed.), (1971), *Proceedings of the Architectural Psychology Conference at Kingston Polytechnic*, RIBA, London.

House, J.S. and Wolf, S. (1978), 'Effects of Urban Residence on Interpersonal Trust and Helping Behavior', in *Journal of Personality and Social Psychology*, 36, pp. 1029–43.

Howell, S.C. (1980), *Designing for Aging*, MIT Press, Cambridge, MA.

Husserl, E. (1960), *Cartesian Mediations*, Martinus Nijhoff, The Hague. (original edn 1929–32).

Husserl, E. (1970), *The Crisis of European Sciences and Transcendental Phenomenology*, Northwestern University Press, Evanston, IL, (original edn 1936–54).

Insel, P.M. and Moos, R.H. (1974), 'Psychological Environments: Expanding the Scope of Human Ecology', in *American Psychologist*, 29, 179–88.

Israel, J. and Tajfel, H. (eds) (1972), *The Context of Social Psychology: A Critical Assessment*, Academic Press, London.

Ittelson, W. (1960), *Some Factors Influencing the Design and Functions of Psychiatric Facilities*, Progress Report, Brooklin College.

Ittelson, W.H. (1961), 'The Constancies in Perceptual Theory', in *Psychological Review*, 58, pp. 285–94.

Ittelson, W.H. (ed.) (1973a), *Environment and Cognition*, Academic Press, New York.

Ittelson, W.H. (1973b), 'Environment Perception and Contemporary Perceptual Theory', in W.H. Ittelson (ed.), *Environment and Cognition*, Academic Press, New York, pp. 1–19.

Ittelson, W.H., Proshansky, H.M. and Rivlin, L.G. (1970), 'Bedroom Size and Social Interaction of the Psychiatric Ward', in *Environment and Behavior*, 2, pp. 255–70.

Ittelson, W.H., Proshansky, H., Rivlin, A. and Winkel, G. (1974), *An Introduction to Environmental Psychology*, Holt, Rinehart & Winston, New York.

Izumi, K. (1957), 'An Analysis for the Design of Hospital Quarters for the Neuropsychiatric Patient', in *Mental Hospitals*, 8, pp. 31–2.

Jackson, J.B. (ed.) (1951–68), *Landscapes*, vol. 1–18.

Jackson, J.B. (1970), *Landscapes: Selected Writings of J.B. Jackson* (ed. E.H. Zube), University of Massachusetts Press, Amherst.

James, L.R. and Jones, A.P. (1974), 'Organizational Climate: a Review of Theory and Research', in *Psychological Bulletin*, 81, pp. 1096–112.

Janis, I.L. and Mann, L. (1977), *Decision Making*, Free Press, New York.

Jaspars, J. and Fraser, C. (1984), 'Attitudes and Social Representations', in M. Farr and S. Moscovici (eds), *Social Representations*, Cambridge University Press, Cambridge, pp. 129–58.

Jodelet, D. (1987), 'The Study of People–Environment Relations in France', in D. Stokols and I. Altman (eds), *Handbook of Environmental Psychology*, vol. 2, Wiley, New York, pp. 1171–94.

Jodelet, D. (1989), *Les representations sociales*, PUF, Paris.

Johansson, T. (1952), *Farg: Den allmanna farglarans grunder*, Natur och Kultur, Stockholm.

Jonsson, A. and Hansson, L. (1977), 'Prolonged Exposure to a Stressful Stimulus (Noise) as a Cause of Raised Blood Pressure in Man', in *Lancet*, 1, pp. 86–7.

Kaminsky, G. (ed.) (1976), *Umweltpsychologie*, Ernst Klett Verlag, Stuttgart.

Kaminsky, G. (1983), 'The Enigma of Ecological Psychology', in *Journal of Environmental Psychology*, 3, pp. 85–94.

Kaminsky, G. and Fleischer, F. (1984), 'Ökologische Psychologie: Ökopsychologische Untersuchung und Beratung', in H.A. Hartman and R. Haubl (eds), *Psychologische Begutachtung*, Urban & Schwarzenberg, Munich, pp. 329–58.

Kantowitz, B.H. (1977), 'Environmental Psychology: Behavior in the Physical World', in R.A. Baron, D. Byrn and B.H. Kantowitz (eds), *Psychology: Understanding Behavior*, W.B. Sanders, Philadelphia.

Kaplan, R. (1973), 'Predictors or Environmental Preferences: Designers and Clients', in W.F.E. Preiser (ed.), *Environmental Design Research*, Dowden, Hutchinson & Ross, Stroudsburg, PA, pp. 145–62.

Kaplan, R. (1977), 'Patterns of Environmental Preference', in *Environment and Behavior*, 9, pp. 195–215.

Kaplan, S. (1982), 'Where Cognition and Affects Meet: a Theoretical Analysis of Preference', in P. Bart, A. Chen and G. Francescato (eds), *Knowledge for Design*, EDRA, Washington, DC. pp. 183–8.

Kaplan, S. (1983), 'A Model of Person–Environment Compatibility', in *Environment and Behavior*, 15, pp. 311–32.

Kaplan, S. and Kaplan, R. (1982), *Cognition and Environment*. Praeger, New York.

Kates, R.W. and Wohlwill, J.F. (eds) (1966), 'Man's Response to the Physical Environment', Special Issue, in *Journal of Social Issues*, 22, pp. 1–140.

Kelly, G.A. (1955), *The Psychology of Personal Constructs*, Norton, New York.

Kelvin, P. (1973), 'A Social-Psychological Examination of Privacy', in *British Journal of Social and Clinical Psychology*, 12, pp. 248–61.

Kilpatrick, F.P. (1954), 'Two Processes of Perceptual Learning', in *Journal of Experimental Psychology*, 47, pp. 362–70.

Kilpatrick, F.P. (1961), Introduction in F.P. Kilpatrick (ed.), *Explorations in Transactional Psychology*, New York University Press, New York, pp. 1–5.

Koffka, K. (1924), 'Introspection and Method of Psychology', in *The British Journal of Psychology*, 15 (2), pp. 149–61.

Koffka, K. (1935), *Principles of Gestalt Psychology*, Harcourt Brace, New York.

Köhler, W. (1929), *Gestalt Psychology*, Liveright, New York.

Köhler, W. (1940), *Dynamics in Psychology*, Liveright, New York.

Korosec-Serfaty, P. (1985), 'Experiences and Uses of the Dwelling', in I. Altman and C.M. Werner (eds), *Home Environments*, Plenum, New York.

Korosec-Serfaty, P. (1988), 'Urban Open Space', in D. Canter, M. Krampen and D. Stea (eds), *Ethnoscapes: vol 1: Environmental Perspectives*, Avebury, Aldershot, pp. 123–50.

Kosslyn, S.M. (1980), *Image and Mind*, Harvard University Press, Cambridge, MA.

Kosslyn, S.M., Pick, H.L., jr and Fariello, G.R. (1974), 'Cognitive Maps in Children and Men', in *Child Development*, 45, pp. 707–16.

Krampen, M. (1979), *Meaning in the Urban Environment*, Pion, London.

Krech, D. and Crutchfield, R.S. (1948), *Theory and Problems of Social Psychology*, McGraw-Hill, New York.

Kromm, D.E., Probald, F. and Wall, G. (1973), 'An International Comparison of Response to Air Pollution', in *Journal of Environment and Man*, 1, pp. 363–75.

Kruse, L. (1978), 'Ökologische Fragestellungen in der Sozialpsychologie', in Grauman (ed.), *Ökologische Perspektiven in der Psychologie*, Huber, Berne, pp. 171–90.

Kruse, L. (1988), 'Behavioral Settings, Cognitive Scripts, Linguistic Frames', in *Proceedings of IAPS 10th Conference*, Delft University Press, Delft, pp. 106–13.

Kruse, L. and Grauman, C. (1987), 'Environmental Psychology in Germany', in D. Stokols and I. Altman (eds), *Handbook of Environmental Psychology*, vol. 2, Wiley, New York, pp. 1195–226.

Kruse, L. and Grauman, C. (1990), 'The Environment: Social Construction and Psychological Problems', in H.T. Himmelweit and G. Garkell (eds), *Societal Psychology*, Sage, London, pp. 212–29.

Kryter, K.D. (1970), *The Effects of Noise on Man*, Academic Press, New York.

Kuethe, J.L. and Weingartner, H. (1964), 'Male–Female Schemata of Homosexual and Non-Homosexual Penitentiary Inmates', in *Journal of Personality*, 32, pp. 23–31.

Kuhn, T.S. (1962), *The Structure of Scientific Revolutions*, Chicago University Press, Chicago.

Kuipers, B. (1978), 'Modeling Spatial Knowledge', in *Cognitive Science*, 2, pp. 129–53.

Kuller, R. (1987), 'Environmental Psychology from a Swedish Perspective', in D. Stokols and I. Altman (eds), *Handbook of Environmental Psychology*, vol. 2, Wiley, New York, pp. 1243–80.

Ladd, F. (1970), 'Black Youths View Their Environment: Neighborhood Maps', in *Environment and Behavior*, 2, pp. 74–99.

Landweher, K. (1988), 'Environmental Perception: an Ecological Perspective', in D. Canter, M. Krampen and D. Stea (eds), *Ethnoscapes: vol. 1. Environmental Perspectives*, Avebury, Aldershot, pp. 18–38.

Lazarus, R.S. (1966), *Psychological Stress and the Coping Process*, McGraw-Hill, New York.

Lazarus, R.S. and Cohen, J. (1977), 'Environmental Stress', in I. Altman and J. Wohlwill (eds), *Human Behavior and Environment: Advances in Theory and Research*, Plenum, New York.

Lazarus, R.S., de Longis, A., Folkman, S. and Gruen, R. (1985), 'Stress and Adaptational Outcomes: the Problem of Confounded Measures', in *American Psychologist*, 40, pp. 770–9.

Lee, T. (1968), 'Urban Neighbourhood as a Socio-Spatial Scheme', in *Human Relations*, 21 (3), pp. 241–67.

Lee, T. (1976), *Psychology and the Environment*, Methuen, London.

Lee, T. (1990), 'Moving House and Home', in S. Fisher and C. Cooper (eds), *On the Move: the Psychology of Change and Transition*, Wiley, New York, pp. 171–89.

Levinson, S.C. (1983), *Pragmatics*, Cambridge University Press, Cambridge.

Levy-Leboyer, C. (1980), *Psychologie et environnement*, Presses Universitaires de France, Paris.

Lewin, K. (1936), *Principles of Topological Psychology*, McGraw-Hill, New York.

Lewin, K. (1943), 'Forces behind Food Habits and Methods of Change', in *Bulletin of the National Research Council*, XVIII, pp. 35–65.

Lewin, K. (1944), 'Constructs in Psychology and Psychological Ecology', in *University of Iowa Studies in Child Welfare*, XX, pp. 17–21.

Lewin, K. (1948), *Resolving Social Conflicts*, Harper Brothers, New York.

Lewin, K. (1951), *Field Theory in Social Science*, Harper, New York.

Little, B.R. (1968), 'Psychospecialization: Functions of Differential Interests in Persons and Things', in *Bulletin of the British Psychological Society*, 21, p. 113 (abstract).

Little, B.R. (1972a), *Person–Thing Orientation: a Provisional Manual for the T–P Scale*, Oxford University, Dept of Experimental Psychology, Oxford.

Little, B.R. (1972b), 'Psychological Man as Scientist, Humanist and Specialist', in *Journal of Experimental Research in Personality*, 6, pp. 95–118.

Little, B.R. (1976), 'Specialization and the Varieties of Environmental Experience: Empirical Studies within the Personality Paradigm', in S. Wapner and S.B. Kaplan (eds), *Experiencing Environment*, Plenum, New York, pp. 81–116.

Little, B.R. (1983), 'Personal Projects: a Rationale and Method of Investigation', in *Environment and Behavior*, 15 (3), pp. 273–309.

Little, B.R. (1987), 'Personality and Environment', in D. Stokols and I. Altman (eds), *Handbook of Environmental Psychology*, vol. 1, Wiley, New York, pp. 205–44.

Lofstedt, B. (1966), 'Human Heat Tolerance', unpublished doctoral dissertation, University of Lund, Lund.

Lorenz, K. (1965), *Evolution and Modification of Behavior*, University of Chicago Press, Chicago.

Lott, B.S. and Sommer, R. (1967), 'Seating Arrangements and Status', in *Journal of Personality and Social Psychology*, 7, pp. 90–5.

Lounsbury, J. and Tornatzky, L.G. (1977), 'A Scale for Assessing Attitude toward Environmental Quality', in *Journal of Social Psychology*, 101, pp. 299–305.

Lowenthal, D. (1961), 'Geography, Experience, and Imagination: toward a Geographical Epistemology', in *Annals of the Association of American Geographers*, 51, pp. 241–60.

Lyman, S.M. and Scott, M.B. (1967), 'Territoriality: a Neglected Sociological Dimension', in *Social Problems*, 15, pp. 236–49.

Lynch, K. (1960), *The Image of the City*, MIT Press, Cambridge, MA.

Lynch, K. (ed.), (1977), *Growing up in Cities*, MIT Press, Cambridge, MA.

MAB Italia (1981), *Urban Ecology Applied to the City of Rome*, UNESCO-MAB Project 11, MAB Italia, Rome.

MAB Italia (1990), *Programma UNESCO Uomo e Biosfera, Rapporto nazionale*, Consiglio Nazionale delle Ricerche, Rome.

McGrath, J.E. (1970), *Social and Psychological Factors in Stress*, Holt, Rinehart & Winston, New York.

McGuire, H. (1983), 'A Contextualist Theory of Knowledge: Its Implications for Innovation and Reform in Psychological Research', in L. Berkowitz (ed.), *Advances in Experimental Social Psychology*, Academic Press, New York.

McKechnie, G.F. (1974), *Manual for the Environmental Response Inventory*, Consulting Psychologists Press, Palo Alto CA.

McKechnie, G.F. (1977), 'The Environmental Response Inventory in Application', in *Environment and Behavior*, 9, pp. 255–76.

McKechnie, G.F. (1978), 'Environmental Dispositions: Concepts and Measures', in P. McReynolds (ed.), *Advances in Psychological Assessment*, vol. 4, Jossey Bass, San Francisco.

Magana, G.R., Evans, G.W. and Romney, A.K. (1981), 'Scaling Techniques in the Analysis of Environmental Cognition Data', in *Professional Geography*, 33, pp. 294–301.

Magenau, E. (ed.) (1959), *Research for Architecture*, American Institute of Architects, Washington, DC.

Magnusson, D. (ed.) (1981), *Toward a Psychology of Situations*, Lawrence Erlbaum, Hillsdale, NJ.

Mainardi Peron, E. (1985), 'Choice and Ordering of Items in Descriptions of Places', paper presented to the 16th Environmental Design Research Association Conference, New York.

Mainardi Peron, E., Baroni, M.R., Job, R. and Salmasco, P. (1985), 'Cognitive Factors and Communicative Strategies in Recalling Unfamiliar Places', in *Journal of Environmental Psychology*, 5, pp. 325–33.

Mainardi Peron, E., Baroni, M.R. and Zucco, G. (1988), 'The Effects of the Salience and Typicality of Objects in Natural Settings upon Their Recollection', *Looking Back to the Future, Proceedings of IAPS 10*, Delft University Press, Delft, pp. 563–82.

Maloney, M.P., Ward, M.P. and Braucht, G.N. (1975), 'A Revised Scale for the Measurement of Ecological Attitudes and Knowledge', in *American Psychologist*, 30, pp. 787–90.

Manicas, P.T. and Secord, P.F. (1983), 'Implications for Psychology of the New Philosophy of Sciences', in *American Psychologist*, 38, pp. 399–413.

Mannetti, L., Tanucci, G., Bonnes, M. and Secchiaroli, G. (1987), 'Environmental Cognition and Action in the City of Rome', poster at the Fourth International Conference on 'Event Perception and Action', Trieste.

Marans, R.W. (1976), 'Perceived Quality of Residential Environments: Some Methodological Issues', in K.H. Craik and E.H. Zube (eds), *Perceiving Environmental Quality*, Plenum, New York.

Mayo, E. (1933), *The Human Problems of an Industrial Civilization*, Macmillan, New York.

Mead, G.H. (1934), *Mind, Self and Society*, University of Chicago Press, Chicago.

Mehrabian, A. (1977), 'Individual Differences in Stimulus Screening and Arousability', in *Journal of Personality*, 45, pp. 237–50.

Mehrabian, A. (1978), 'Characteristic Individual Reactions to Preferred and Unpreferred Environments', in *Journal of Personality*, 46, pp. 717–31.

Mehrabian, A. and Russell, J.A. (1974), *An Approach to Environmental Psychology*, MIT Press, Cambridge, MA.

Mehrabian, A. and Russell, J.A. (1975), 'Environmental Effects on Affiliation among Strangers', in *Humanitas*, 11, pp. 219–30.

Mercer, G.W. and Benjamin, M.L. (1980), 'Spatial Behavior of University Undergraduates in Double Occupancy Resident Rooms: an Inventory of Effects', in *Journal of Applied Social Psychology*, 10, pp. 32–44.

Merleau-Ponty, M. (1945), *Phénoménologie de la perception*, Gallimard, Paris.

Merleau-Ponty, M. (1951), *Les sciences de l'homme et la phénoménologie*, CDU, Paris.

Michelson, W. (1970), *Man and His Urban Environment*, Addison-Wesley, Reading, MA.

Michelson, W. (1987), 'Measuring Macroenvironment and Behavior: the Time Budget and Time Geography', in R. Bechtel, R. Marans and W. Michelson (eds), *Methods in Environment and Behavior Research*, Van Nostrand Reinhold, New York, pp. 216–46.

Midden, C.J.H. and Verplanken, R. (1990), 'The Stability of Nuclear Attitudes after Chernobyl', in *Journal of Environmental Psychology*, 10, pp. 111–9.

Milgram, S. (1984), 'Cities as Social Representations', in R. Farr and S. Moscovici (eds), *Social Representations*, Cambridge University Press, Cambridge.

Milgram, S. and Jodelet, D. (1976), 'Psychological Maps of Paris', in H.M. Proshansky, W.H. Ittelson and L.G. Rivlin (eds), *Environmental Psychology: People and their Physical Settings*, (2nd edn), Holt, Rinehart & Winston, New York, pp. 104–24.

Milgram, S., Greenwald, J., Keesler, S., McKenna, W. and Waters, J. (1972), 'A Psychological Map of New York City', in *American Scientist*, 60, pp. 194–200.

Miller, G.A., Galanter, F. and Pribram, K.H. (1960), *Plans and Structure of Behavior*, Holt, Rinehart & Winston, New York.

Milne, A.A. (1928), *The House at Pooh Corner*, Methuen, London.

Mischel, W. (1968), *Personality and Assessment*, Academic Press, New York.

Moar, I and Bowers, G.H. (1983), 'Inconsistency in Spatial Knowledge', in *Memory & Cognition*, 11, pp. 107–13.

Moore, G. (1974), 'The Development of Environmental Knowledge: an Overview of an Interactional-Constructivist Theory and Some Data on Within-Individual Development Variations', in D. Canter and T. Lee (eds), *Psychology and the Built Environment*, Architectural Press, London.

Moore, G. (1976), 'Theory and Research on the Development of Environmental Knowing', in G. Moore and R.G. Golledge (eds), *Environmental Knowing*, Dowden, Hutchison and Ross, Stroudsburg, PA, pp. 138–64.

Moore, G. (1986), 'A Framework for Theories of Environment and Behavior: Unit of Analysis and the Locus of Control of Behavior', paper presented to the 21st International Congress of Applied Psychology, Jerusalem.

Moore, G. (1987), 'Environment and Behavior Research in North America: History, Developments, and Unresolved Issues', in D. Stokols and I. Altman (eds), *Handbook of Environmental Psychology*, vol. 2, Wiley, New York, pp. 1371–410.

Moore, G. and Golledge, R.G. (1976), 'Environmental Knowing Concepts and Theories', in G. Moore R.G. Golledge (eds), *Environmental Knowing*, Dowden, Hutchison and Ross, Stroudsburg, PA, pp. 3–24.

Moore, G., Tuttle, D. and Howell, S.C. (1985), *Environmental Design Research Directions*, Praeger, New York.

Moos, R.H. (1973), 'Conceptualizations of Human Environment', in *American Psychologist*, 28, pp. 652–5.

Moos, R.H. (1975), *Evaluating Correctional and Community Settings*, Wiley, New York.

Moos, R.H. and Lemke, S. (1984), 'Multiphasic Environmental Assessment Procedure', unpublished manuscript, Stanford University, Social Ecology Laboratory, Palo Alto, CA.

Moscovici, S. (1961–76), *La psychanalyse: Son image et son public*, Presses Universitaires de France, Paris.

Moscovici, S. (1963), 'Attitudes and Opinions', in *Annual Review of Psychology*, 14, pp. 231–60.

Moscovici, S. (1973), 'Forward', in C. Herzlich (ed.), *Health and Illness: a Social Psychological Analysis*, Academic Press, London, pp. ix–xiv. (original edn 1969).

Moscovici, S. (1976), 'La psychologie des représentations sociales', in *Cahiers Vilfredo Pareto*, 14, pp. 409–16.

Moscovici, S. (1981), 'On Social Representations', in J.P. Forgas (ed.), *Social Cognition: Perspectives in Everyday Understanding*, Academic Press: Longon, pp. 181–209.

Moscovici, S. (1982), 'The Coming Era of Representations', in J.P. Codol and J.P. Leyens (eds), *Cognitive Approaches to Social Behavior*, Nijoff, The Hague, pp. 115–50.

Moscovici, S. (1984a), 'The Phenomenon of Social Representations', in R. Farr and S. Moscovici (eds), *Social Representations*, Cambridge University Press, Cambridge, pp. 3–69.

Moscovici, S. (1984b), *Psychologie sociale*, Presses Universitaires de France, Paris.

Murphy, G. (1947), *Personality: a Biosocial Approach to Origins and Structure*, Harper, New York.

Murray, H.A. (1938), *Explorations in Personality*, Oxford University Press, New York.

Neisser, U. (1976), *Cognition and Reality*, Freeman, San Francisco.

Neisser, U. (1987), 'Introduction: the Ecological and Intellectual Bases in Categorization', in U. Neisser (ed.), *Concepts and Conceptual Development: Ecological and Intellectual Factors in Categorization*, Cambridge University Press, Cambridge, pp. 1–23.

Neisser, U. (1988), 'Five Kinds of Self-Knowledge', in *Philosophical Psychology*, 1, pp. 35–59.

Neisser, U. (1990), 'The Ecological Approach to Cognitive Psychology', in *Comunicazioni Scientifische di Psicologia Generale*, 1, pp. 11–22.

Newman, O. (1972), *Defensible Space: Crime Prevention through Urban Design*, Macmillan, New York.

Niit, T., Heidmets, M. and Kruusvall, J. (1987), 'Environmental Psychology in the Soviet

Union', in D. Stokols and I. Altman (eds), *Handbook of Environmental Psychology*, vol. 2, Wiley, New York, pp. 1311–36.

Norberg-Schulz, C. (1971), *Existence, Space, and Architecture*, Praeger, New York.

Norberg-Schulz, C. (1980), *Genius Loci: Toward a Phenomenology of Architecture*, Academy Editions, London.

Normoyle, J. and Lavrakas, P.J. (1984), 'Fear of Crime in Elderly Women: Perceptions of Control, Predictability and Territoriality', in *Personality and Social Psychology Bulletin*, 10, pp. 191–202.

Onibokun, A.G. (1974), 'Evaluating Consumers' Satisfaction with Housing: an Application of a System Approach', in *Journal of the American Institute of Planning*, 40, pp. 189–200.

Orleans, P. (1973), 'Differential Cognition of Urban Residents: Effects of Social Scale on Mapping', in R.M. Downs and D. Stea (eds), *Image and Environment: Cognitive Mapping and Spatial Behavior*, Aldine, Chicago, pp. 78–96.

Osmond, H. (1957), 'Function as the Basis of Psychiatric Ward Design', in *Mental Hospital*, 8, pp. 23–30.

Oxley, D., Haggard, I., Werner, C. and Altman, I. (1986), 'Transactional Qualities of Neighbourhood Social Networks: a Case Study of "Christmas Street"', in *Environment and Behavior*, 18, pp. 640–77.

Palmonari, A. (1989), *Processi simbolici e dinamiche sociali*, Il Mulino, Bologna.

Palmonari, A., Carugati, F., Ricci-Bitti, P.E. and Sarchielli, G. (1979), *Identità imperfette*, Il Mulino, Bologna.

Parkes, D.N. and Thrift, N.J. (1980), *Time, Space, and Places*, Wiley, New York.

Pastalan, L.A. (1970), 'Privacy as an Expression of Human Territoriality', in L.A. Pastalan and D.H. Parson (eds), *Spatial Behavior of Older People*, University of Michigan, Ann Arbor.

Perussia, F. (1983), 'A Critical Approach to Environmental Psychology in Italy', in *Journal of Environmental Psychology*, 3 (3), pp. 263–77.

Peters, H.P., Albrecht, J., Hennen, I. and Stegelmann, H.U. (1990), 'Chernobyl and the Nuclear Power Issue in West German Public Opinion', in *Journal of Environmental Psychology*, 10, pp. 121–34.

Piaget, J. and Inhelder, R. (1947), *La représentation de l'espace chez l'enfant*, PUF, Paris.

Piaget, J. and Inhelder, R. (1968), *Mémoire et intelligence*, PUF, Paris.

Postman, R., Bruner, J. and McGuinnies, E. (1948), 'Personal Values as Selective Factors in Perception', in *Journal of Abnormal and Social Psychology*, 43, pp. 142–54.

Potter, J. and Wetherell, M. (1987), *Discourse and Social Psychology*, Sage, London.

Proshansky, H.M. (1976), 'Environmental Psychology and the Real World', in *American Psychologist*, 4, pp. 303–10.

Proshansky, H.M. (1978), 'The City and Self-Identity', in *Environment and Behavior*, 10, pp. 147–69.

Proshansky, H.M. (1987), 'The Field of Environmental Psychology: Securing Its Future', in D. Stokols and I. Altman (eds), *Handbook of Environmental Psychology*, vol. 2, Wiley, New York, pp. 1467–88.

Proshansky, H.M. and Fabian, K. (1987), 'The Development of Place Identity in the Child', in C.S. Weinstein and T.G. David (eds), *Spaces for Children*, Plenum, New York, pp. 21–40.

Proshansky, H.M. and Kaminoff, R.D. (1982), 'The Built Environment of the Young Adult', in S. Messick (ed.), *Development in Young Adulthood: Characteristics and Competences in Education, Work and Social Life*, Jossey Bass, San Francisco.

Proshansky, H.M. and O'Hanlon, T. (1977), 'Environmental Psychology: Origins and Development', in D. Stokols (ed.), *Perspectives on Environment and Behavior*, Plenum, New York, pp. 101–27.

Proshansky, H.M., Ittelson, W. and Rivlin, L.G. (eds) (1970), *Environmental Psychology: Man and His Physical Settings* (1st edn), Holt, Rinehart & Winston, New York.

Proshansky, H.M., Nelson-Schulman, Y. and Kaminoff, R.D. (1979), 'The Role of Physical

Setting in Life Crisis Experiences', in I. Sharon and C. Spielberger (eds), *Stress and Anxiety*, vol. 6, Hemisphere, Washington, DC, pp. 3–26.

Proshansky, H.M., Fabian, A.K. and Kaminoff, R. (1983), 'Place-Identity: Physical World Socialization of the Self', in *Journal of Environmental Psychology*, 3, pp. 57–83.

Rapoport, A. (1964–5), 'The Architecture of Isphahan', in *Landscape*, 14 (2), pp. 4–11.

Rapoport, A. (1982), *The Meaning of the Built Environment: A Non-Verbal Communication Approach*, Sage, Beverly Hills, CA.

Rapoport, A. (1986), 'The Use and Design of Open Spaces in Urban Neighbourhoods', in D. Frick (ed.), *The Quality of Urban Life*, de Gruyter, Berlin, pp. 159–76.

Rapoport, A. (1990), 'Systems of Activities and Systems of Settings', in S. Kent (ed.), *Domestic Architecture and the Use of Space*, Cambridge University Press, Cambridge, pp. 9–19.

Ratner, S. et al. (eds) (1964), *John Dewey and Arthur Bentley: A Philosophical Correspondence, 1932–1951*, Rutgers University Press, New Brunswick, NJ.

Reed, E. and Jones, R. (1982), *Reasons for Realism: Selected Essays of James J. Gibson*, Lawrence Erlbaum, Hillsdale NJ.

Relph, E. (1970), 'An Inquiry of the Relationship between Phenomenology and Geography', in *Canadian Geographer*, 14, pp. 437–51.

Relph, E. (1976), *Place and Placelessness*, Pion, London.

Renn, O. (1990), 'Public Responses to the Chernobyl Accident', in *Journal of Environmental Psychology*, 10, pp. 151–67.

Roethlisberger, F.J. and Dickinson, W.J. (1939), *Management and the Worker*, Harvard University Press, Cambridge, MA.

Romney, A.K. and D'Andrade, R.G. (1964), 'Transcultural Studies in Cognition', in *American Anthropologist*, 66, pp. 146–70.

Rosemberg, M. (1979), *Conceiving the Self*, Basic Books, New York.

Russell, J.A. and Lanius, U.F. (1984), 'Adaptation Level and the Affective Appraisal of Environments', in *Journal of Environmental Psychology*, 4, pp. 119–35.

Russell, J.A. and Mehrabian, A. (1978), 'Approach-Avoidance and Affiliation as Functions of Emotion-Eliciting Quality of an Environment', in *Environment and Behavior*, 10, pp. 355–87.

Russell, J.A. and Pratt, G. (1980), 'A Description of the Affective Quality Attributed to Environments', in *Journal of Personality and Social Psychology*, 38, pp. 311–22.

Russell, J.A. and Ward, L.M. (1981), 'On the Psychological Reality of Experimental Meaning: Reply to Daniel and Ittelson', in *Journal of Experimental Psychology: General*, 110, pp. 163–8.

Russell, J.A. and Ward, L.M. (1982), 'Environmental Psychology', in *Annual Review of Psychology*, 33, pp. 259–88.

Russell, J.A., Ward, L.M. and Pratt, G. (1981), 'Affective Quality Attributed to Environments: a Factor Analytic Study', in *Environment and Behavior*, 13, pp. 259–88.

Saarinen, T.F. (1966), *Perception of Drought Hazard on the Great Plains*, research paper 106, University of Chicago, Department of Geography, Chicago.

Saarinen, T.F. (1969), *Perception of Environment. Commission on College Geography*, research paper 5, Association of American Geographers, Washington, DC.

Saarinen, T.F., Seamon, D. and Sell, J.L. (eds) (1984), *Environmental Perception and Behavior*, research paper 209, University of Chicago, Department of Geography, Chicago.

Saegert, S. (1987), 'Environmental Psychology and Social Change', in D. Stokols and I. Altman (eds), *Handbook of Environmental Psychology*, vol. 1, Wiley, New York, pp. 99–128.

Saegert, S. and Winkel, G. (1990), 'Environmental Psychology', in *Annual Review of Psychology*, 41, pp. 441–77.

Saegert, S., Mackintosh, E. and West, S. (1975), 'Two Studies of Crowding in Urban Public Spaces', in *Environment and Behavior*, 7, pp. 159–84.

Sarbin, T.R. (1976), 'Contextualism: a World View From Modern Psychology', in M.M. Page (ed.), *Nebraska Symposium on Motivation*, University of Nebraska Press, Lincoln, pp. 1–41.

Sauer, C.O. (1925), 'The Morphology of Landscape', in J. Leighlet (ed.), *Land and Life: A Selection from the Writings of Carl Ortwin Sauer*, University of California Press, Berkeley, 1969, pp. 315–50.

Schank, R. and Abelson, R. (1977), *Scripts, Plans, Goals, and Understanding*, Lawrence Erlbaum, Hillsdale, NJ.

Schoggen, P. (1989), *Behavioral Settings*, Stanford University Press, Stanford, CA.

Schütz, A. (1962–6), *Collected Papers*, 3 vols., Martinus Nijhoff, The Hague.

Schütz, A. (1967), *The Phenomenology of the Social World*, Northwestern University Press, Evanston, IL.

Seamon, D. (1979), *A Geography of the Life World*, Croom Helm, London.

Seamon, D. (1982), 'The Phenomenological Contribution to Environmental Psychology', in *Journal of Environmental Psychology*, 2, pp. 119–40.

Sebba, R. and Churchman, A. (1983), 'Territories and Territoriality in the Home', in *Environment and Behavior*, 15, pp. 191–210.

Secchiaroli, G. (1979a), 'Progettazione dell'ambiente per l'uomo e psicologia ambientale: una nuova prospettiva', in *Psicologia Contemporanea*, 33, pp. 30–5.

Secchiaroli, G. (1979b), 'Gli psicologi alla scoperta dell'ambiente', in *Sociologia Urbana e Rurale*, 1, pp. 15–22.

Secchiaroli, G. (1979c), 'Andiamo in centro', in *Bologna Incontri*, 9, pp. 18–20.

Secchiaroli, G. (1981), 'Psychologie et environnement: Problèmes et perspectives par rapport au context italien', paper presented to the International Symposium on 'Toward a Social Psychology of the Environment', Maison des Sciences de l'Homme, Paris.

Secchiaroli, G. (1986), 'Immaginabilità sociale dell'ambiente urbano e processi di costruzione delle realtà ambientali', in *Sociologia Urbana e Rurale*, 19, pp. 179–86.

Secchiaroli, G. (1987a), 'Comportamenti e pratiche turistiche tra rappresentazioni ambientali e costruzione di significati', in P. Guidicini and A. Savelli (eds), *Leggere il turismo in una società che cambia*, Franco Angeli, Milan, pp. 62–75.

Secchiaroli, G. (1987b), 'Costruzioni cognitive e immaginabilità sociale dei luoghi urbani: Quartiere, centro e periferia nella città di Roma', in E. Bianchi, F. Perussia and M.F. Rossi (eds), *Immagine soggettiva e ambiente, problemi, applicazioni e strategie di ricerca*, UNICOPLI, Milan, pp. 18–33.

Secchiaroli, G. and Bonnes, M. (1983), *Complessità dell'ambiente urbano e rappresentazioni cognitive degli abitanti*, rapporto tecnico no. 315, Istituto di Psicologia, CNR, Rome.

Segall, M.H., Campbell, D.T. and Herskovitz, M. (1966), *The Influence of Culture on Visual Perception*, Bobbs-Merrill, Indianapolis, IN.

Seligman, M.E.P. (1973), 'Fall into Helplessness', in *Psychology Today*, June, pp. 43–8.

Seligman, M.E.P. (1974), 'Depression and Learned Helplessness', in R.J. Friedman and M.M. Katz (eds), *The Psychology of Depression: Contemporary Theory and Research*, Wiley, New York, pp. 114–29.

Seligman, M.E.P. (1975), *Helplessness*, Freeman, San Francisco.

Selye, H. (1956), *The Stress of Life*, McGraw-Hill, New York.

Sherrod, D.R. and Downs, R. (1974), 'Environmental Determinants of Altruism: the Effects of Stimulus Overload and Perceived Control of Helping', in *Journal of Experimental Social Psychology*, 10, pp. 468–79.

Sherrod, D.R., Hage, J.N., Halpern, P.L. and Moore, B.S. (1977), 'Effects of Personal Causation and Perceived Control on Responses to an Adverse Environment: the More Control, the Better', in *Journal of Experimental Social Psychology*, 13, pp. 14–27.

Shumaker, S.A. and Taylor, R.B. (1983), 'Toward a Clarification of People–Place Relationship: a Mode of Attachment to Place', in N.R. Feimer and E.S. Geller (eds), *Environmental Psychology: Directions and Perspectives*, Praeger, New York, pp. 219–51.

Siegel, A.W. and White, S.H. (1975), 'The Development of Spatial Representations of Large-Scale Environments', in H.W. Reese (ed.), *Advances in Child Development and Behavior*, vol. 10, Academic Press, New York, pp. 8–55.

Smith, C.J. (1976), 'Residential Neighbourhoods as Human Environments', in *Environmental Planning*, 8, pp. 311–26.

Smith, H.W. (1983), 'Territorial Spacing on a Beach Revisited: a Cross-National Exploration', in *Social Psychology Quarterly*, 44, pp. 132–7.

Sommer, R. (1959), 'Studies in Personal Space', in *Sociometry*, 22, pp. 247–60.

Sommer, R. (1969), *Personal Space: the Behavioral Basis of Design*, Prentice-Hall, Englewood Cliffs, NJ.

Sommer, R. (1987), 'Dream, Reality, and the Future of Environmental Psychology', in D. Stokols and I. Altman, (eds), *Handbook of Environmental Psychology*, vol. 2, Wiley, New York, pp. 1489–512.

Sommer, R. and Ross, H. (1958), 'Social Interaction on a Geriatric Ward', in *International Journal of Social Psychiatry*, 4, pp. 128–33.

Sonnenfeld, J. (1969), 'Personality and Behavior in Environment', in *Proceedings of the Association of American Geographers*, 1, pp. 136–40.

Stea, D. (1967), 'Reasons for Our Moving', in *Landscape*, 17, pp. 27–8.

Stea, D. (1969), 'The Measurement of Mental Maps: an Experimental Model for Studying Conceptual Space', in K.R. Cox and R.G. Golledge (eds), *Behavioral Problems in Geography: a Symposium*, Northwestern University Press, Evanston, IL, pp. 228–53.

Stokols, D. (1978), 'Environmental Psychology', in *Annual Review of Psychology*, 29, pp. 253–95.

Stokols, D. (1979), 'A Congruence Analysis of Stress', in I. Saranson and C. Spielberger (eds), *Stress and Anxiety*, vol. 6, Hemisphere, New York, pp. 27–53.

Stokols, D. (1981), 'Group X Place Transactions: Some Neglected Issues in Psychological Research on Settings', in D. Magnusson (ed.), *Towards a Psychology of Situations: an Interactional Perspective*, Lawrence Erlbaum, Hillsdale, NJ, pp. 393–415.

Stokols, D. (1987), 'Conceptual Strategies of Environmental Psychology', in D. Stokols and I. Altman, (eds), *Handbook of Environmental Psychology*, vol. 1, Wiley, New York, pp. 41–70.

Stokols, D. and Altman, I. (eds) (1987), *Handbook of Environmental Psychology*, Wiley, New York, vols. 1 and 2.

Stokols, D. and Shumaker, S. (1981), 'People in Place: a Transactional View of Settings', in J. Harvey (ed.), *Cognition, Social Behavior, and the Environment*, Lawrence Erlbaum, Hillsdale, NJ, pp. 441–88.

Stokols, D., Rall, M., Pinner, B. and Schopler, J. (1973), 'Physical, Social, and Personal Determinants of the Perception of Crowding', in *Environment and Behavior*, 5, pp. 87–117.

Stokols, D., Ohlig, W. and Resnick, S.M. (1978), 'Perception of Residential Crowding, Classroom Experiences and Student Health', in *Human Ecology*, 6, pp. 233–52.

Strauss, A.L. (1961), *Images of the American City*, Free Press, New York.

Stringer, P. and Kremer, A. (1987), 'Environmental Psychology in the Netherlands' in D. Stokols and I. Altman (eds), *Handbook of Environmental Psychology*, vol. 2, Wiley, New York, pp. 1227–42.

Sundstrom, E. (1975), 'An Experimental Study of Crowding: Effects of Room Size, Intrusion and Goal-Blocking on Non-Verbal Behaviors, Self-Disclosure and Self-Reported Stress', in *Journal of Personality and Social Psychology*, 32, pp. 645–54.

Sundstrom, E., Town, J.P., Brown, D.W., Forman, A. and McGee, C. (1982), 'Privacy and Communication in an Open-Plan Office: a Case Study', in *Environment and Behavior*, 14, pp. 379–92.

Tajfel, H. (1969), 'Social and Cultural Factors in Perception', in G. Lindzey and E. Aronson (eds), *Handbook of Social Psychology*, Addison-Wesley, Reading, MA, pp. 315–94.

Tajfel, H. (1981), *Human Groups and Social Categories*, Cambridge University Press, Cambridge.

Tajfel, H. (ed.) (1984), *The Social Dimension*, vols. 1–2, Cambridge University Press, Cambridge.

Tangenes, B., Marek, J. and Hellesoy, O.H. (1981), *Work and Physical Environment on a North Sea Platform*, Mobil Exploration Norway Inc., Bergen.

Taylor, C.W., Bailey, R. and Branch, C.H. (eds) (1967), *Second National Conference on Architectural Psychology*, University of Utah, Salt Lake City.

Taylor, R.B., Gottfredson, S.D. and Brower, S. (1980), 'The Defensibility of Defensible Space: a Critical Review and a Synthetic Framework for Future Research', in T. Hirschi and M. Gottfredson (eds), *Understanding Crime*, Sage, Beverly Hills, CA, pp. 48–69.

Taylor, R.B., Gottfredson, S. and Brower, S. (1984), 'Understanding Block Crime and Fear', in *Journal of Research in Crime and Delinquency*, 21, pp. 303–31.

Theologus, G.S., Wheaton, G.R. and Fleishman, E.A. (1974), 'Effects of Intermitent Moderate Intensity Noise on Human Performance', in *Journal of Applied Psychology*, 59, pp. 539–47.

Tolman, E.C. (1932), *Purposive Behavior in Animals and Men*, Century Co., New York.

Tolman, E.C. (1948), 'Cognitive Maps in Rats and Men', in *Psychological Review*, 55, pp. 189–208.

Tolman, E.C. and Brunswik, E. (1935), 'The Organism and the Causal Texture of the Environment', in *Psychological Review*, 42, pp. 43–7.

Tuan, Y.F. (1961), 'Topophilia', in *Landscape*, 11, pp. 29–32.

Tuan, Y.F. (1974), *Topophilia: a Study of Environmental Perception, Attitudes and Values*, Prentice Hall, Englewood Cliffs, NJ.

Tuan, Y.F. (1977), *Space and Place: the Perspective of Experience*, University of Minnesota Press, Minneapolis.

Tuan, Y.F. (1979), *Landscapes of Fear*, Pantheon, New York.

Tuan, Y.F. (1980), 'Rootedness versus Sense of Place', in *Landscape*, 24, pp. 3–8.

Turner, J. (1981), 'Toward a Cognitive Redefinition of the Social Group', in *Cahiers de Psychologie Cognitive*, 2, pp. 93–118.

UNESCO-MAB (1973), *Expert Panel on MAB Project 13: Perception of Environmental Quality*, MAB report series no. 17, UNESCO, Paris.

UNESCO-MAB (1988), *Man Belongs to the Earth*, UNESCO, Paris.

Valsiner, J. and Benigni, I. (1986), 'Naturalistic Research and Ecological Thinking in the Study of Child Development', in *Developmental Review*, 6 (3), pp. 203–23.

Van der Plight, J. and Midden, C.J.H. (1990), 'Chernobyl: Four Years Later. Attitudes, Risk, Management and Communication', in *Journal of Environmental Psychology*, 10, pp. 91–9.

Van Liere, K.D. and Dunlap, R.E. (1981), 'Environmental Concern: Does it Make a Difference How It's Measured?', in *Environment and Behavior*, 13, pp. 651–76.

Veroff, J. (1983), 'Contextual Determinants of Personality', in *Personality and Social Psychology Bulletin*, 9, pp. 331–43.

Wapner, S. (1987), 'A Holistic, Developmental, System-Oriented Environmental Psychology: Some Beginnings', in D. Stokols and I. Altman (eds), *Handbook of Environmental Psychology*, vol. 2, Wiley, New York, pp. 1433–66.

Wapner, S. and Kaplan, B. (eds) (1983), *Toward a Holistic Developmental Psychology*, Lawrence Erlbaum, Hillsdale, NJ.

Ward, L.M., Snodgrass, J., Chew, B. and Russell, J. (1988), 'The Role of Plans in Cognitive and Affective Responses to Places', in *Journal of Environmental Psychology*, 8, pp. 1–8.

Warner, H.D. (1969), 'Effects of Intermittent Noise on Human Target Detection', in *Human Factors*, 11, pp. 245–50.

Weick, K.E. (1979), *The Social Psychology of Organization*, Addison-Wesley, Reading, MA.

Weinstein, N.D. (1978), 'Individual Differences in Reactions to Noise: A Longitudinal Study in a College Dormitory', in *Journal of Applied Psychology*, 63, pp. 456–66.

Werner, C.M., Altman, I. and Oxley, D. (1985), 'Temporal Aspects of Home: A Transactional Perspective', in I. Altman and C.M. Werner (eds), *Home Environments*, vol. 8, *Human Behavior and Environment*, Plenum, New York, pp. 1–32.

Werner, C.M., Altman, I. and Oxley, D. (1987), 'People, Places, and Time: a Transactional Analysis of Neighborhood', in W.J. Jones and D. Perlman (eds), *Advances in Personal Relationships*, JAI Press, New York, pp. 243–75.

Werner, H. (1948), *Comparative Psychology of Mental Development*, International University Press, New York.

Wertheimer, M. (1945), *Produktives Denken*, Kramer, Frankfurt a. M.

Whyte, A. (1977), *Guidelines for Field Studies in Environmental Perception*, MAB technical note 5, UNESCO, Paris.

Whyte, A. (1984), 'Integration of Natural and Social Sciences in Environmental Research: a Case Study of the MAB Programme', in F. di Castri, F.W. Barker and M. Hadley (eds), *Ecology in Practice*, vol. 2, Tycooly, Dublin, pp. 298–323.

Wicker, A.W. (1969), 'Cognitive Complexity, School Size, and Participation in School Behavior Settings: a Test of the Frequency Interactional Hypothesis', in *Journal of Educational Psychology*, 60, pp. 200–3.

Wicker, A.W. (1979), *An Introduction to Ecological Psychology*, Brooks/Cole, Monterey, CA.

Wicker, A.W. (1987), 'Behavioral Settings Reconsidered: Temporal Stages, Resources, Internal Dynamics, Context', in D. Stokols and I. Altman, (eds), *Handbook of Environmental Psychology*, vol. 1, Wiley, New York, pp. 613–53.

Wineman, J.D. (1982a), 'The Office Environment as a Source of Stress', in G.W. Evans (ed.), *Environmental Stress*, Cambridge University Press, New York, pp. 256–83.

Wineman, J.D. (1982b), 'Office Design and Evaluation: an Over-View', in *Environment and Behavior*, 14, pp. 271–98.

Winkel, G.H. (ed.) (1969), *Environment and Behavior*, Sage, Beverly Hills, CA.

Wohlwill, J.F. (1970), 'The Emerging Discipline of Environmental Psychology', in *American Psychologist*, 25, pp. 303–12.

Wohlwill, J.F. (1976), 'Environmental Aesthetics: the Environment as a Source of Affect', in I. Altman and J. Wohlwill (eds), *Human Behavior and Environment: Advances in Theory and Research*, vol. 1, Plenum Press, New York, pp. 37–86.

Wolf, C.P. (1974), 'Social Impact Assessment: the State of the Art, Man–Environment Interaction: Evaluations and Applications', vol. 2, *Proceedings of the 5th International Environmental Design Research Association Conference*, Environmental Design Research Association, Washington, DC.

Wolf, C.P. (ed.) (1975), *Environment and Behavior*, 7, Special Issue on Social Impact Assessment.

Worchel, S. and Lollis, M. (1982), 'Reactions to Territorial Contamination as a Function of Culture', in *Personality and Social Psychology Bulletin*, 8, pp. 370–5.

Wright, G. (1947), 'Terrae Incognitae: the Place of Imagination in Geography', in *Annals of the Association of American Geographers*, 37, pp. 1–15.

Zajonc, R.B. (1980), 'Cognition and Social Cognition: a Historical Perspective', in L. Festinger (ed.), *Retrospection on Social Psychology*, Oxford University Press, New York, pp. 151–75.

Zube, E.H. (ed.) (1980), *Social Sciences: Interdisciplinary Research and the US Man and Biosphere Program: Workshop Proceedings*, Department of State, US MAB, Washington, DC.

Zube, E.H., Sell, J.L. and Taylor, J.G. (1982), 'Landscape Perception: Research, Application and Theory', in *Landscape Planning*, 9, pp. 1–33.

Index

Compiled by Jackie McDermott